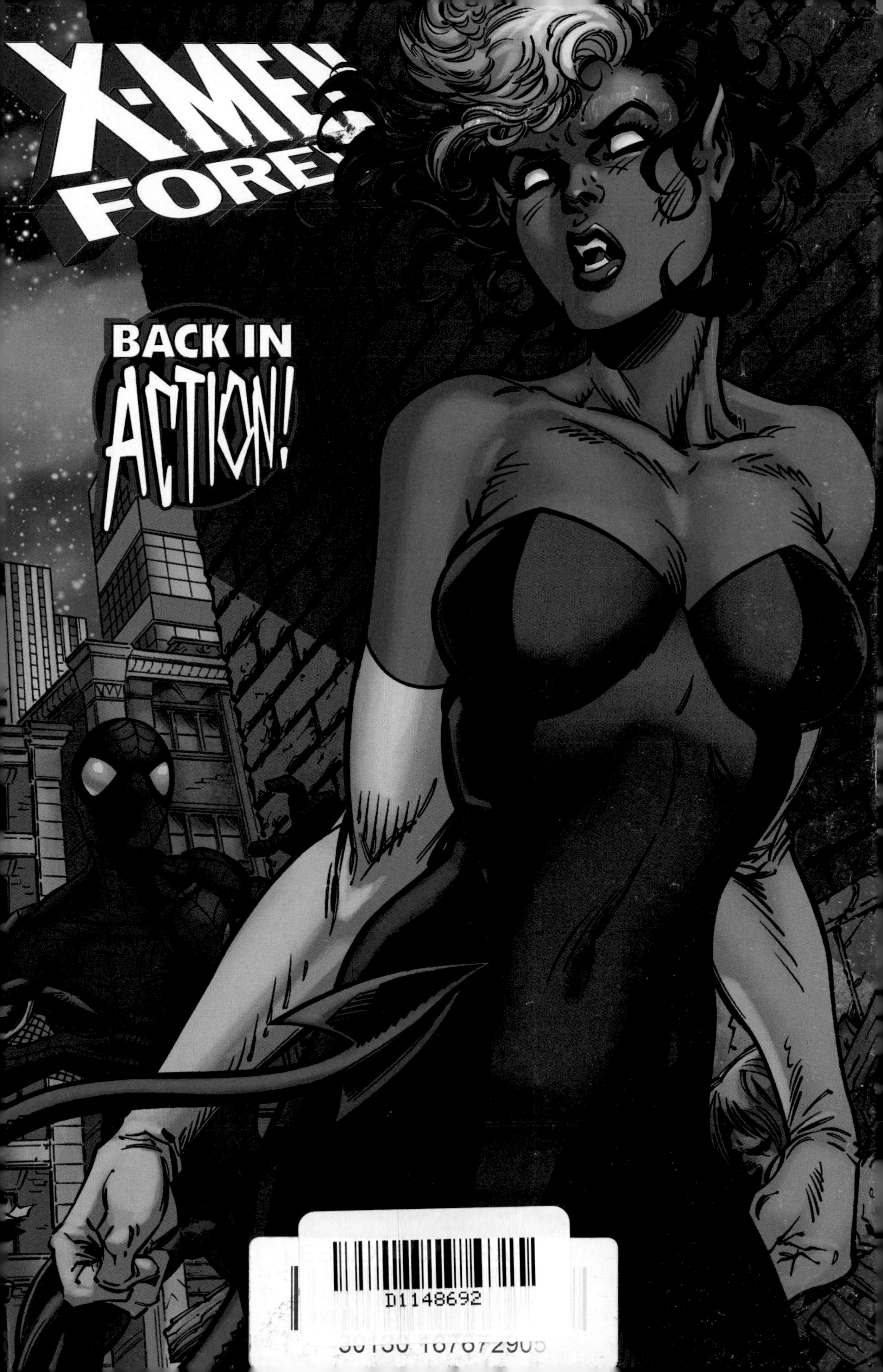
X-ME
FORE
BACK IN
ACTION!

X-MEN FOREVER

BACK IN ACTION!

Writer:
CHRIS CLAREMONT

Pencilers:
TOM GRUMMETT (ISSUES #1-3)
& RODNEY BUCHEMI (ISSUES #4-5)

Inkers:
CORY HAMSCHER (ISSUES #1-3)
& GREG ADAMS (ISSUES #4-5)

Colorist:
WILFREDO QUINTANA

Letterer:
TOM ORZECHOWSKI

Cover Art:
**TOM GRUMMETT, CORY HAMSCHER, TERRY AUSTIN
& WILFREDO QUINTANA**

Editors:
CHARLIE BECKERMAN & MICHAEL HORWITZ

Consulting Editor:
MARC SUMERAK

Senior Editor:
MARK PANICCIA

Collection Editor: **JENNIFER GRÜNWALD**
Editorial Assistants: **JAMES EMMETT & JOE HOCHSTEIN**
Assistant Editors: **ALEX STARBUCK & NELSON RIBEIRO**
Editor, Special Projects: **MARK D. BEAZLEY** • Senior Editor, Special Projects: **JEFF YOUNGQUIST**
Senior Vice President of Sales: **DAVID GABRIEL**

Editor in Chief: **JOE QUESADA** • Publisher: **DAN BUCKLEY**
Executive Producer: **ALAN FINE**

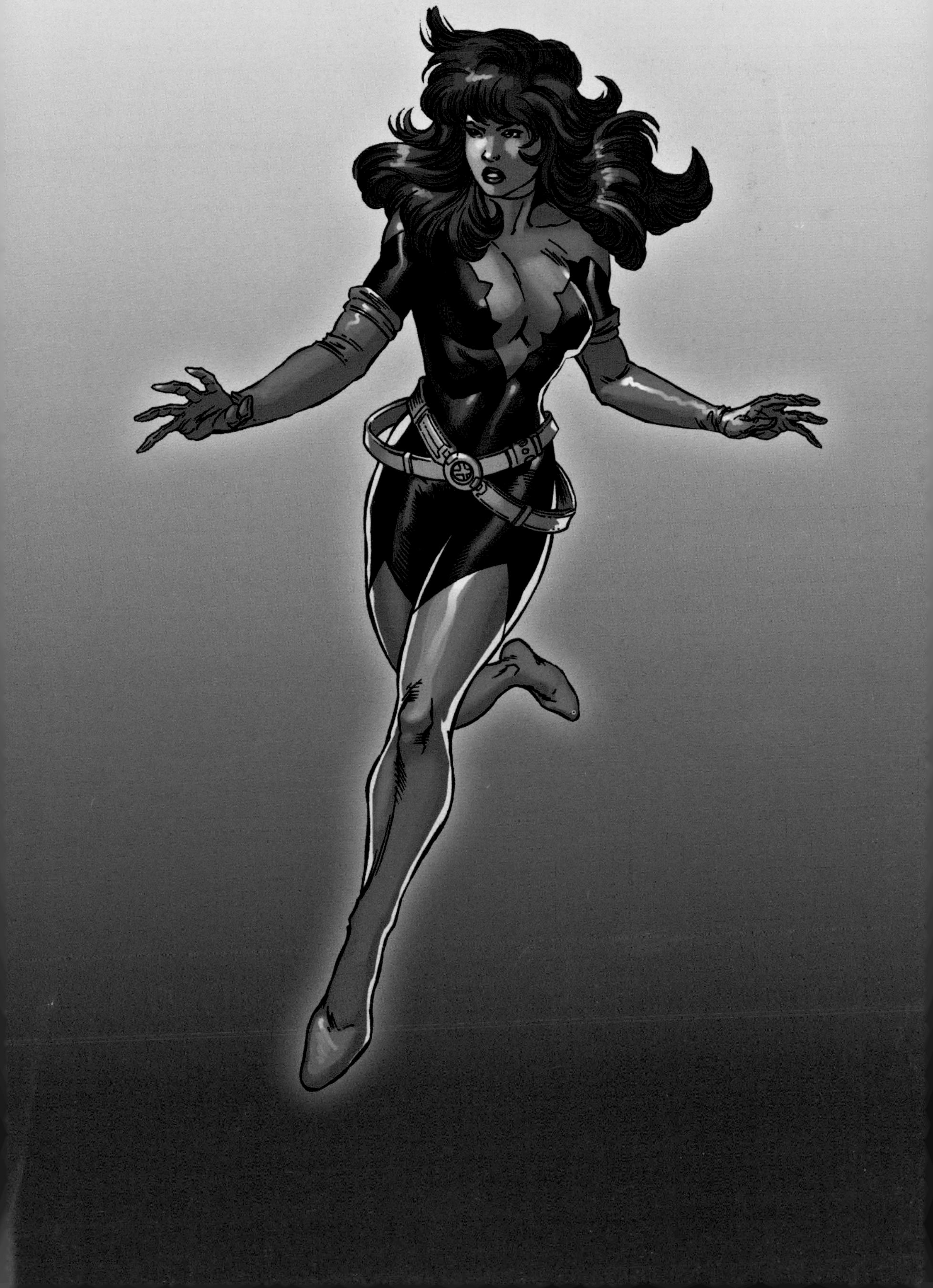

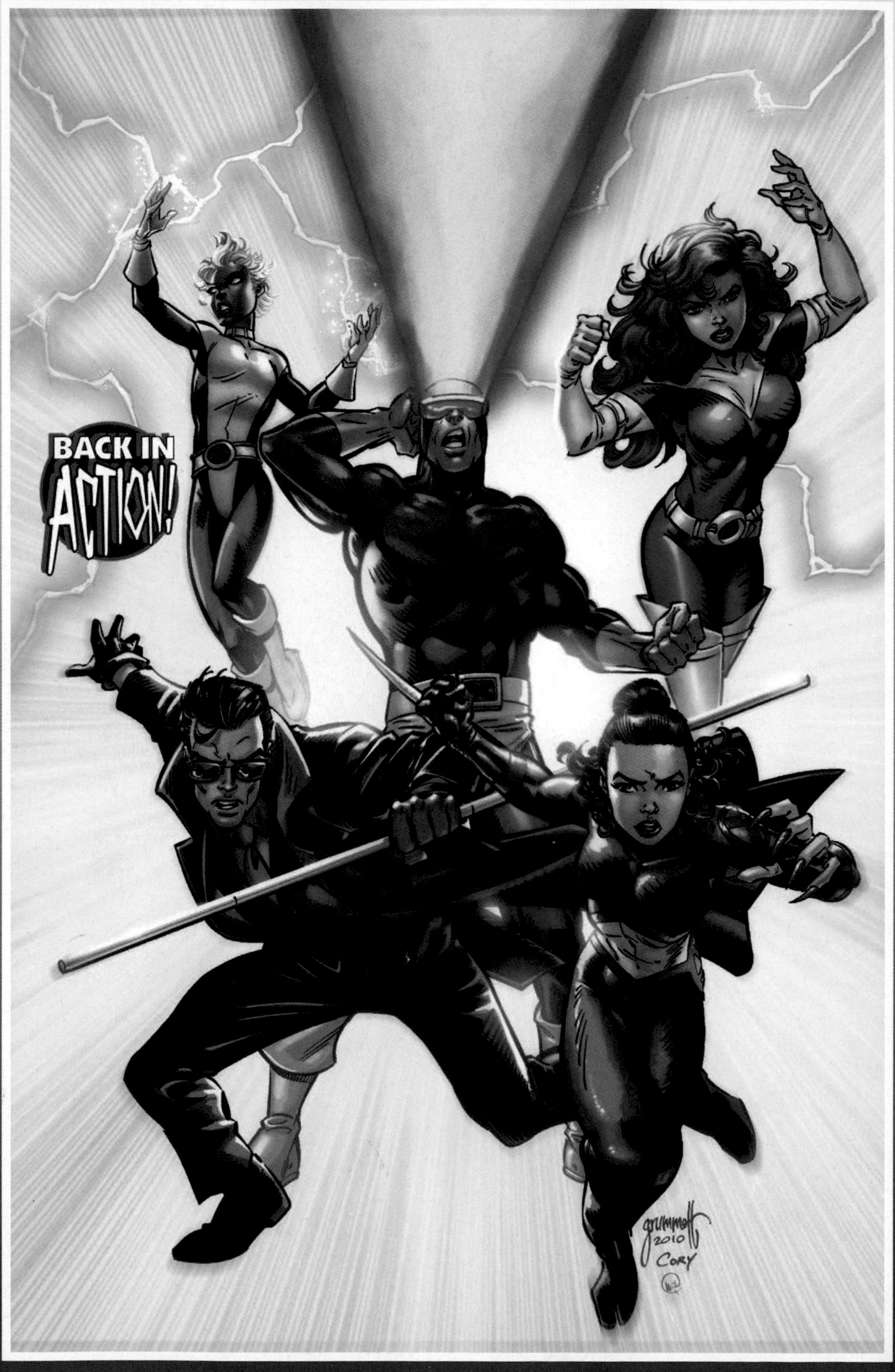
BACK IN ACTION!
grummett 2010
CORY

ONE

Comics legend Chris Claremont had an epic 16-year run on **X-MEN**, *which concluded with* **X-MEN: MUTANT GENESIS** *#1-3 in 1991. Now, in an unprecedented comics event, Claremont returns to his iconic run on the* **X-MEN**.

Previously, in

X-MEN FOREVER

The X-Men live in a different world than the one they used to know.

Wolverine is dead, killed by Storm at the behest of a secret organization known only as the Consortium. Storm now rules Wakanda, having violently overthrown the Black Panther.

The Beast, a.k.a. Hank McCoy, is dead, killed in the line of duty while attempting to disarm a genetic bomb aboard a Consortium satellite. He gave his life to save billions on Earth… working side-by-side with a rogue Consortium member and former Avengers colleague, Tony Stark.

Professor Charles Xavier is gone, taken into custody by the Imperial Guard and sentenced to live out his life in Shi'ar space. The founder of the X-Men leaves behind his students who must now take up his mantle and lead.

Amidst all this, the specter of Mutant Burnout—the condition that sentences mutants to an early death—continues to weigh heavily on the shoulders of the X-Men. All of them could probably use a breather, some time to reflect…

…unfortunately, time waits for no one, man or mutant.

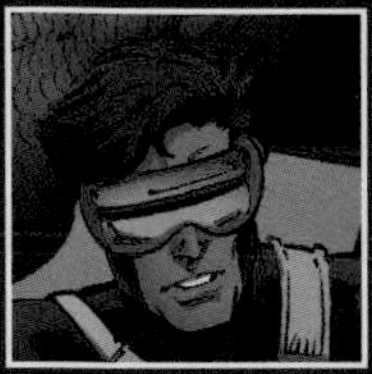

CYCLOPS
Scott Summers

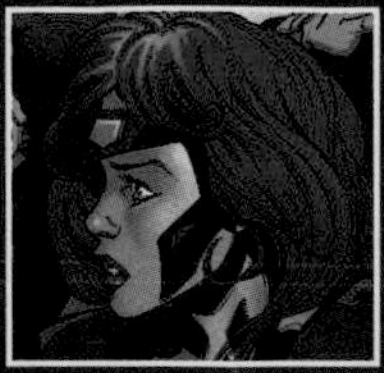

JEAN GREY

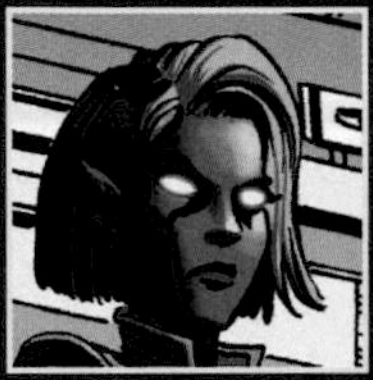

ROGUE
Anna Marie Raven

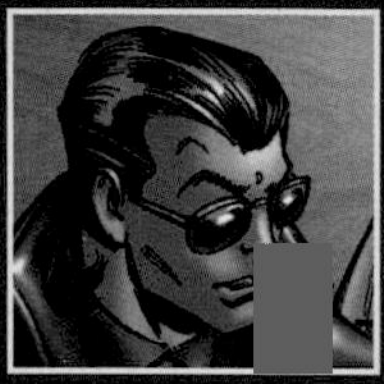

GAMBIT
Remy Picard

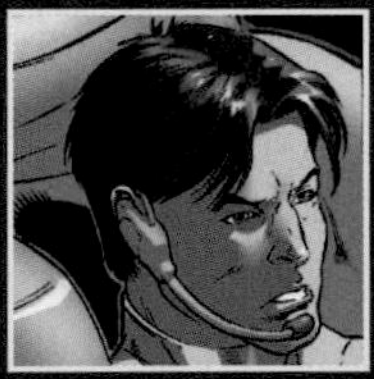

NIGHTCRAWLER
Kurt Wagner

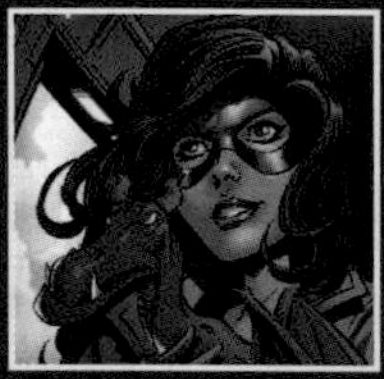

SHADOWCAT
Kitty Pryde

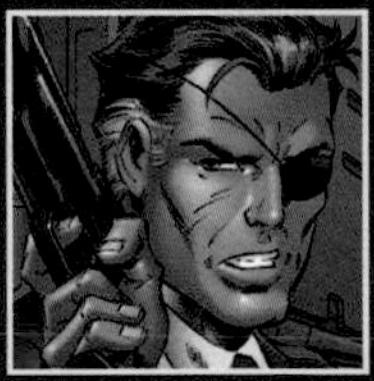

NICK FURY
Director of S.H.I.E.L.D.

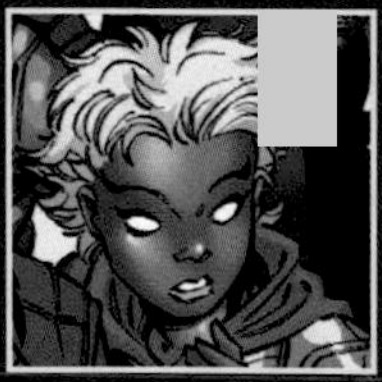

LIL' 'RO
Ororo Munroe?

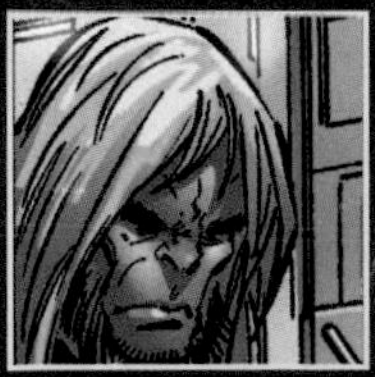

SABRETOOTH
'Nuff Said

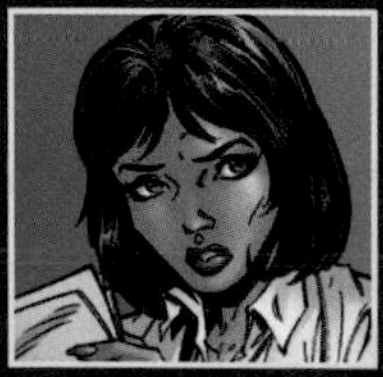

MOIRA MACTAGGERT
Top Geneticist

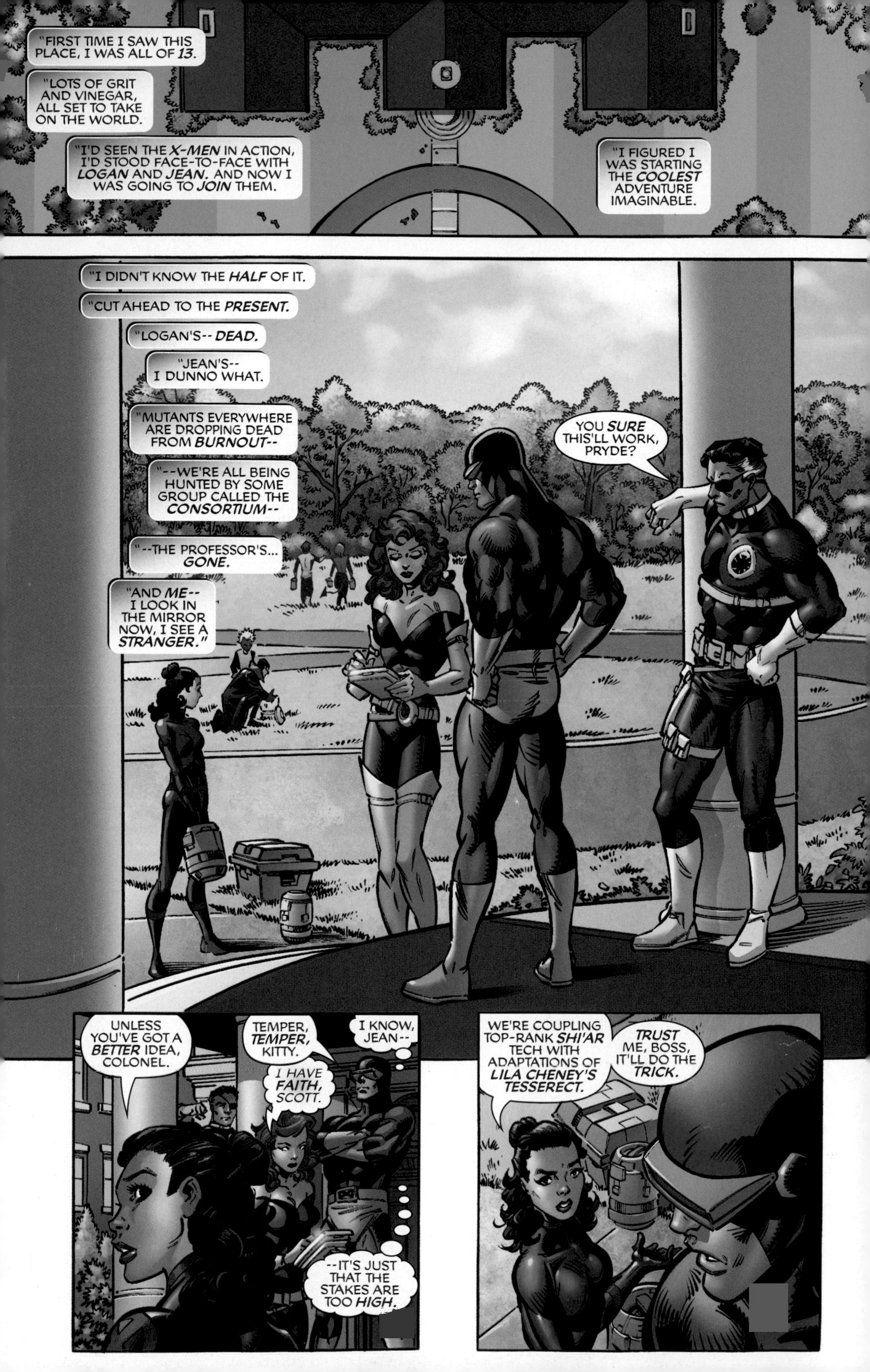
"FIRST TIME I SAW THIS PLACE, I WAS ALL OF 13.
"LOTS OF GRIT AND VINEGAR, ALL SET TO TAKE ON THE WORLD.
"I'D SEEN THE X-MEN IN ACTION, I'D STOOD FACE-TO-FACE WITH LOGAN AND JEAN. AND NOW I WAS GOING TO JOIN THEM.
"I FIGURED I WAS STARTING THE COOLEST ADVENTURE IMAGINABLE.
"I DIDN'T KNOW THE HALF OF IT.
"CUT AHEAD TO THE PRESENT.
"LOGAN'S-- DEAD.
"JEAN'S-- I DUNNO WHAT.
"MUTANTS EVERYWHERE ARE DROPPING DEAD FROM BURNOUT--
"--WE'RE ALL BEING HUNTED BY SOME GROUP CALLED THE CONSORTIUM--
"--THE PROFESSOR'S... GONE.
"AND ME-- I LOOK IN THE MIRROR NOW, I SEE A STRANGER."
YOU SURE THIS'LL WORK, PRYDE?
UNLESS YOU'VE GOT A BETTER IDEA, COLONEL.
TEMPER, TEMPER, KITTY.
I KNOW, JEAN--
I HAVE FAITH, SCOTT.
--IT'S JUST THAT THE STAKES ARE TOO HIGH.
WE'RE COUPLING TOP-RANK SHI'AR TECH WITH ADAPTATIONS OF LILA CHENEY'S TESSERECT.
TRUST ME, BOSS, IT'LL DO THE TRICK.

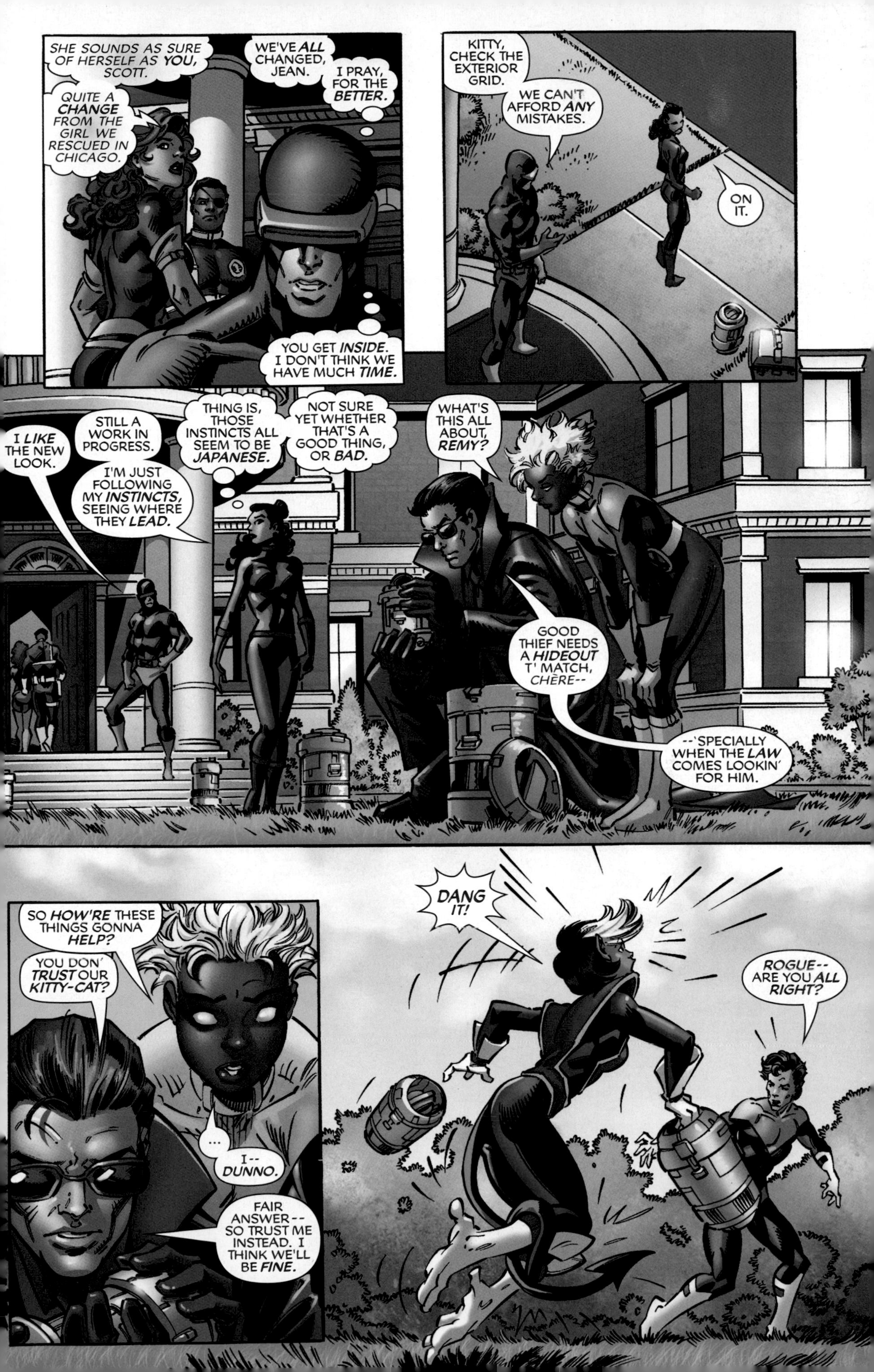

SHE SOUNDS AS SURE OF HERSELF AS YOU, SCOTT.
QUITE A CHANGE FROM THE GIRL WE RESCUED IN CHICAGO.
WE'VE ALL CHANGED, JEAN.
I PRAY, FOR THE BETTER.
YOU GET INSIDE. I DON'T THINK WE HAVE MUCH TIME.
KITTY, CHECK THE EXTERIOR GRID.
WE CAN'T AFFORD ANY MISTAKES.
ON IT.
I LIKE THE NEW LOOK.
STILL A WORK IN PROGRESS.
I'M JUST FOLLOWING MY INSTINCTS, SEEING WHERE THEY LEAD.
THING IS, THOSE INSTINCTS ALL SEEM TO BE JAPANESE.
NOT SURE YET WHETHER THAT'S A GOOD THING, OR BAD.
WHAT'S THIS ALL ABOUT, REMY?
GOOD THIEF NEEDS A HIDEOUT T' MATCH, CHÈRE--
--'SPECIALLY WHEN THE LAW COMES LOOKIN' FOR HIM.
SO HOW'RE THESE THINGS GONNA HELP?
YOU DON' TRUST OUR KITTY-CAT?
...
I-- DUNNO.
FAIR ANSWER-- SO TRUST ME INSTEAD. I THINK WE'LL BE FINE.
DANG IT!
ROGUE-- ARE YOU ALL RIGHT?

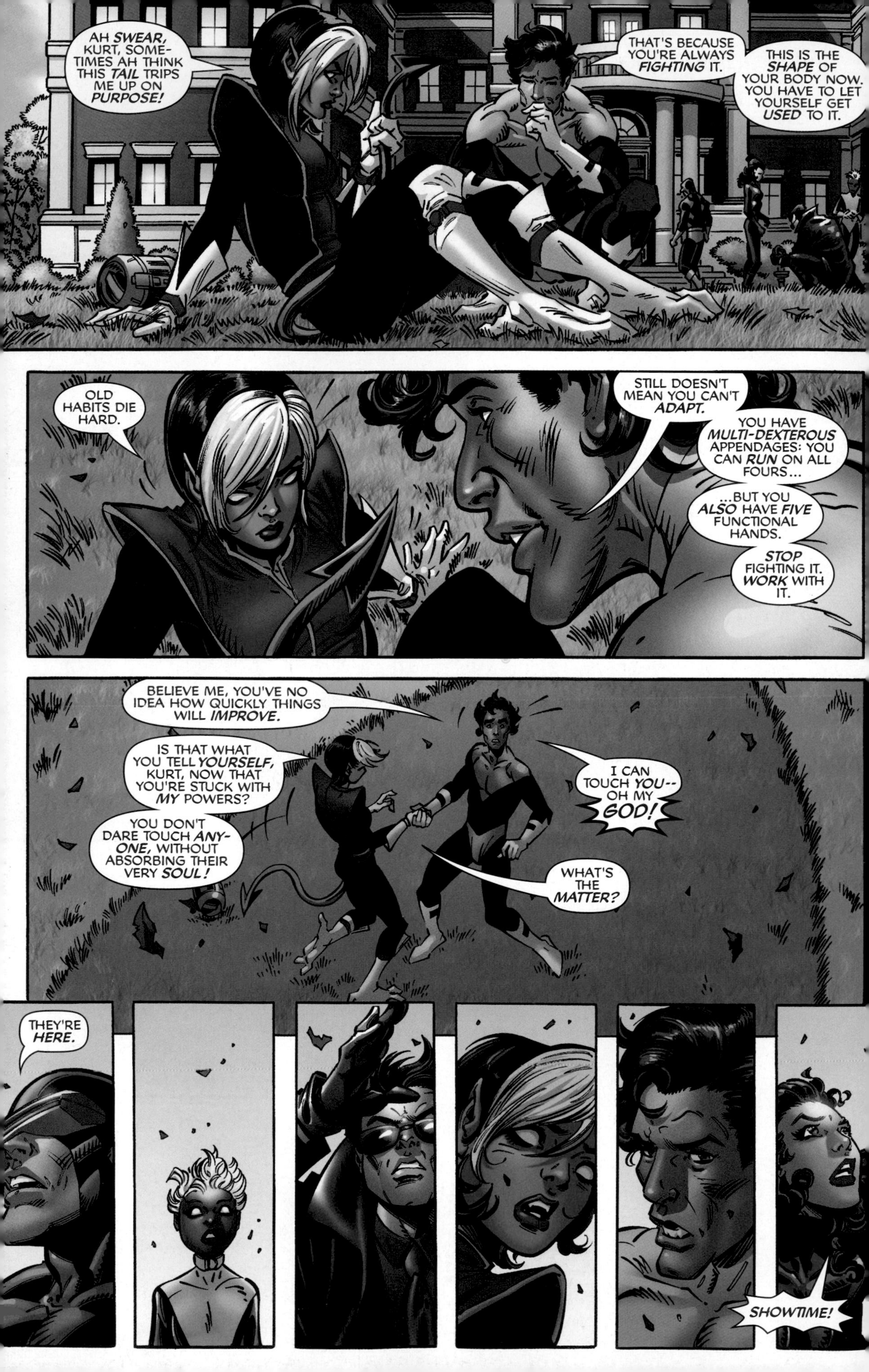
AH SWEAR, KURT, SOMETIMES AH THINK THIS TAIL TRIPS ME UP ON PURPOSE!
THAT'S BECAUSE YOU'RE ALWAYS FIGHTING IT.
THIS IS THE SHAPE OF YOUR BODY NOW. YOU HAVE TO LET YOURSELF GET USED TO IT.
OLD HABITS DIE HARD.
STILL DOESN'T MEAN YOU CAN'T ADAPT.
YOU HAVE MULTI-DEXTEROUS APPENDAGES: YOU CAN RUN ON ALL FOURS...
...BUT YOU ALSO HAVE FIVE FUNCTIONAL HANDS.
STOP FIGHTING IT. WORK WITH IT.
BELIEVE ME, YOU'VE NO IDEA HOW QUICKLY THINGS WILL IMPROVE.
IS THAT WHAT YOU TELL YOURSELF, KURT, NOW THAT YOU'RE STUCK WITH MY POWERS?
YOU DON'T DARE TOUCH ANYONE, WITHOUT ABSORBING THEIR VERY SOUL!
I CAN TOUCH YOU-- OH MY GOD!
WHAT'S THE MATTER?
THEY'RE HERE.
SHOWTIME!

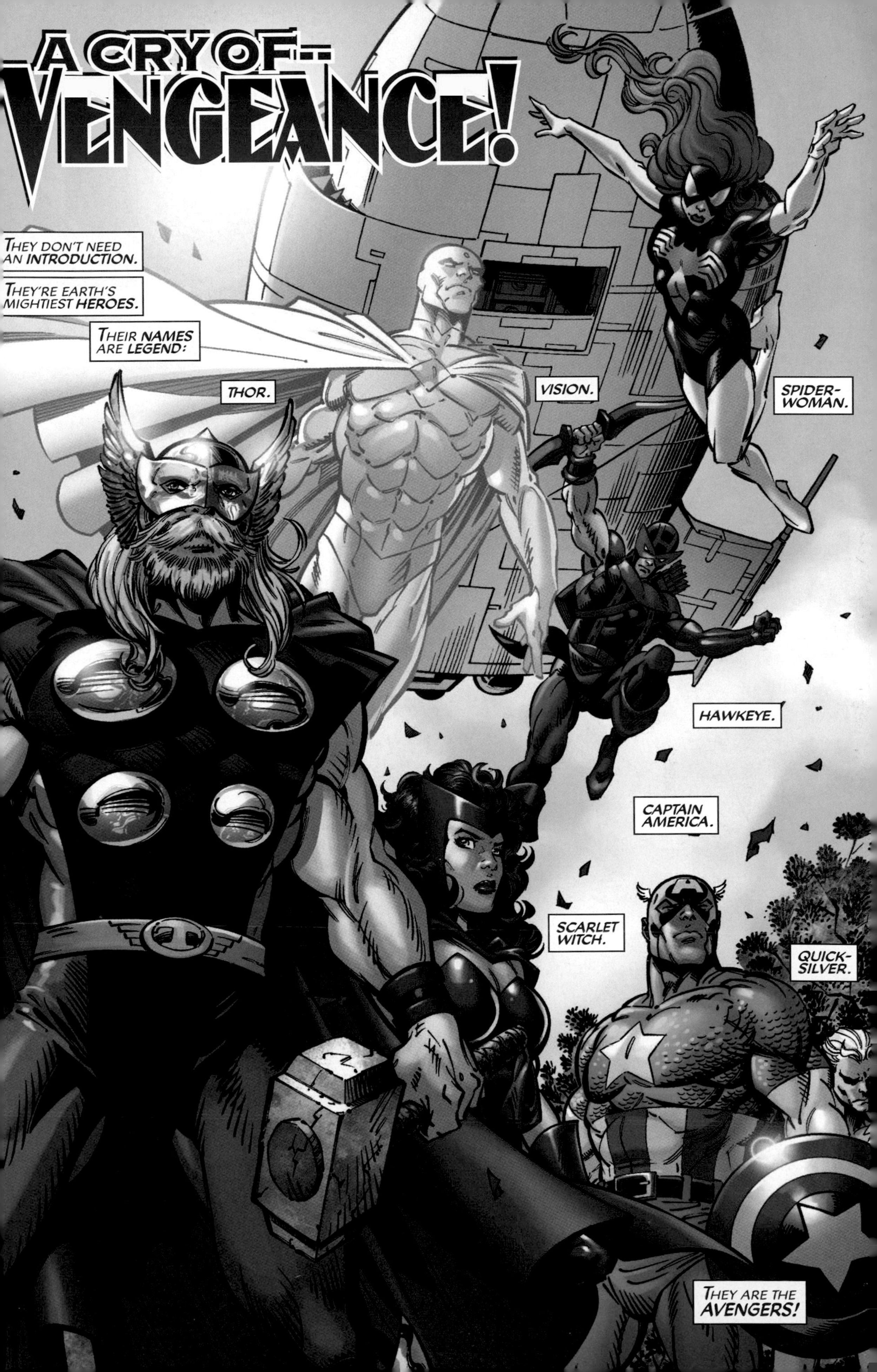
A CRY OF--
VENGEANCE!
THEY DON'T NEED AN INTRODUCTION.
THEY'RE EARTH'S MIGHTIEST HEROES.
THEIR NAMES ARE LEGEND:
THOR.
VISION.
SPIDER-WOMAN.
HAWKEYE.
CAPTAIN AMERICA.
SCARLET WITCH.
QUICK-SILVER.
THEY ARE THE AVENGERS!

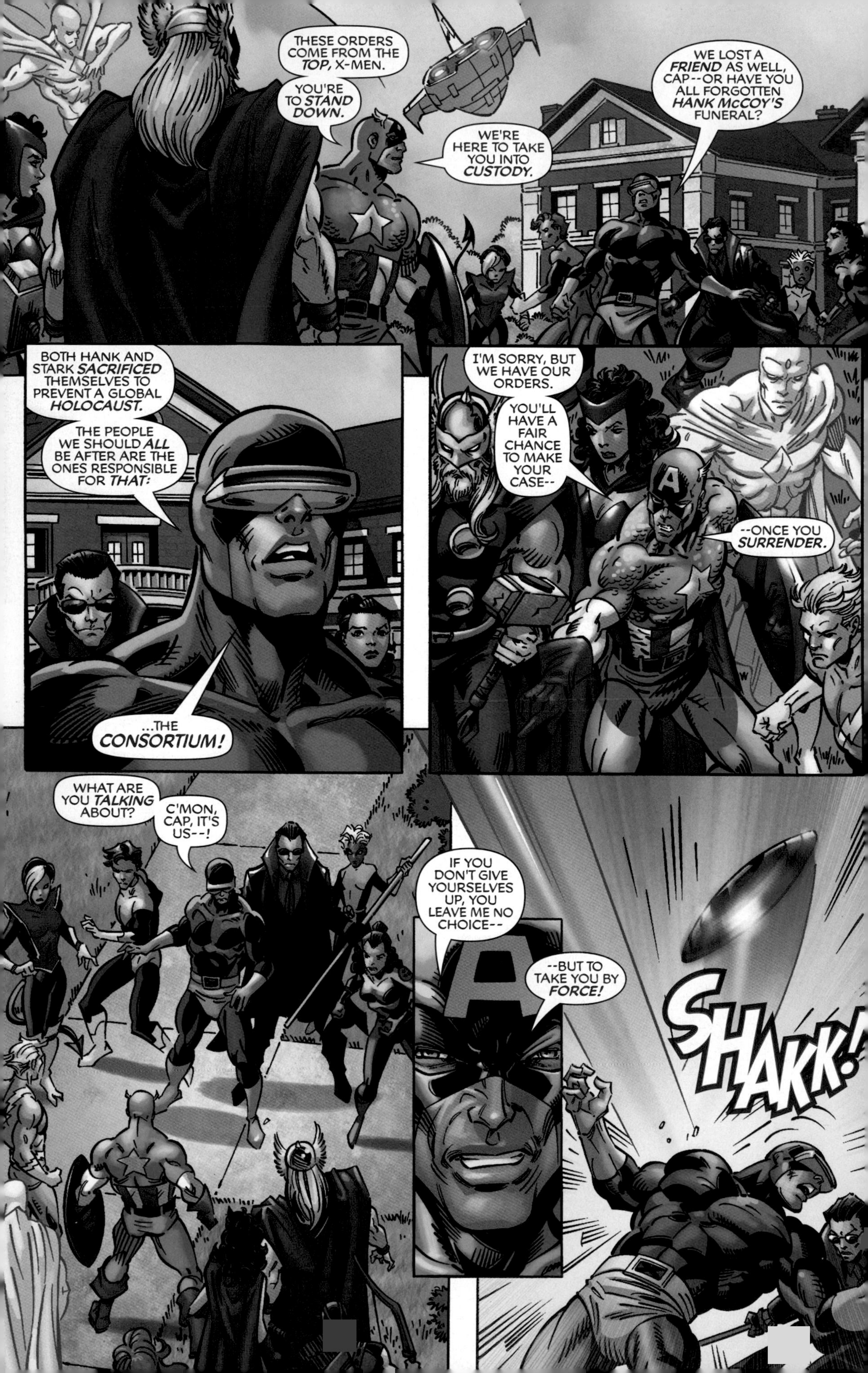
THESE ORDERS COME FROM THE TOP, X-MEN.
YOU'RE TO STAND DOWN.
WE'RE HERE TO TAKE YOU INTO CUSTODY.
WE LOST A FRIEND AS WELL, CAP--OR HAVE YOU ALL FORGOTTEN HANK McCOY'S FUNERAL?
BOTH HANK AND STARK SACRIFICED THEMSELVES TO PREVENT A GLOBAL HOLOCAUST.
THE PEOPLE WE SHOULD ALL BE AFTER ARE THE ONES RESPONSIBLE FOR THAT:
...THE CONSORTIUM!
I'M SORRY, BUT WE HAVE OUR ORDERS.
YOU'LL HAVE A FAIR CHANCE TO MAKE YOUR CASE--
--ONCE YOU SURRENDER.
WHAT ARE YOU TALKING ABOUT?
C'MON, CAP, IT'S US--!
IF YOU DON'T GIVE YOURSELVES UP, YOU LEAVE ME NO CHOICE--
--BUT TO TAKE YOU BY FORCE!
SHAKK!

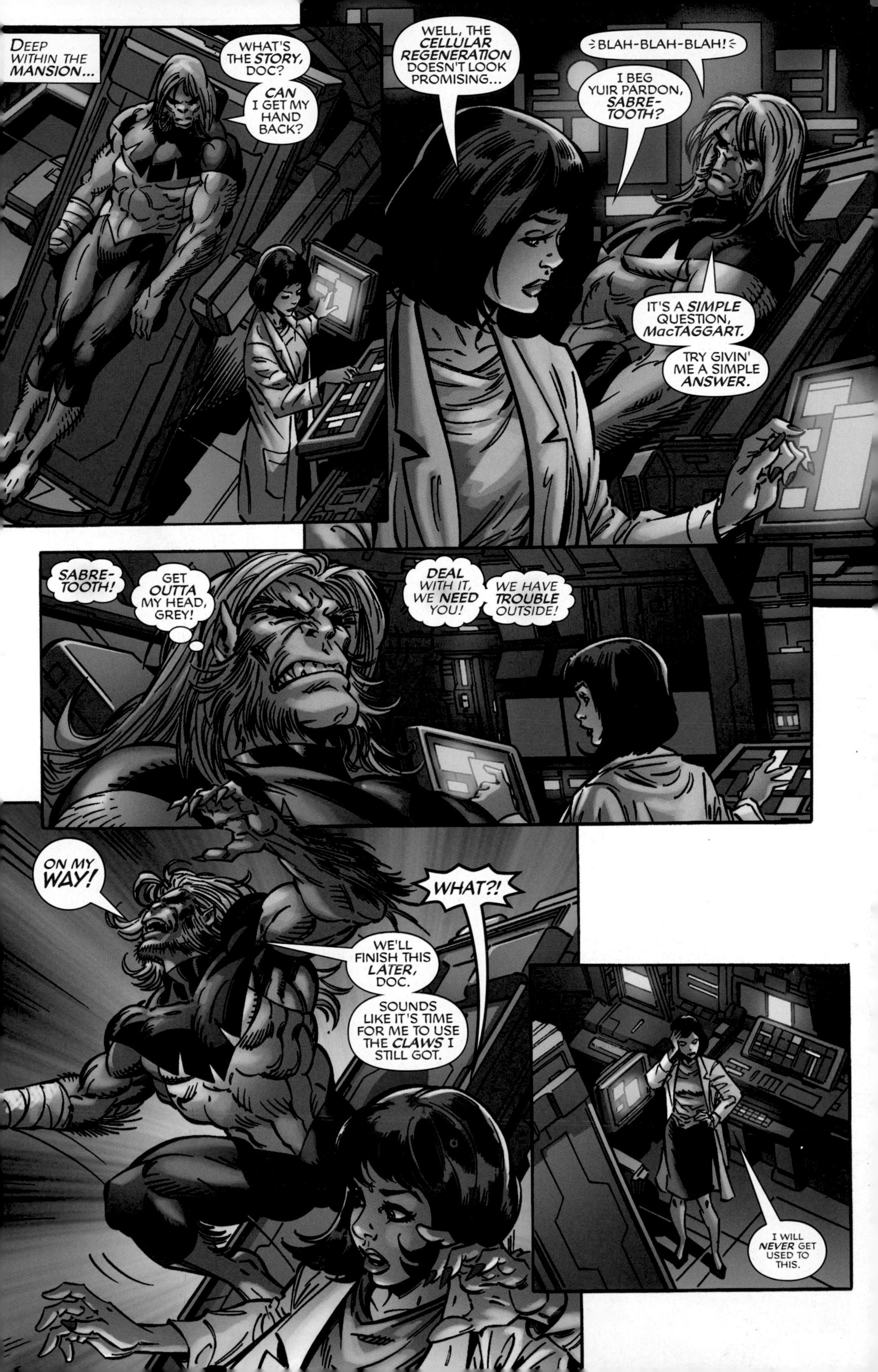
DEEP WITHIN THE MANSION...
WHAT'S THE STORY, DOC?
CAN I GET MY HAND BACK?
WELL, THE CELLULAR REGENERATION DOESN'T LOOK PROMISING...
BLAH-BLAH-BLAH!
I BEG YUIR PARDON, SABRE-TOOTH?
IT'S A SIMPLE QUESTION, MacTAGGART.
TRY GIVIN' ME A SIMPLE ANSWER.
SABRE-TOOTH!
GET OUTTA MY HEAD, GREY!
DEAL WITH IT, WE NEED YOU!
WE HAVE TROUBLE OUTSIDE!
ON MY WAY!
WHAT?!
WE'LL FINISH THIS LATER, DOC.
SOUNDS LIKE IT'S TIME FOR ME TO USE THE CLAWS I STILL GOT.
I WILL NEVER GET USED TO THIS.

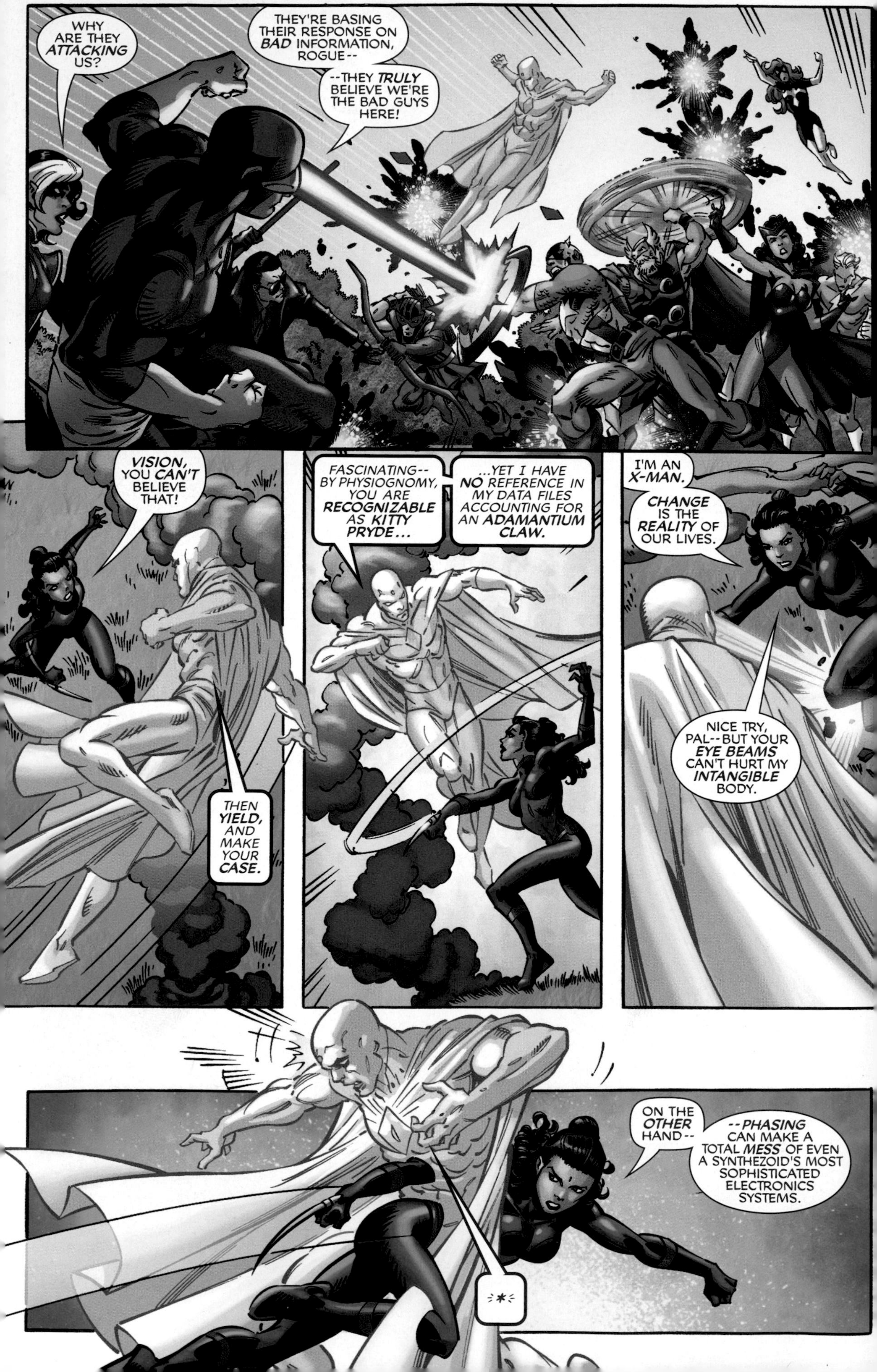
WHY ARE THEY ATTACKING US?
THEY'RE BASING THEIR RESPONSE ON BAD INFORMATION, ROGUE--
--THEY TRULY BELIEVE WE'RE THE BAD GUYS HERE!
VISION, YOU CAN'T BELIEVE THAT!
THEN YIELD, AND MAKE YOUR CASE.
FASCINATING-- BY PHYSIOGNOMY, YOU ARE RECOGNIZABLE AS KITTY PRYDE...
...YET I HAVE NO REFERENCE IN MY DATA FILES ACCOUNTING FOR AN ADAMANTIUM CLAW.
I'M AN X-MAN.
CHANGE IS THE REALITY OF OUR LIVES.
NICE TRY, PAL--BUT YOUR EYE BEAMS CAN'T HURT MY INTANGIBLE BODY.
ON THE OTHER HAND--
--PHASING CAN MAKE A TOTAL MESS OF EVEN A SYNTHEZOID'S MOST SOPHISTICATED ELECTRONICS SYSTEMS.
*

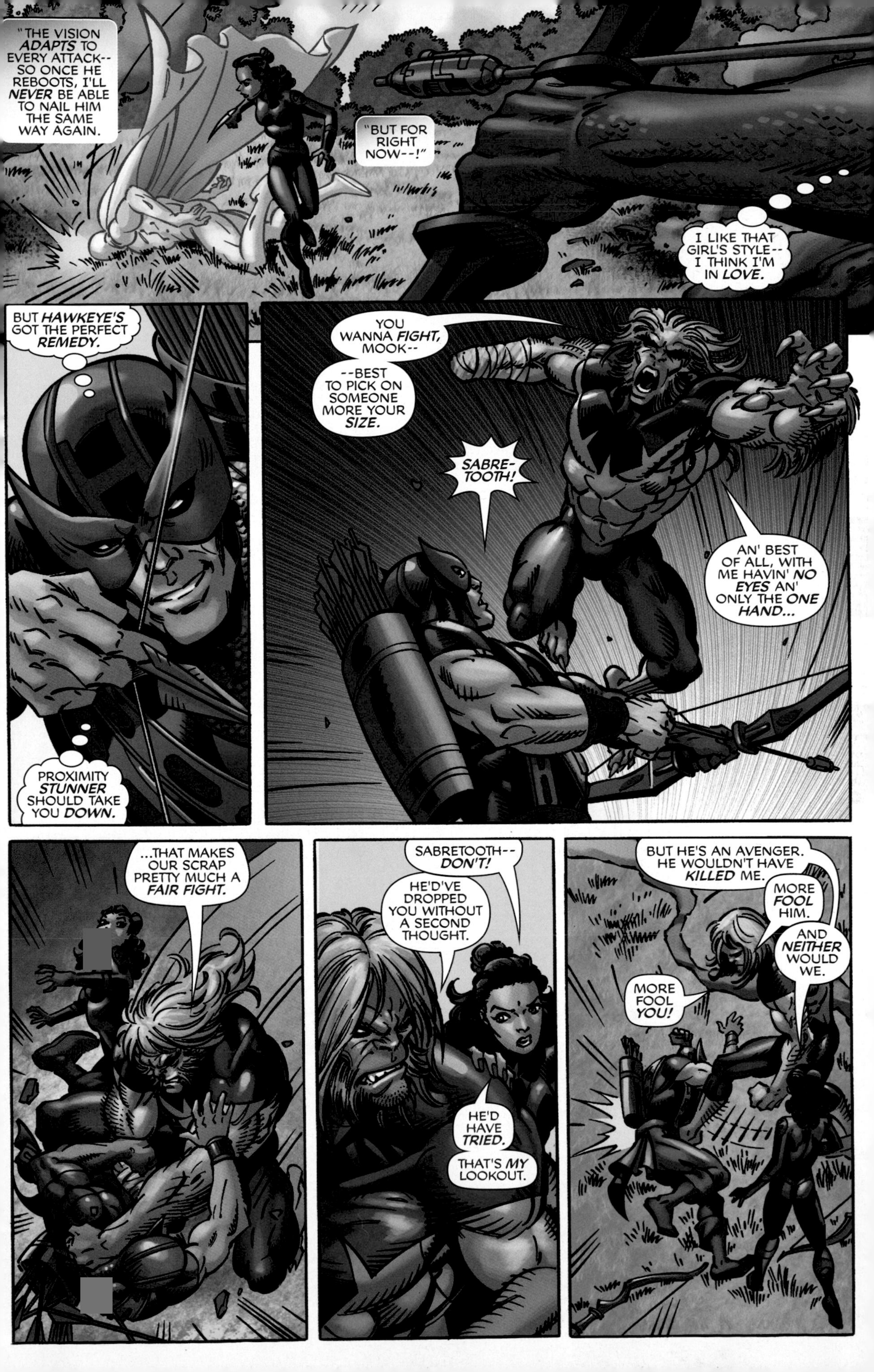
"THE VISION ADAPTS TO EVERY ATTACK-- SO ONCE HE REBOOTS, I'LL NEVER BE ABLE TO NAIL HIM THE SAME WAY AGAIN.
"BUT FOR RIGHT NOW--!"
I LIKE THAT GIRL'S STYLE-- I THINK I'M IN LOVE.
BUT HAWKEYE'S GOT THE PERFECT REMEDY.
PROXIMITY STUNNER SHOULD TAKE YOU DOWN.
YOU WANNA FIGHT, MOOK--
--BEST TO PICK ON SOMEONE MORE YOUR SIZE.
SABRE-TOOTH!
AN' BEST OF ALL, WITH ME HAVIN' NO EYES AN' ONLY THE ONE HAND...
...THAT MAKES OUR SCRAP PRETTY MUCH A FAIR FIGHT.
SABRETOOTH-- DON'T!
HE'D'VE DROPPED YOU WITHOUT A SECOND THOUGHT.
HE'D HAVE TRIED.
THAT'S MY LOOKOUT.
BUT HE'S AN AVENGER. HE WOULDN'T HAVE KILLED ME.
MORE FOOL HIM.
AND NEITHER WOULD WE.
MORE FOOL YOU!

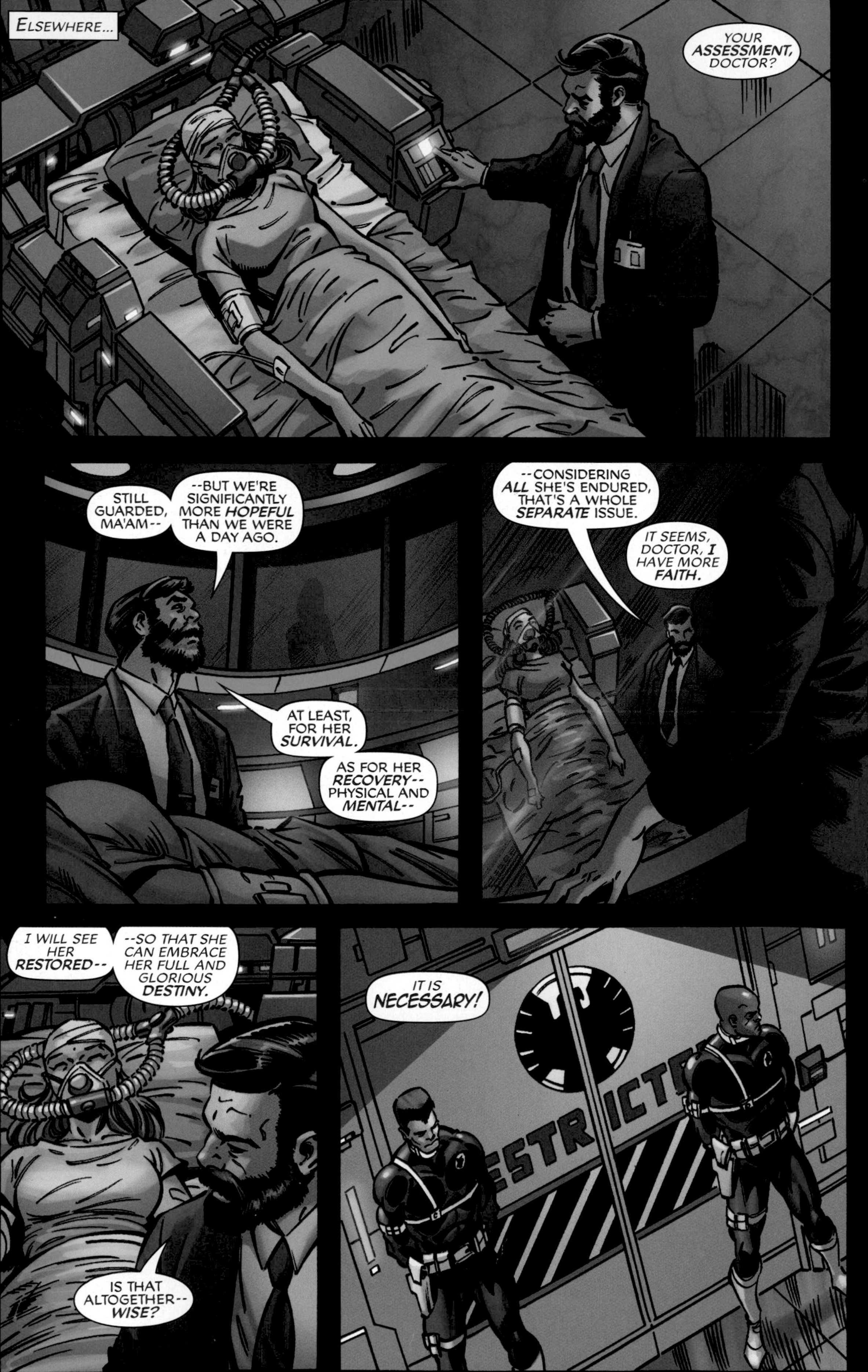
ELSEWHERE...
YOUR ASSESSMENT, DOCTOR?
STILL GUARDED, MA'AM--
--BUT WE'RE SIGNIFICANTLY MORE HOPEFUL THAN WE WERE A DAY AGO.
AT LEAST, FOR HER SURVIVAL.
AS FOR HER RECOVERY-- PHYSICAL AND MENTAL--
--CONSIDERING ALL SHE'S ENDURED, THAT'S A WHOLE SEPARATE ISSUE.
IT SEEMS, DOCTOR, I HAVE MORE FAITH.
I WILL SEE HER RESTORED--
--SO THAT SHE CAN EMBRACE HER FULL AND GLORIOUS DESTINY.
IS THAT ALTOGETHER-- WISE?
IT IS NECESSARY!

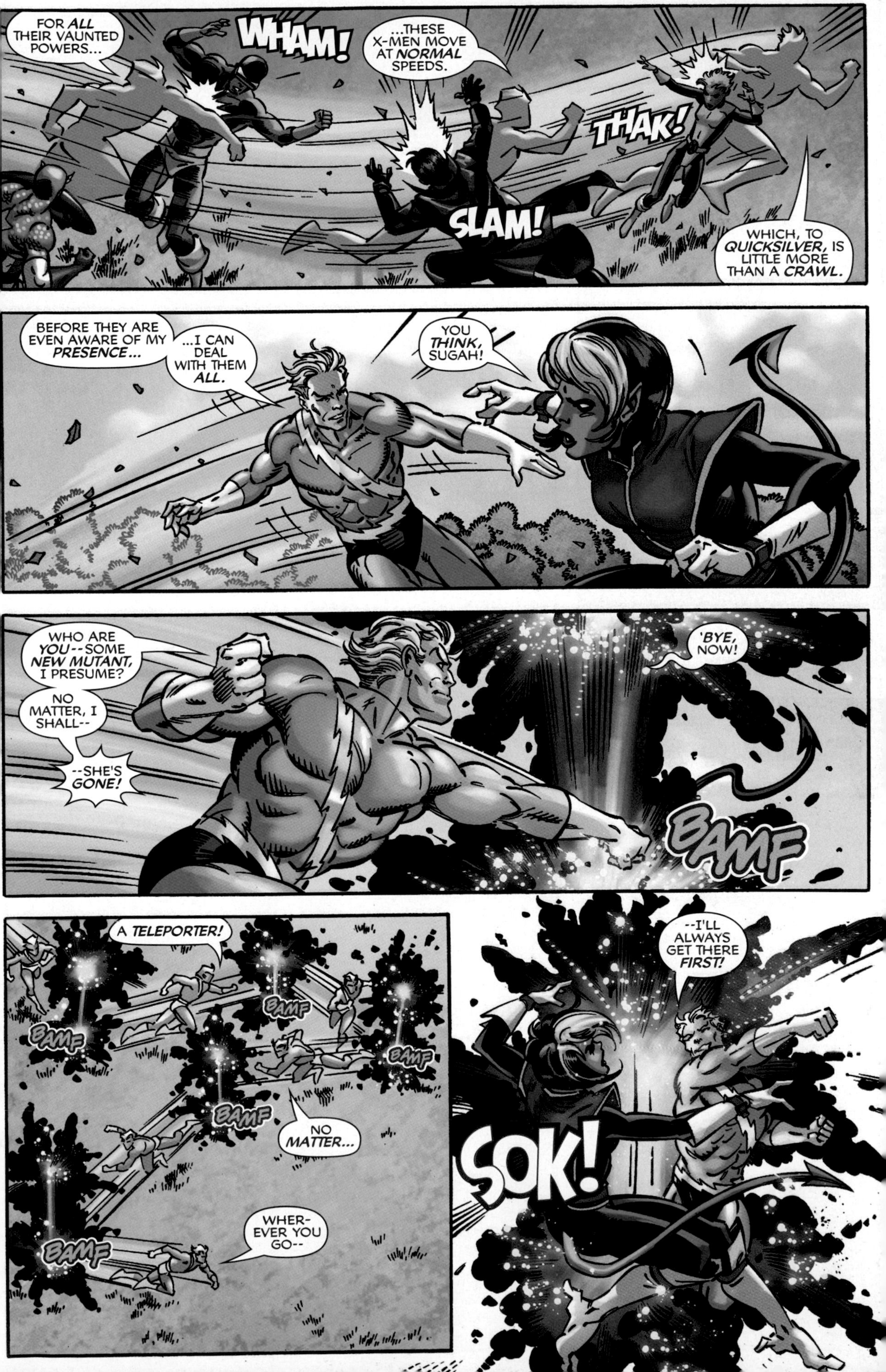

FOR ALL THEIR VAUNTED POWERS...
WHAM!
...THESE X-MEN MOVE AT NORMAL SPEEDS.
THAK!
SLAM!
WHICH, TO QUICKSILVER, IS LITTLE MORE THAN A CRAWL.
BEFORE THEY ARE EVEN AWARE OF MY PRESENCE...
...I CAN DEAL WITH THEM ALL.
YOU THINK, SUGAH!
WHO ARE YOU--SOME NEW MUTANT, I PRESUME?
NO MATTER, I SHALL--
--SHE'S GONE!
'BYE, NOW!
BAMF
A TELEPORTER!
BAMF
BAMF
BAMF
BAMF
BAMF
NO MATTER...
WHER-EVER YOU GO--
--I'LL ALWAYS GET THERE FIRST!
SOK!

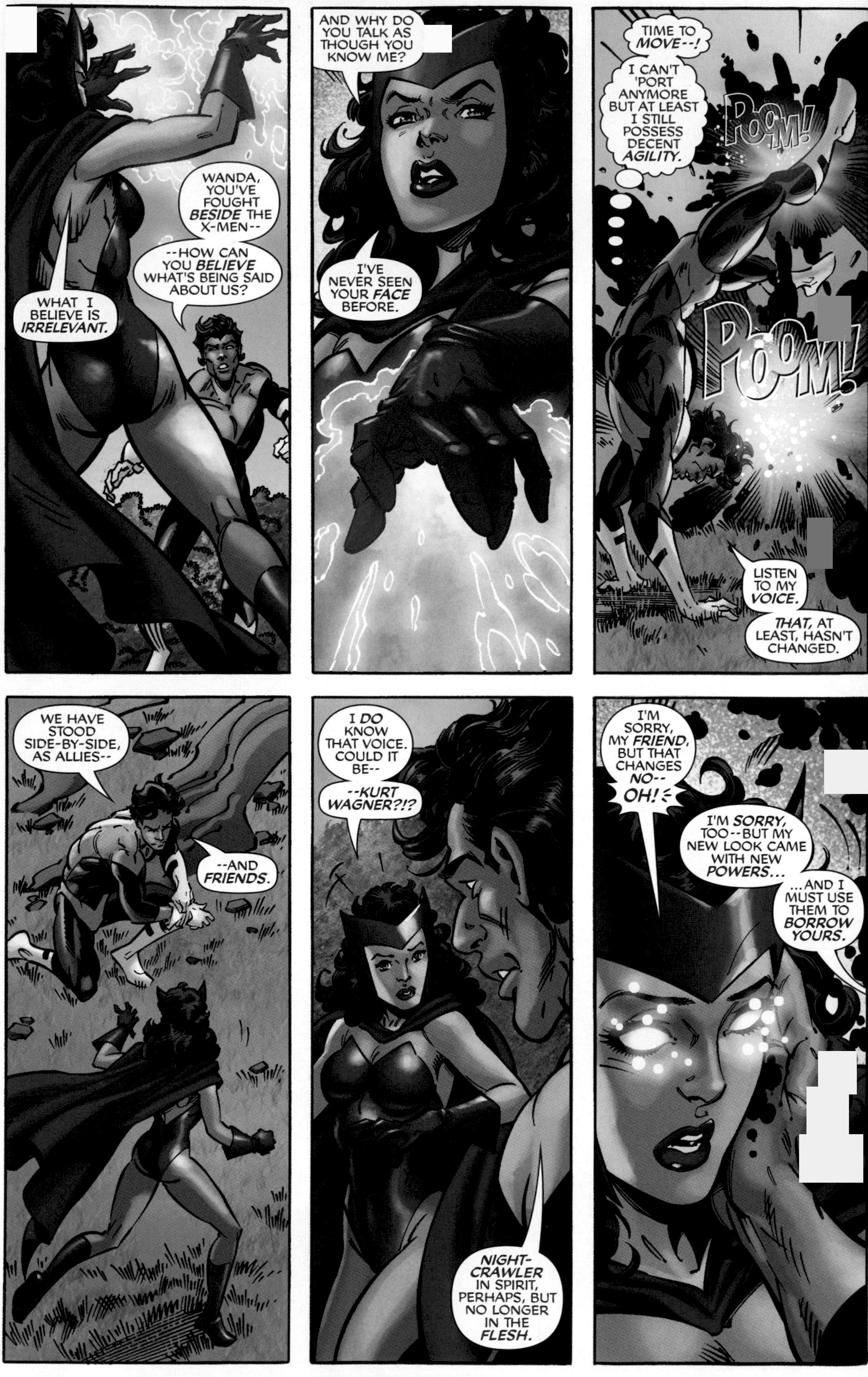
WANDA, YOU'VE FOUGHT BESIDE THE X-MEN--
--HOW CAN YOU BELIEVE WHAT'S BEING SAID ABOUT US?
WHAT I BELIEVE IS IRRELEVANT.
AND WHY DO YOU TALK AS THOUGH YOU KNOW ME?
I'VE NEVER SEEN YOUR FACE BEFORE.
TIME TO MOVE--!
I CAN'T 'PORT ANYMORE BUT AT LEAST I STILL POSSESS DECENT AGILITY.
POOM!
POOOM!
LISTEN TO MY VOICE.
THAT, AT LEAST, HASN'T CHANGED.
WE HAVE STOOD SIDE-BY-SIDE, AS ALLIES--
--AND FRIENDS.
I DO KNOW THAT VOICE. COULD IT BE--
--KURT WAGNER?!?
NIGHT-CRAWLER IN SPIRIT, PERHAPS, BUT NO LONGER IN THE FLESH.
I'M SORRY, MY FRIEND, BUT THAT CHANGES NO-- OH!
I'M SORRY, TOO--BUT MY NEW LOOK CAME WITH NEW POWERS...
...AND I MUST USE THEM TO BORROW YOURS.

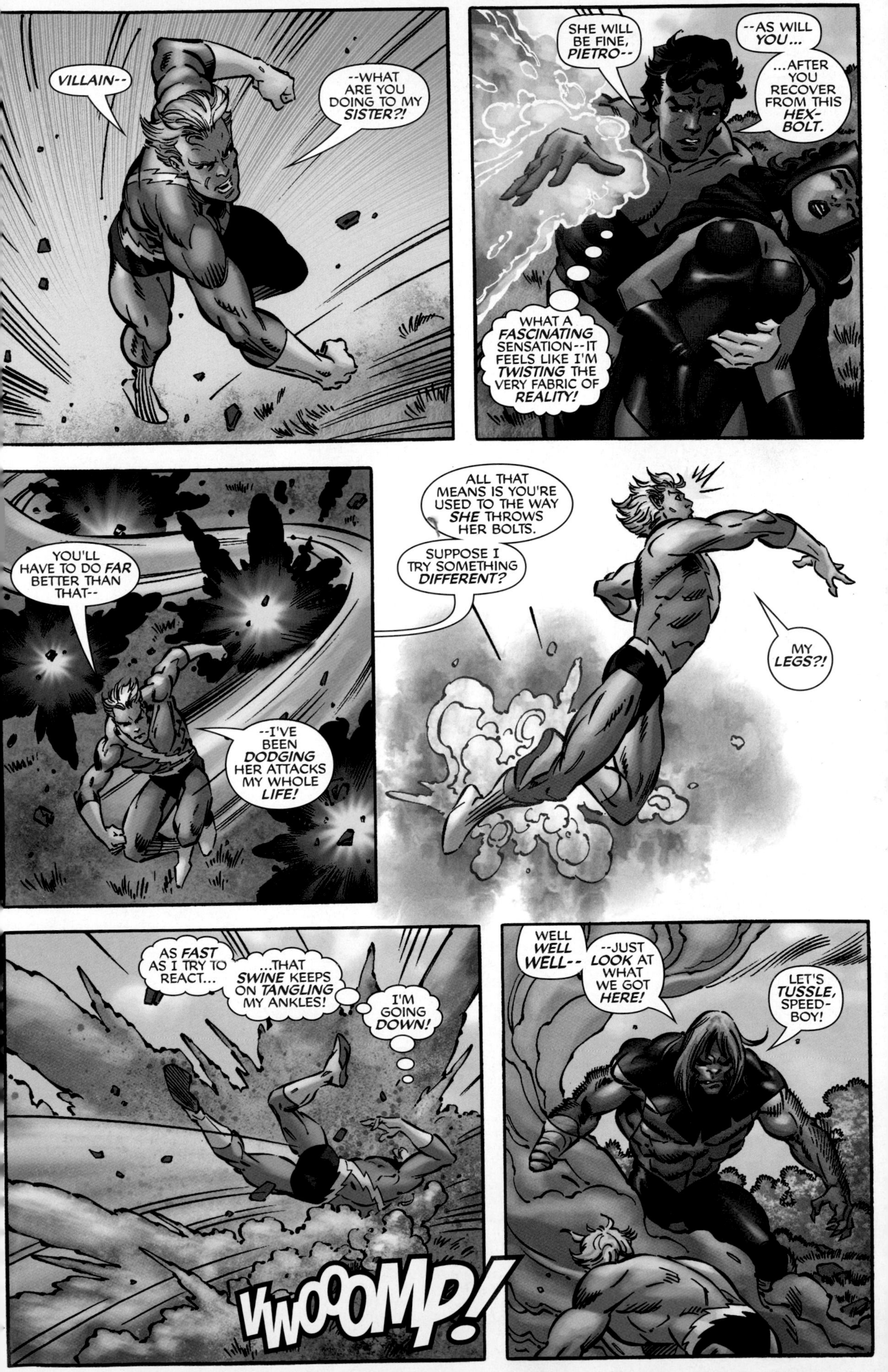
VILLAIN--
--WHAT ARE YOU DOING TO MY SISTER?!
SHE WILL BE FINE, PIETRO--
--AS WILL YOU...
...AFTER YOU RECOVER FROM THIS HEX-BOLT.
WHAT A FASCINATING SENSATION--IT FEELS LIKE I'M TWISTING THE VERY FABRIC OF REALITY!
YOU'LL HAVE TO DO FAR BETTER THAN THAT--
--I'VE BEEN DODGING HER ATTACKS MY WHOLE LIFE!
ALL THAT MEANS IS YOU'RE USED TO THE WAY SHE THROWS HER BOLTS.
SUPPOSE I TRY SOMETHING DIFFERENT?
MY LEGS?!
AS FAST AS I TRY TO REACT...
...THAT SWINE KEEPS ON TANGLING MY ANKLES!
I'M GOING DOWN!
VWOOOMP!
WELL WELL WELL--
--JUST LOOK AT WHAT WE GOT HERE!
LET'S TUSSLE, SPEED-BOY!

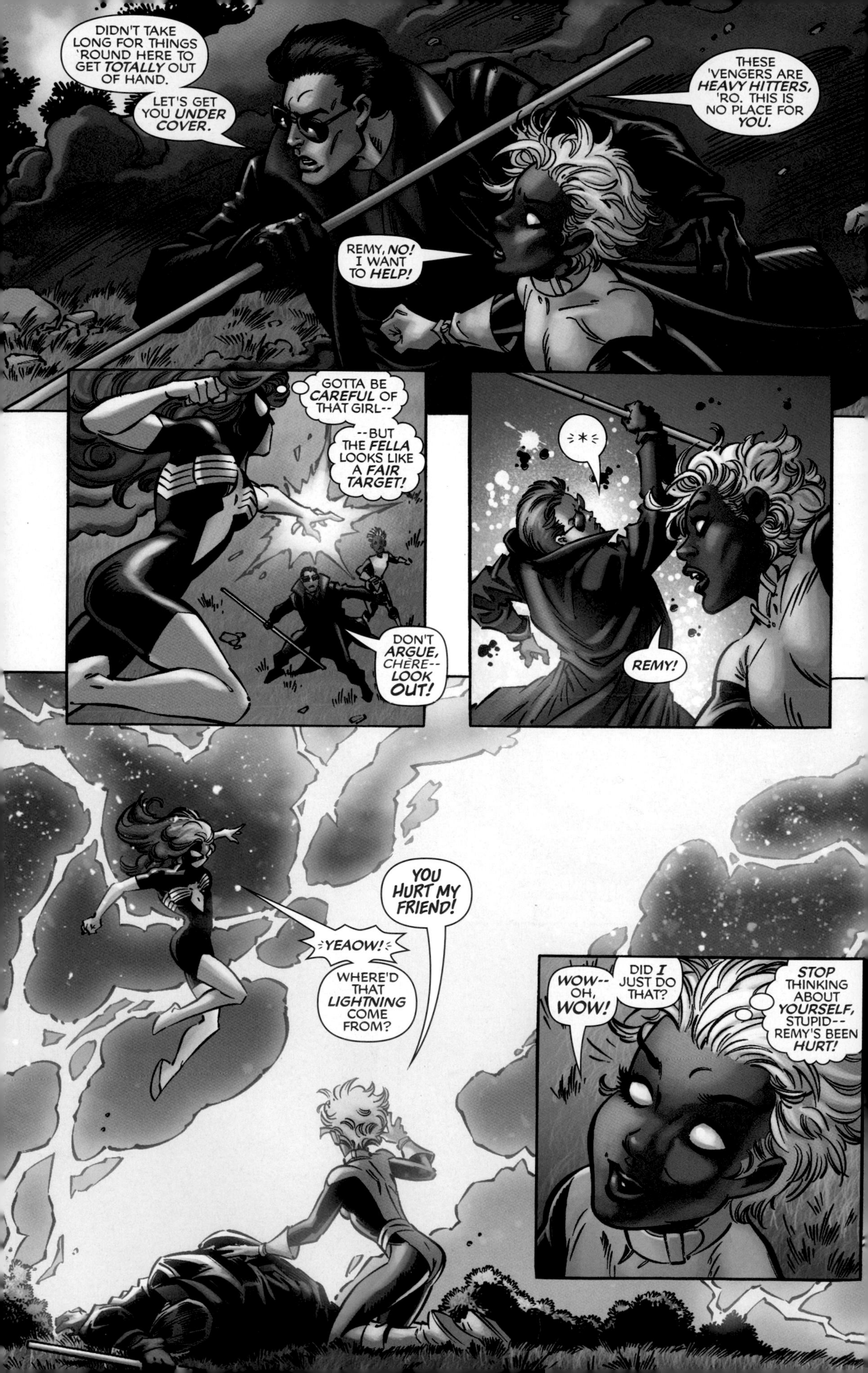

DIDN'T TAKE LONG FOR THINGS 'ROUND HERE TO GET TOTALLY OUT OF HAND.
LET'S GET YOU UNDER COVER.
THESE 'VENGERS ARE HEAVY HITTERS, 'RO. THIS IS NO PLACE FOR YOU.
REMY, NO! I WANT TO HELP!
GOTTA BE CAREFUL OF THAT GIRL--
--BUT THE FELLA LOOKS LIKE A FAIR TARGET!
DON'T ARGUE, CHÈRE-- LOOK OUT!
REMY!
YOU HURT MY FRIEND!
YEAOW!
WHERE'D THAT LIGHTNING COME FROM?
WOW-- OH, WOW!
DID I JUST DO THAT?
STOP THINKING ABOUT YOURSELF, STUPID-- REMY'S BEEN HURT!

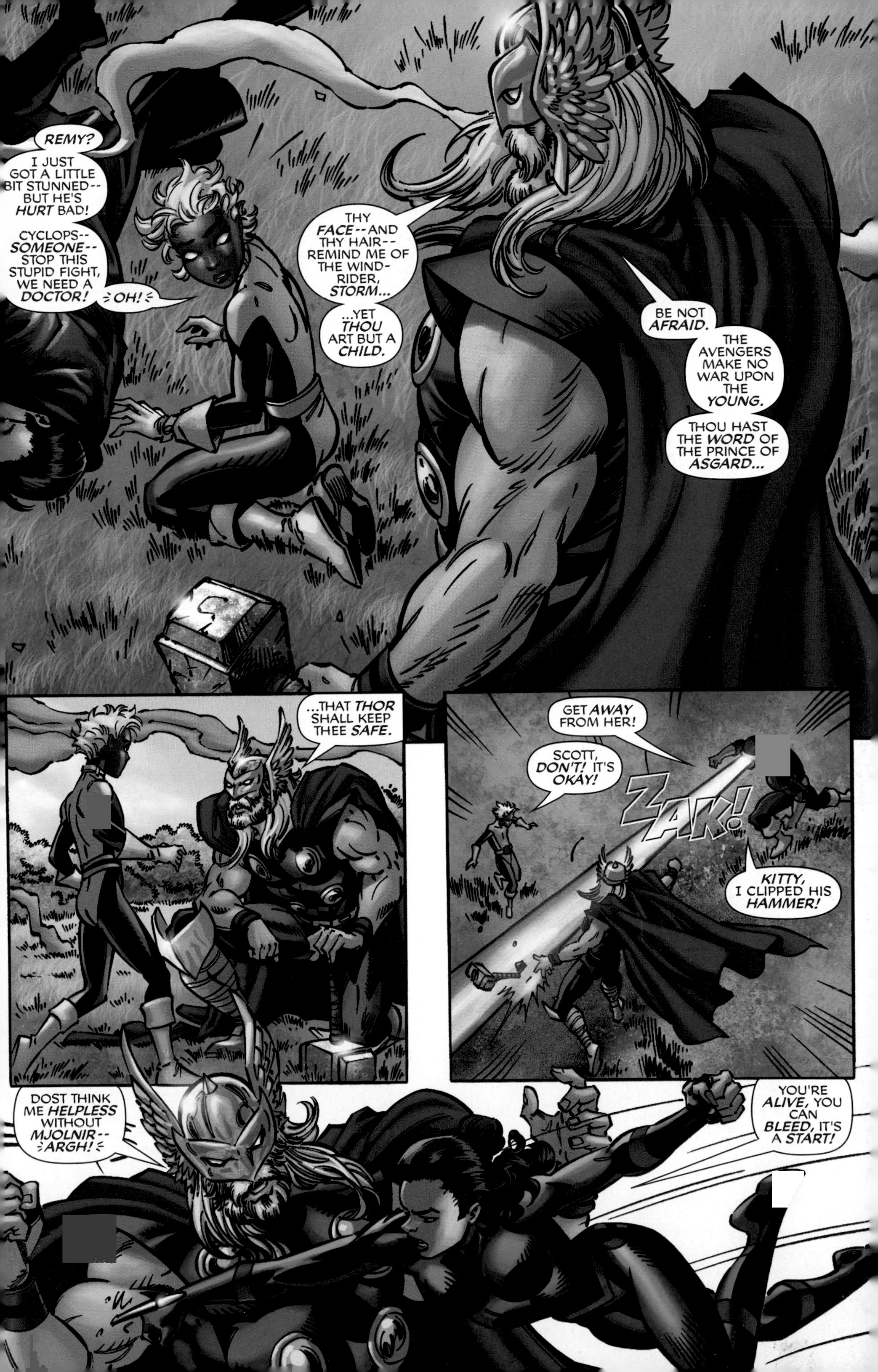
REMY?
I JUST GOT A LITTLE BIT STUNNED-- BUT HE'S HURT BAD!
CYCLOPS-- SOMEONE-- STOP THIS STUPID FIGHT, WE NEED A DOCTOR!
OH!
THY FACE--AND THY HAIR-- REMIND ME OF THE WIND-RIDER, STORM...
...YET THOU ART BUT A CHILD.
BE NOT AFRAID.
THE AVENGERS MAKE NO WAR UPON THE YOUNG.
THOU HAST THE WORD OF THE PRINCE OF ASGARD...
...THAT THOR SHALL KEEP THEE SAFE.
GET AWAY FROM HER!
SCOTT, DON'T! IT'S OKAY!
ZAK!
KITTY, I CLIPPED HIS HAMMER!
DOST THINK ME HELPLESS WITHOUT MJOLNIR-- ARGH!
YOU'RE ALIVE, YOU CAN BLEED, IT'S A START!

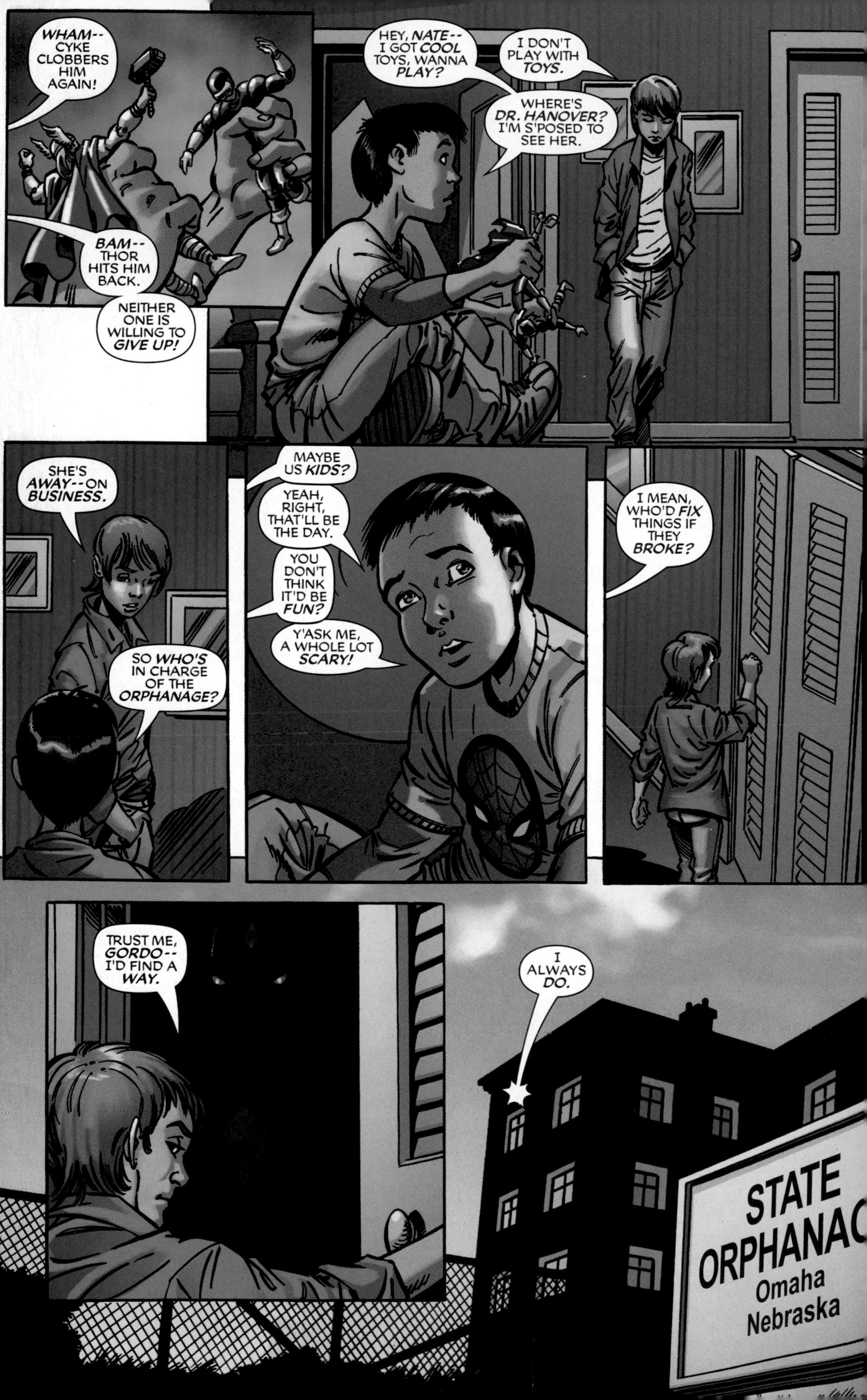
WHAM-- CYKE CLOBBERS HIM AGAIN!
BAM-- THOR HITS HIM BACK.
NEITHER ONE IS WILLING TO GIVE UP!
HEY, NATE-- I GOT COOL TOYS, WANNA PLAY?
I DON'T PLAY WITH TOYS.
WHERE'S DR. HANOVER? I'M S'POSED TO SEE HER.
SHE'S AWAY--ON BUSINESS.
SO WHO'S IN CHARGE OF THE ORPHANAGE?
MAYBE US KIDS?
YEAH, RIGHT, THAT'LL BE THE DAY.
YOU DON'T THINK IT'D BE FUN?
Y'ASK ME, A WHOLE LOT SCARY!
I MEAN, WHO'D FIX THINGS IF THEY BROKE?
TRUST ME, GORDO-- I'D FIND A WAY.
I ALWAYS DO.
STATE ORPHANAG
Omaha
Nebraska

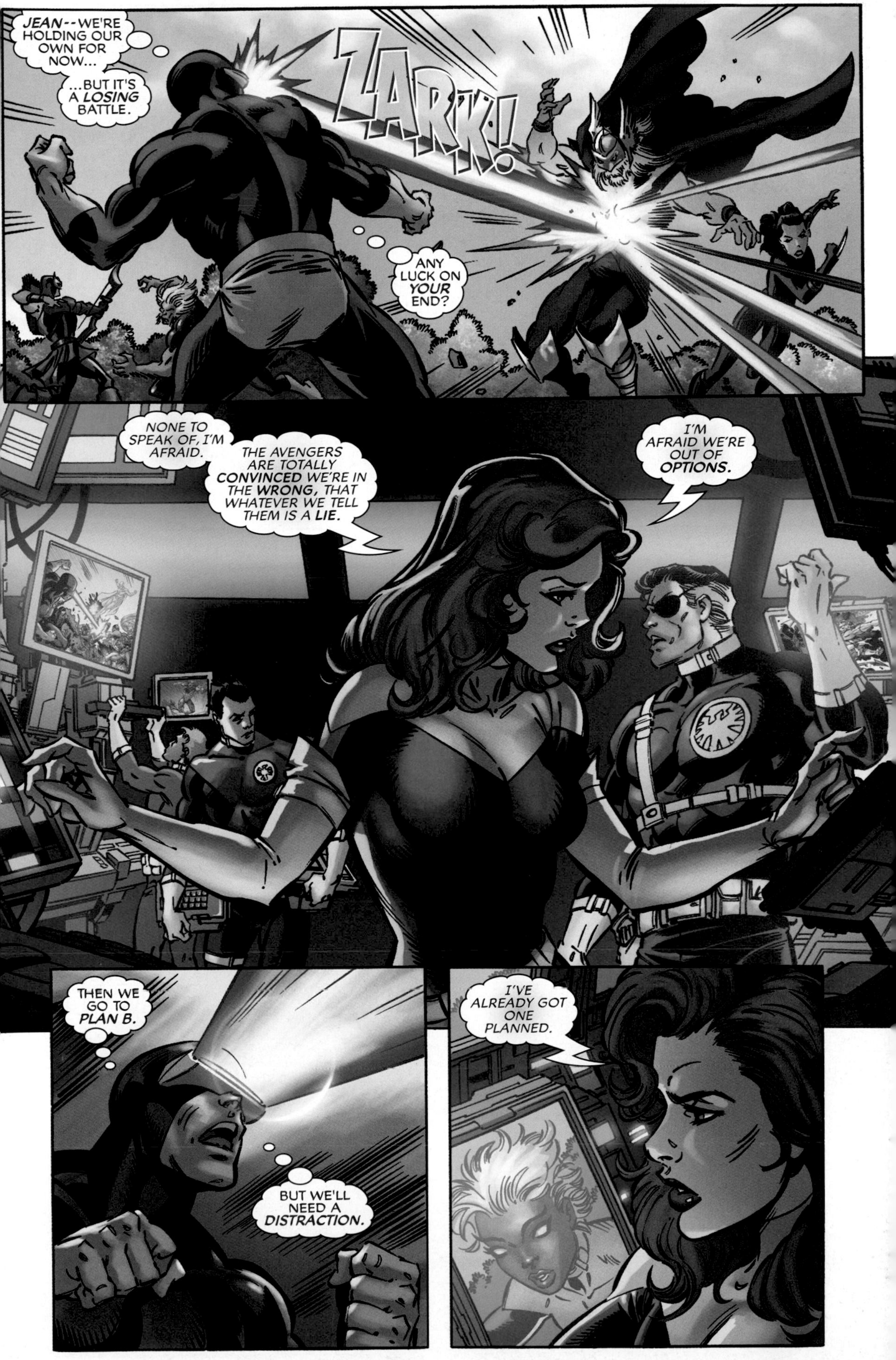
JEAN--WE'RE HOLDING OUR OWN FOR NOW...
...BUT IT'S A LOSING BATTLE.
ZARK!
ANY LUCK ON YOUR END?
NONE TO SPEAK OF, I'M AFRAID.
THE AVENGERS ARE TOTALLY CONVINCED WE'RE IN THE WRONG, THAT WHATEVER WE TELL THEM IS A LIE.
I'M AFRAID WE'RE OUT OF OPTIONS.
THEN WE GO TO PLAN B.
BUT WE'LL NEED A DISTRACTION.
I'VE ALREADY GOT ONE PLANNED.

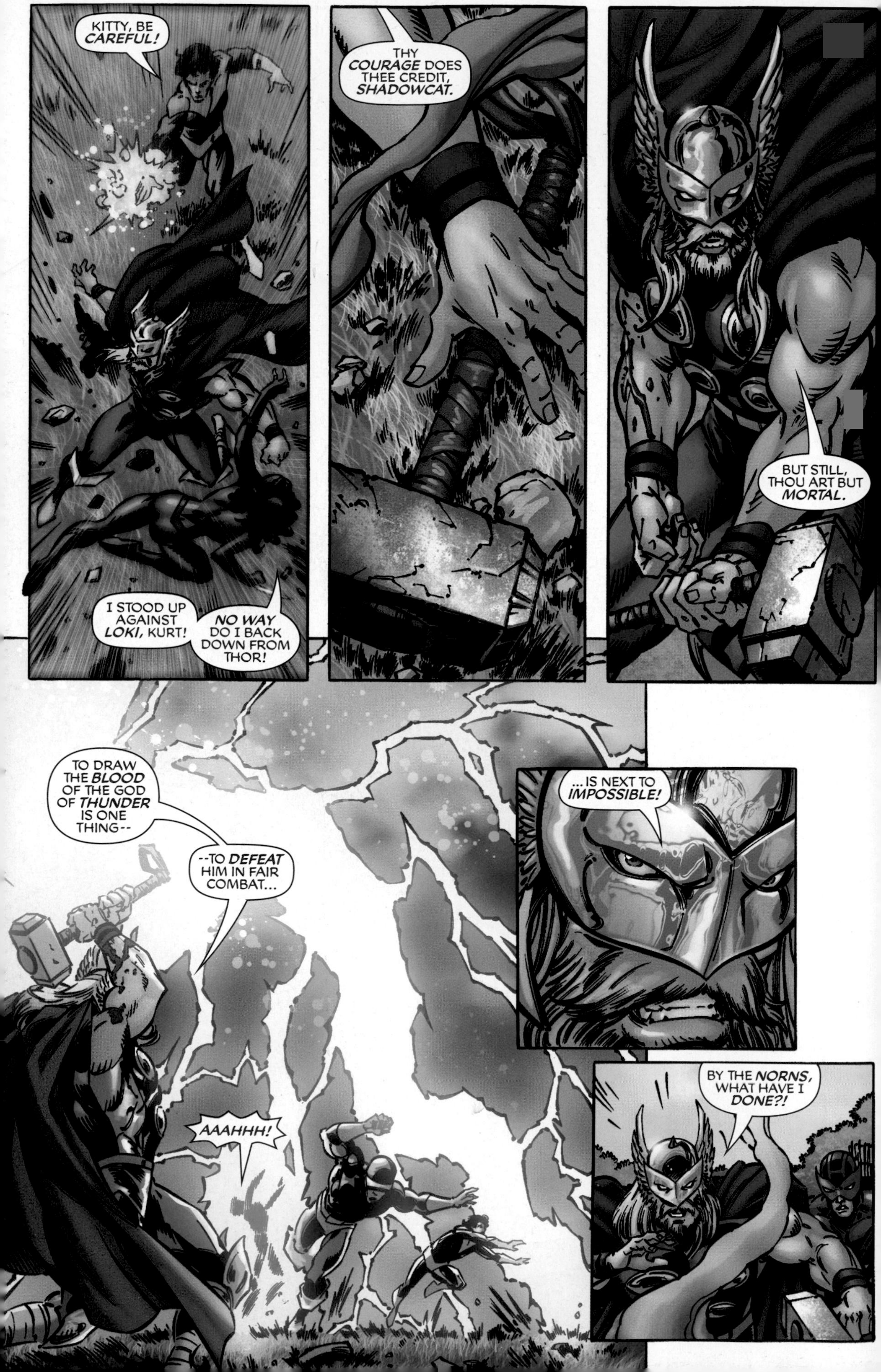
KITTY, BE CAREFUL!
I STOOD UP AGAINST LOKI, KURT!
NO WAY DO I BACK DOWN FROM THOR!
THY COURAGE DOES THEE CREDIT, SHADOWCAT.
BUT STILL, THOU ART BUT MORTAL.
TO DRAW THE BLOOD OF THE GOD OF THUNDER IS ONE THING--
--TO DEFEAT HIM IN FAIR COMBAT...
AAAHHH!
...IS NEXT TO IMPOSSIBLE!
BY THE NORNS, WHAT HAVE I DONE?!

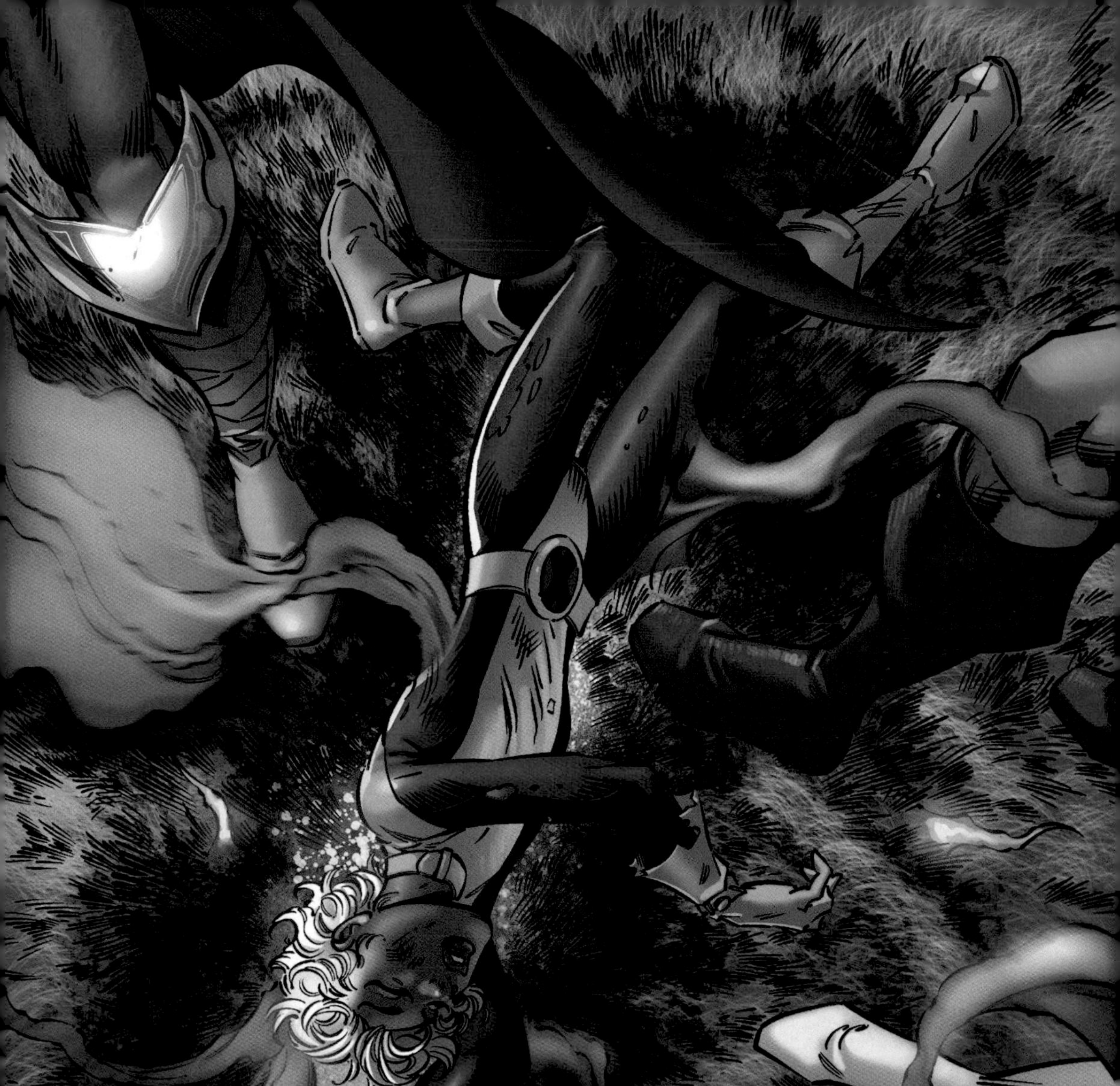
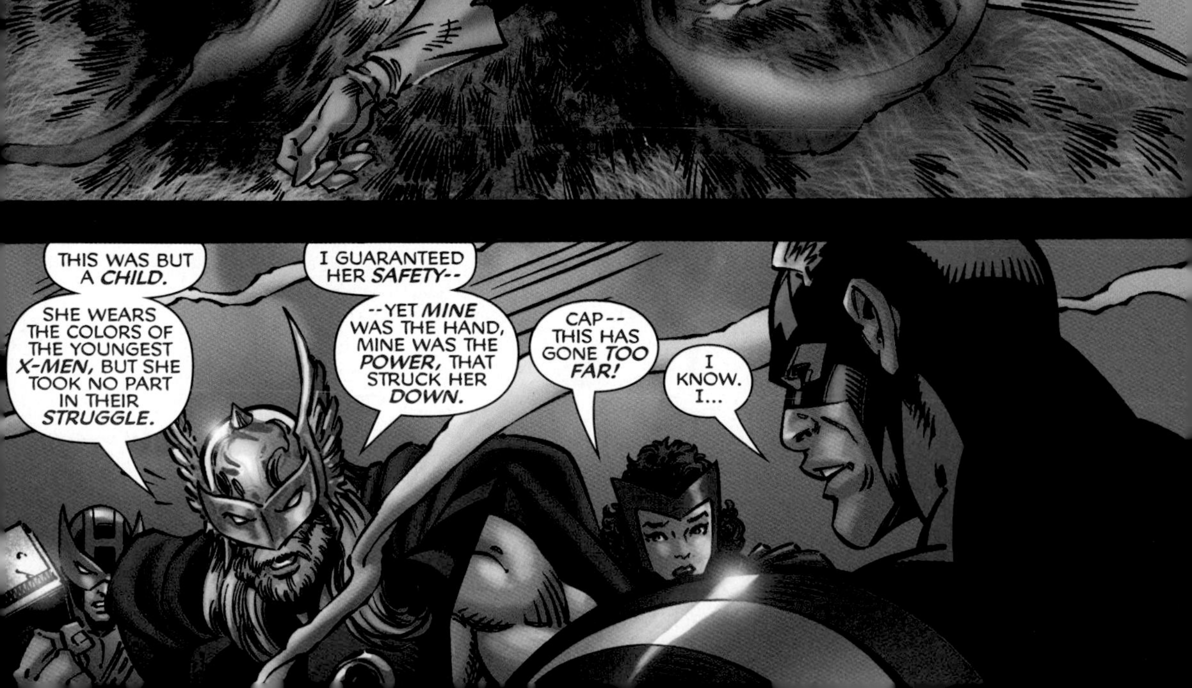
THIS WAS BUT A CHILD.
SHE WEARS THE COLORS OF THE YOUNGEST X-MEN, BUT SHE TOOK NO PART IN THEIR STRUGGLE.
I GUARANTEED HER SAFETY--
--YET MINE WAS THE HAND, MINE WAS THE POWER, THAT STRUCK HER DOWN.
CAP-- THIS HAS GONE TOO FAR!
I KNOW. I...

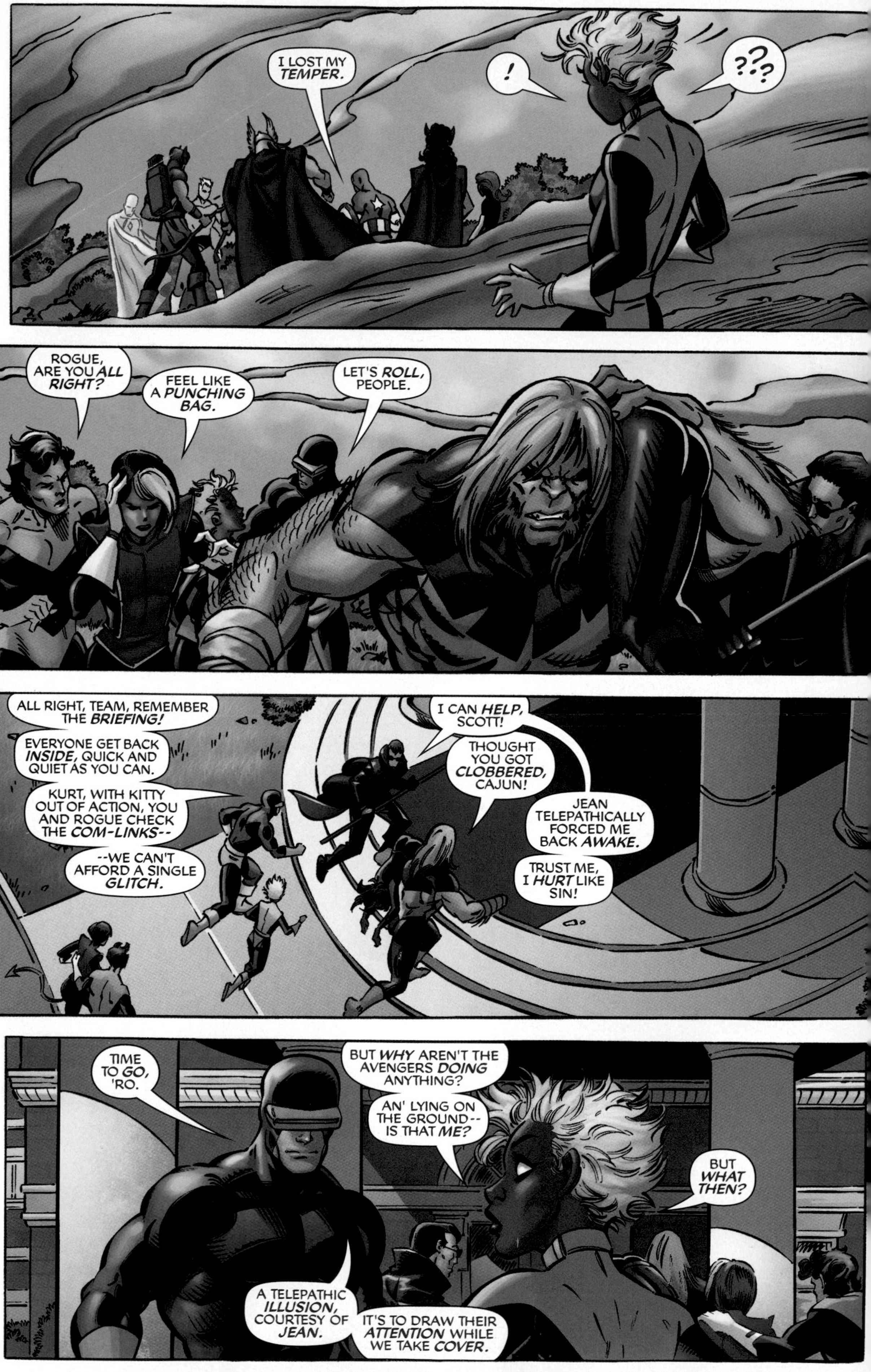
I LOST MY TEMPER.
!
???
ROGUE, ARE YOU ALL RIGHT?
FEEL LIKE A PUNCHING BAG.
LET'S ROLL, PEOPLE.
ALL RIGHT, TEAM, REMEMBER THE BRIEFING!
EVERYONE GET BACK INSIDE, QUICK AND QUIET AS YOU CAN.
KURT, WITH KITTY OUT OF ACTION, YOU AND ROGUE CHECK THE COM-LINKS--
--WE CAN'T AFFORD A SINGLE GLITCH.
I CAN HELP, SCOTT!
THOUGHT YOU GOT CLOBBERED, CAJUN!
JEAN TELEPATHICALLY FORCED ME BACK AWAKE.
TRUST ME, I HURT LIKE SIN!
TIME TO GO, 'RO.
BUT WHY AREN'T THE AVENGERS DOING ANYTHING?
AN' LYING ON THE GROUND-- IS THAT ME?
A TELEPATHIC ILLUSION, COURTESY OF JEAN.
IT'S TO DRAW THEIR ATTENTION WHILE WE TAKE COVER.
BUT WHAT THEN?

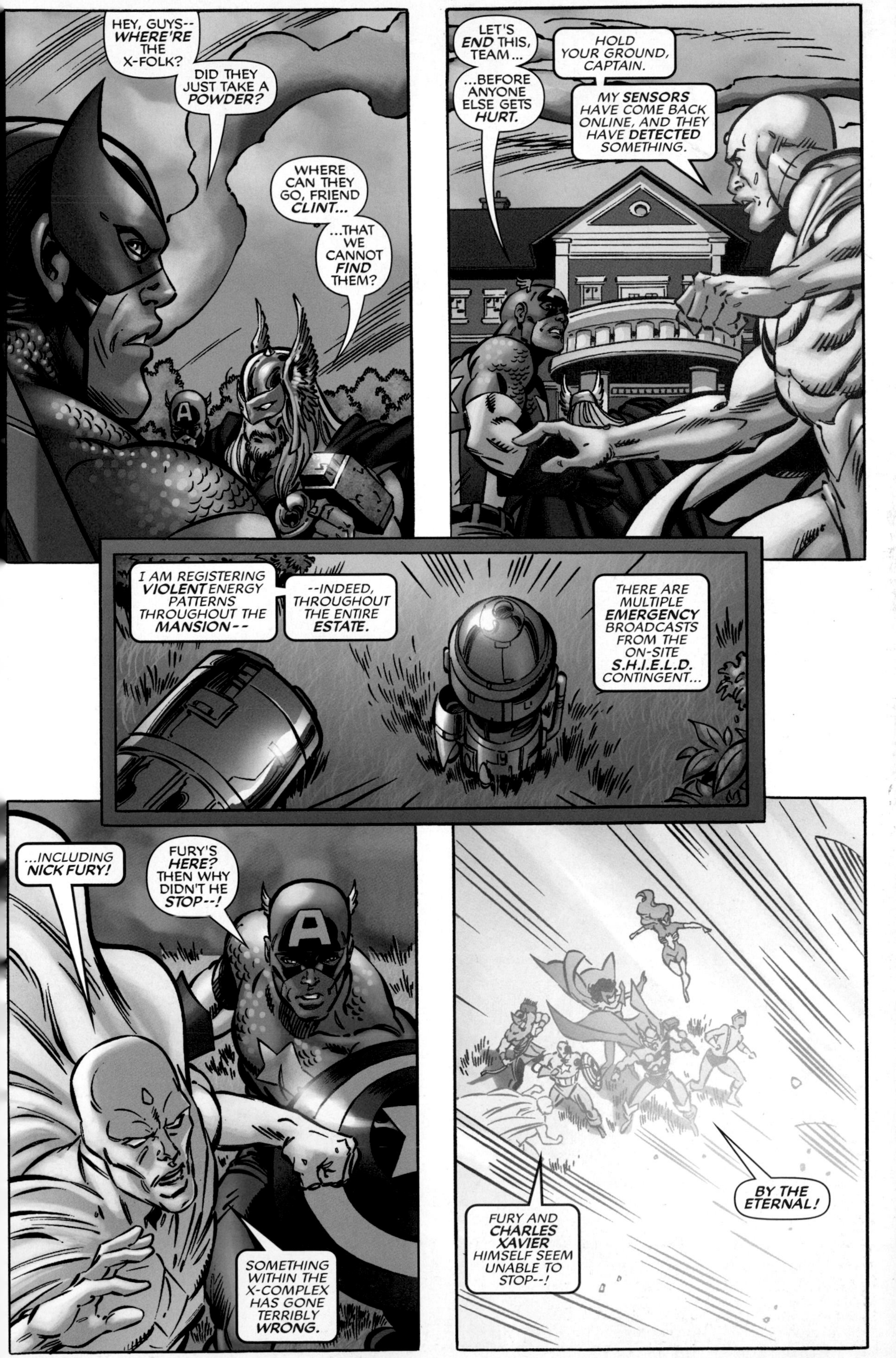
HEY, GUYS-- WHERE'RE THE X-FOLK?
DID THEY JUST TAKE A POWDER?
WHERE CAN THEY GO, FRIEND CLINT...
...THAT WE CANNOT FIND THEM?
LET'S END THIS, TEAM...
...BEFORE ANYONE ELSE GETS HURT.
HOLD YOUR GROUND, CAPTAIN.
MY SENSORS HAVE COME BACK ONLINE, AND THEY HAVE DETECTED SOMETHING.
I AM REGISTERING VIOLENT ENERGY PATTERNS THROUGHOUT THE MANSION--
--INDEED, THROUGHOUT THE ENTIRE ESTATE.
THERE ARE MULTIPLE EMERGENCY BROADCASTS FROM THE ON-SITE S.H.I.E.L.D. CONTINGENT...
...INCLUDING NICK FURY!
FURY'S HERE? THEN WHY DIDN'T HE STOP--!
SOMETHING WITHIN THE X-COMPLEX HAS GONE TERRIBLY WRONG.
FURY AND CHARLES XAVIER HIMSELF SEEM UNABLE TO STOP--!
BY THE ETERNAL!

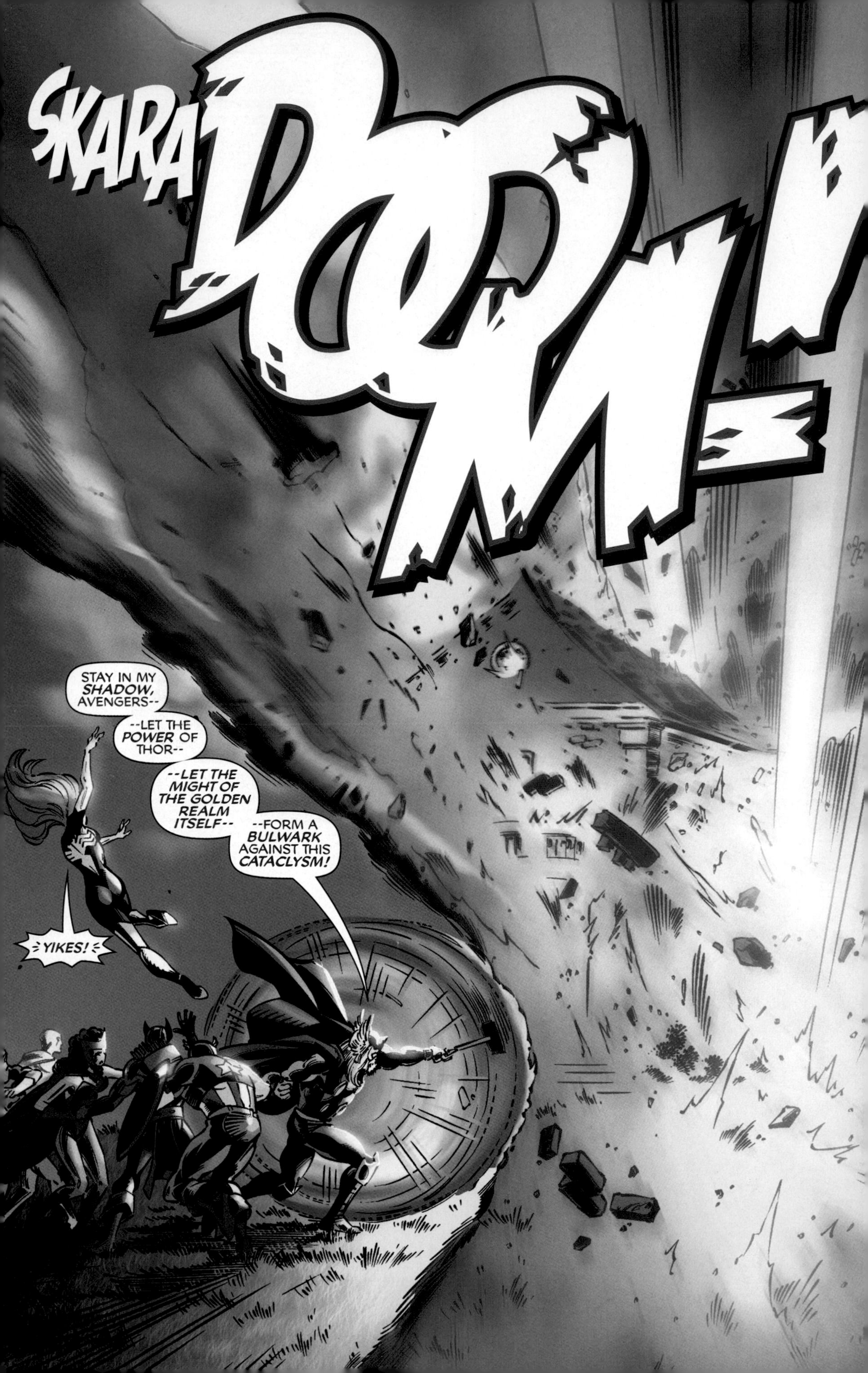
SKARA-DOOM!
STAY IN MY SHADOW, AVENGERS--
--LET THE POWER OF THOR--
--LET THE MIGHT OF THE GOLDEN REALM ITSELF--
--FORM A BULWARK AGAINST THIS CATACLYSM!
YIKES!

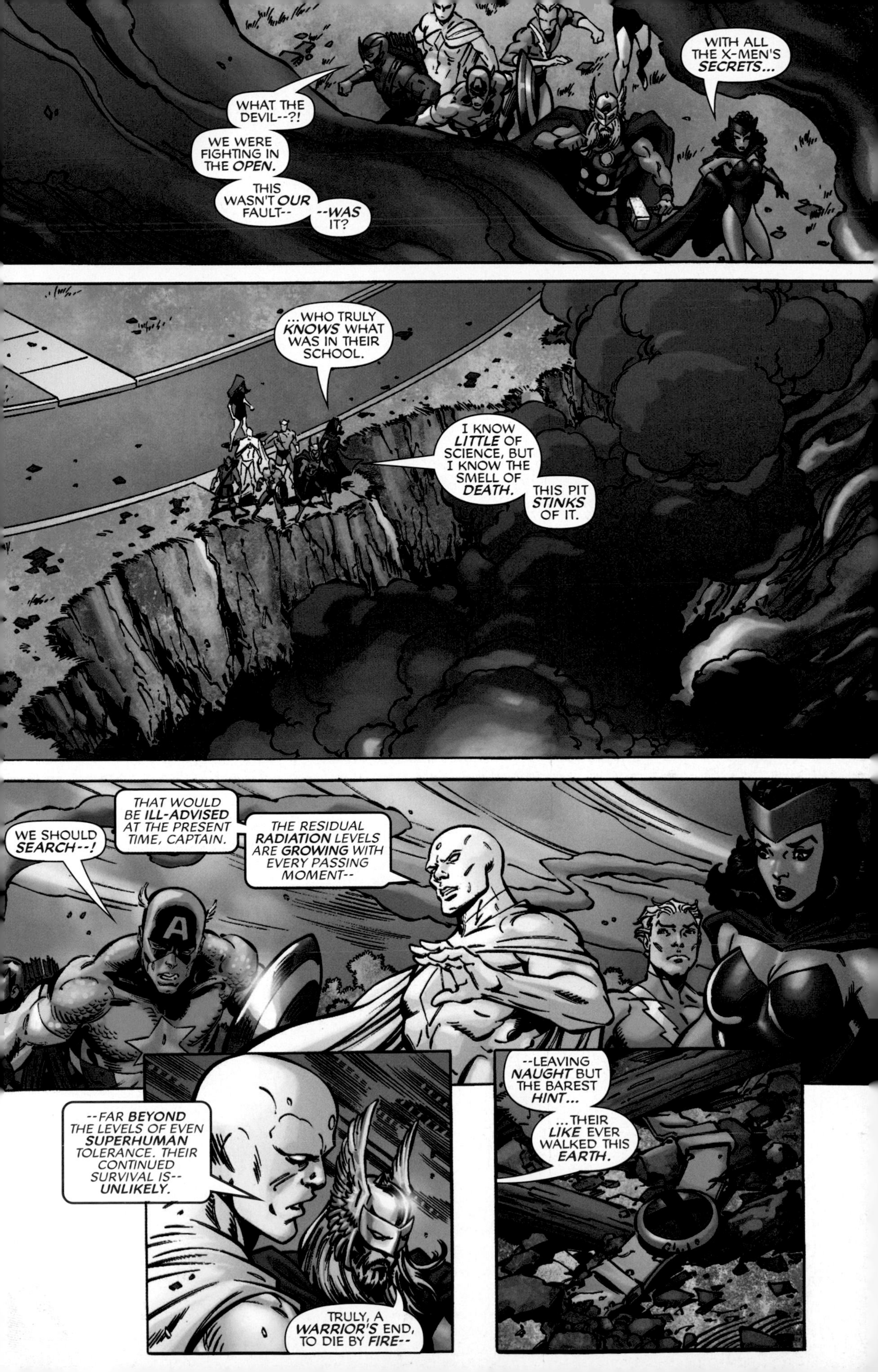
WHAT THE DEVIL--?!
WE WERE FIGHTING IN THE OPEN.
THIS WASN'T OUR FAULT--
--WAS IT?
WITH ALL THE X-MEN'S SECRETS...
...WHO TRULY KNOWS WHAT WAS IN THEIR SCHOOL.
I KNOW LITTLE OF SCIENCE, BUT I KNOW THE SMELL OF DEATH.
THIS PIT STINKS OF IT.
WE SHOULD SEARCH--!
THAT WOULD BE ILL-ADVISED AT THE PRESENT TIME, CAPTAIN.
THE RESIDUAL RADIATION LEVELS ARE GROWING WITH EVERY PASSING MOMENT--
--FAR BEYOND THE LEVELS OF EVEN SUPERHUMAN TOLERANCE. THEIR CONTINUED SURVIVAL IS-- UNLIKELY.
TRULY, A WARRIOR'S END, TO DIE BY FIRE--
--LEAVING NAUGHT BUT THE BAREST HINT...
...THEIR LIKE EVER WALKED THIS EARTH.

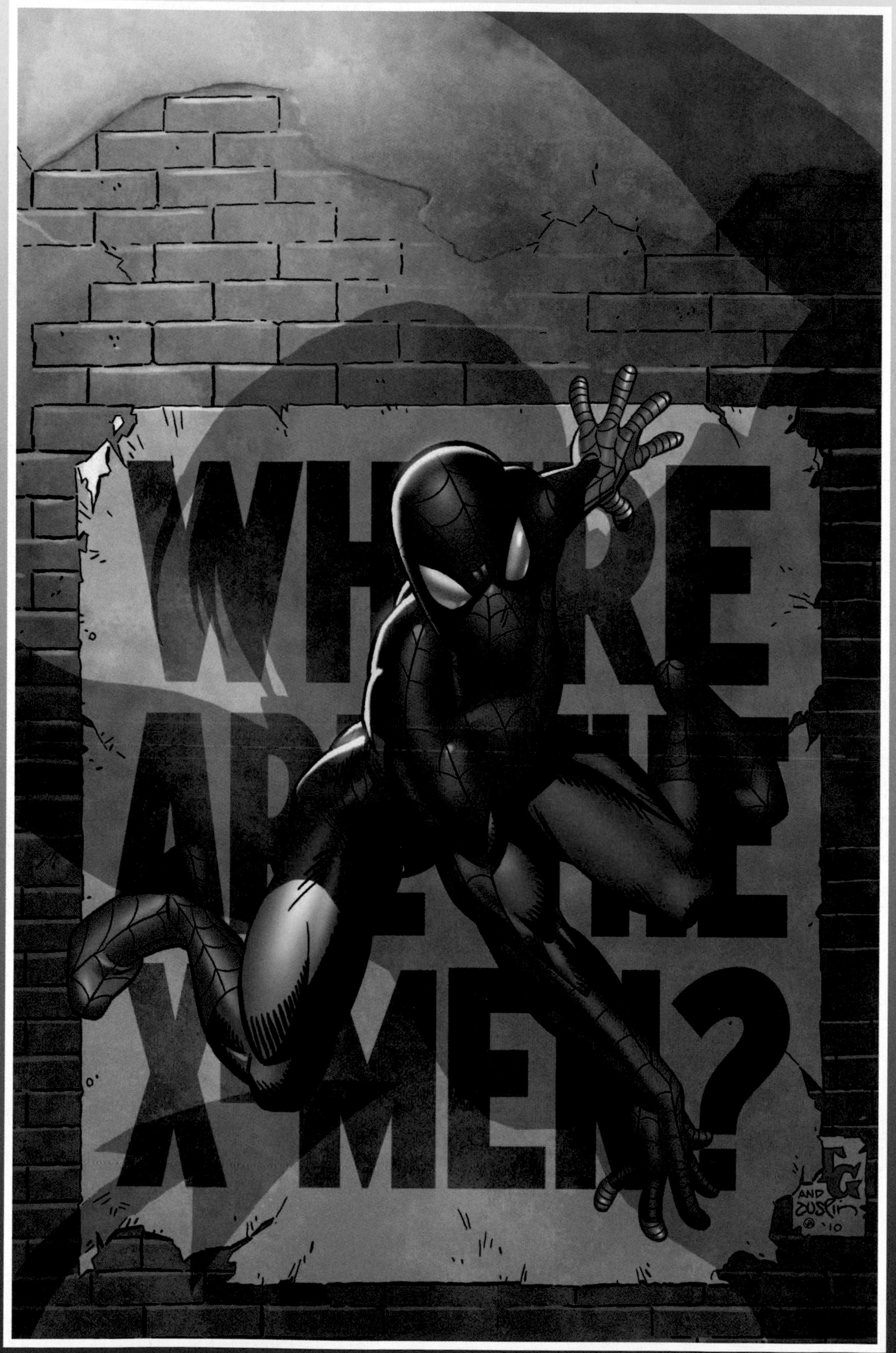

TWO

SIX WEEKS AGO, THIS WAS THE MAIN ENTRANCE OF PROFESSOR CHARLES XAVIER'S SCHOOL FOR GIFTED YOUNGSTERS--

--A WELL-REGARDED, ALBEIT EXTREMELY PRIVATE SCHOOL THAT FOR ALMOST A GENERATION HAS BEEN PART OF THE WESTCHESTER COUNTY COMMUNITY OF SALEM CENTER.

THEN, WITHOUT WARNING...

DANGEROUS PROPERTY-- CONDEMNED

KEEP OUT

AVIER'S CHOOL OR GIFTED OUNGSTERS

X-MEI FORE

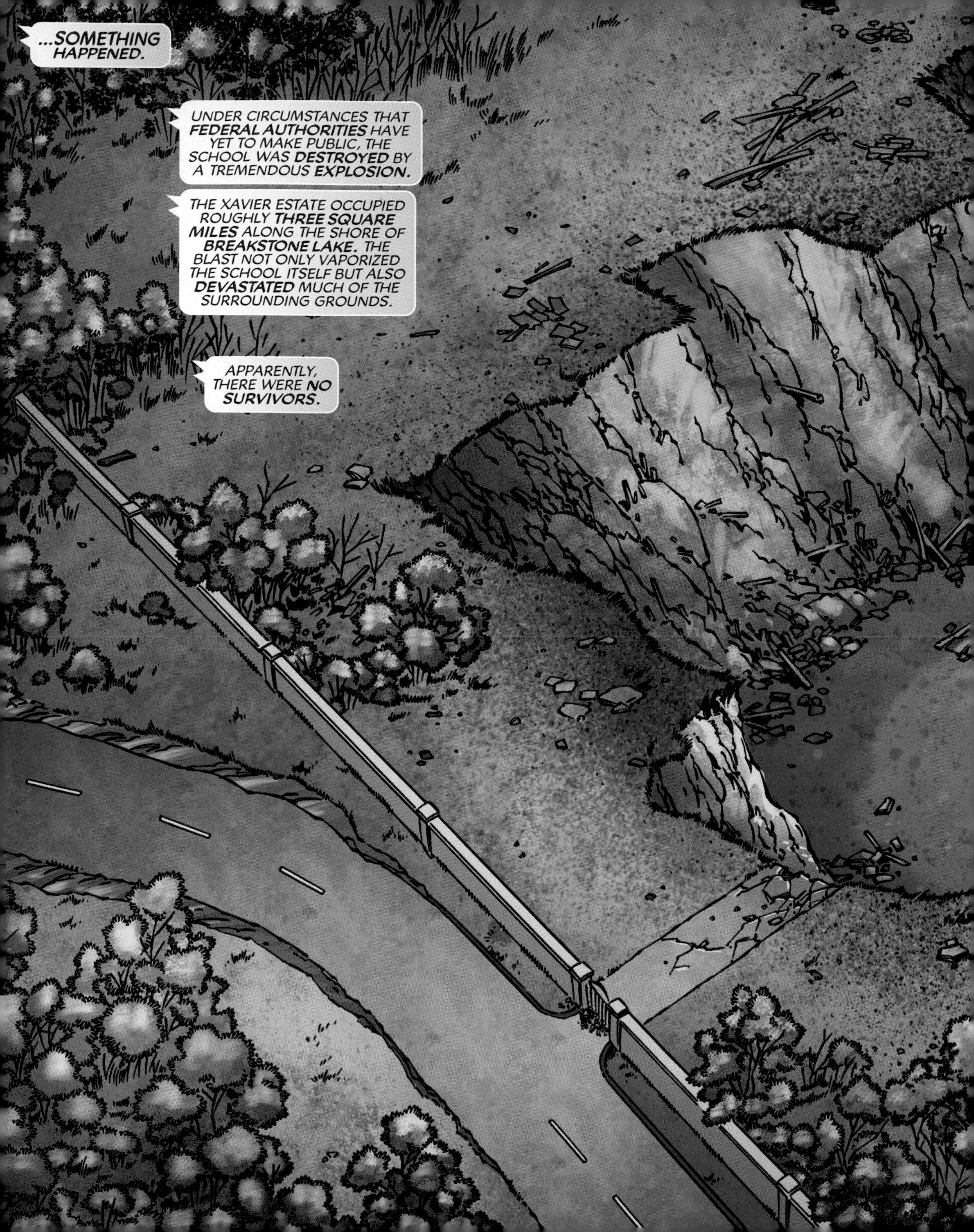
...SOMETHING HAPPENED.
UNDER CIRCUMSTANCES THAT FEDERAL AUTHORITIES HAVE YET TO MAKE PUBLIC, THE SCHOOL WAS DESTROYED BY A TREMENDOUS EXPLOSION.
THE XAVIER ESTATE OCCUPIED ROUGHLY THREE SQUARE MILES ALONG THE SHORE OF BREAKSTONE LAKE. THE BLAST NOT ONLY VAPORIZED THE SCHOOL ITSELF BUT ALSO DEVASTATED MUCH OF THE SURROUNDING GROUNDS.
APPARENTLY, THERE WERE NO SURVIVORS.

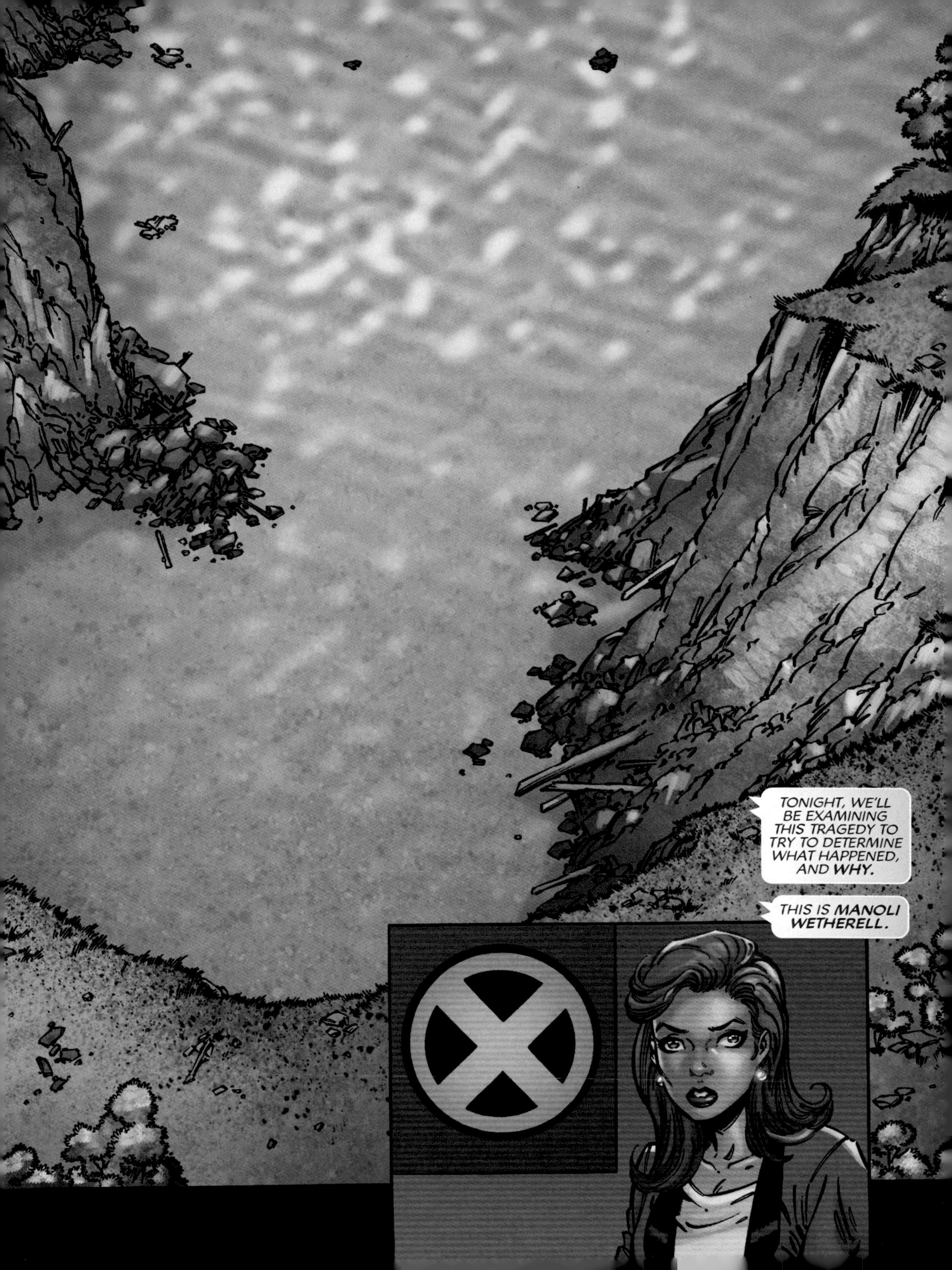
TONIGHT, WE'LL BE EXAMINING THIS TRAGEDY TO TRY TO DETERMINE WHAT HAPPENED, AND WHY.
THIS IS MANOLI WETHERELL.

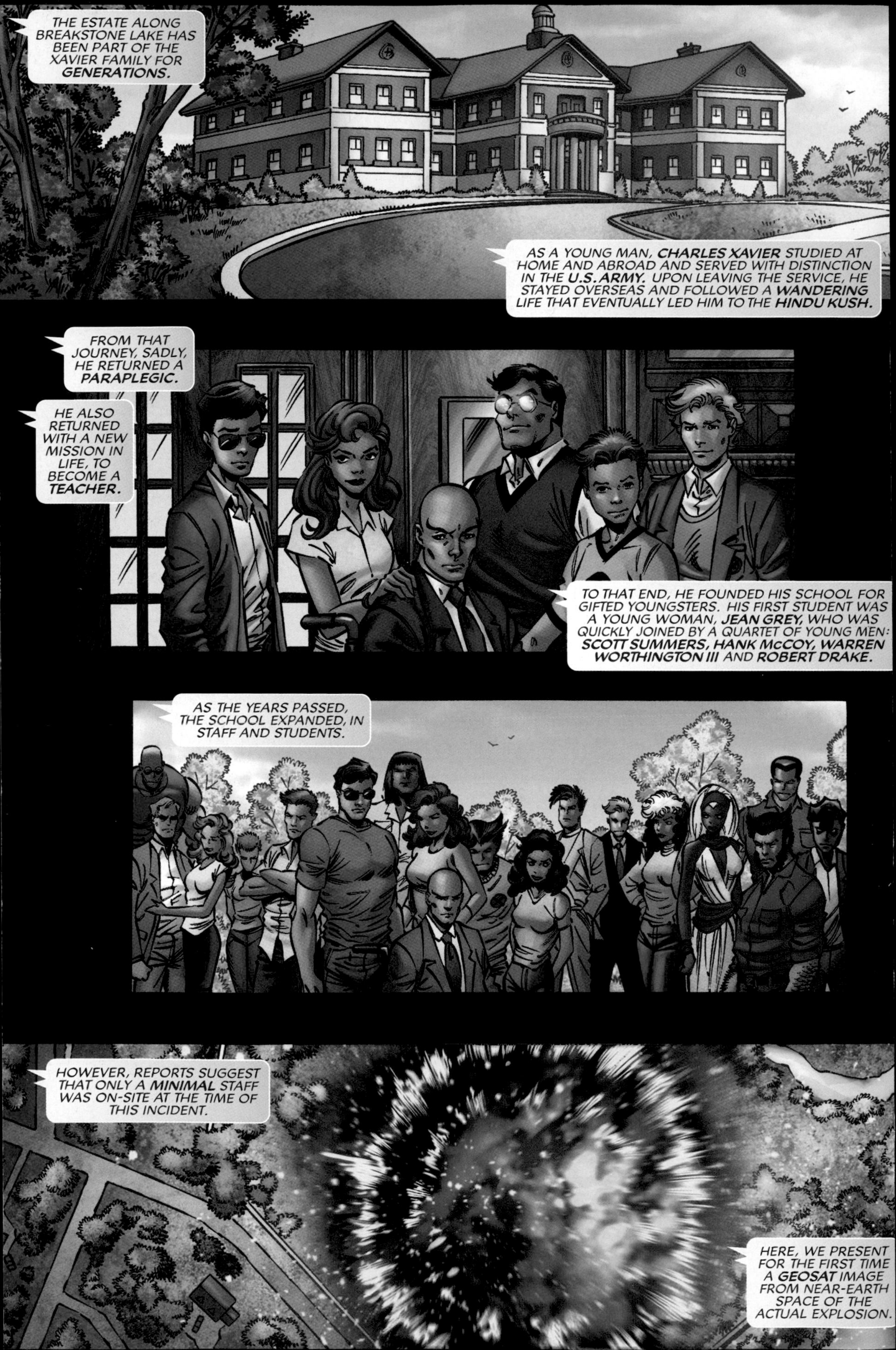

THE ESTATE ALONG BREAKSTONE LAKE HAS BEEN PART OF THE XAVIER FAMILY FOR GENERATIONS.
AS A YOUNG MAN, CHARLES XAVIER STUDIED AT HOME AND ABROAD AND SERVED WITH DISTINCTION IN THE U.S. ARMY. UPON LEAVING THE SERVICE, HE STAYED OVERSEAS AND FOLLOWED A WANDERING LIFE THAT EVENTUALLY LED HIM TO THE HINDU KUSH.
FROM THAT JOURNEY, SADLY, HE RETURNED A PARAPLEGIC.
HE ALSO RETURNED WITH A NEW MISSION IN LIFE, TO BECOME A TEACHER.
TO THAT END, HE FOUNDED HIS SCHOOL FOR GIFTED YOUNGSTERS. HIS FIRST STUDENT WAS A YOUNG WOMAN, JEAN GREY, WHO WAS QUICKLY JOINED BY A QUARTET OF YOUNG MEN: SCOTT SUMMERS, HANK McCOY, WARREN WORTHINGTON III AND ROBERT DRAKE.
AS THE YEARS PASSED, THE SCHOOL EXPANDED, IN STAFF AND STUDENTS.
HOWEVER, REPORTS SUGGEST THAT ONLY A MINIMAL STAFF WAS ON-SITE AT THE TIME OF THIS INCIDENT.
HERE, WE PRESENT FOR THE FIRST TIME A GEOSAT IMAGE FROM NEAR-EARTH SPACE OF THE ACTUAL EXPLOSION.

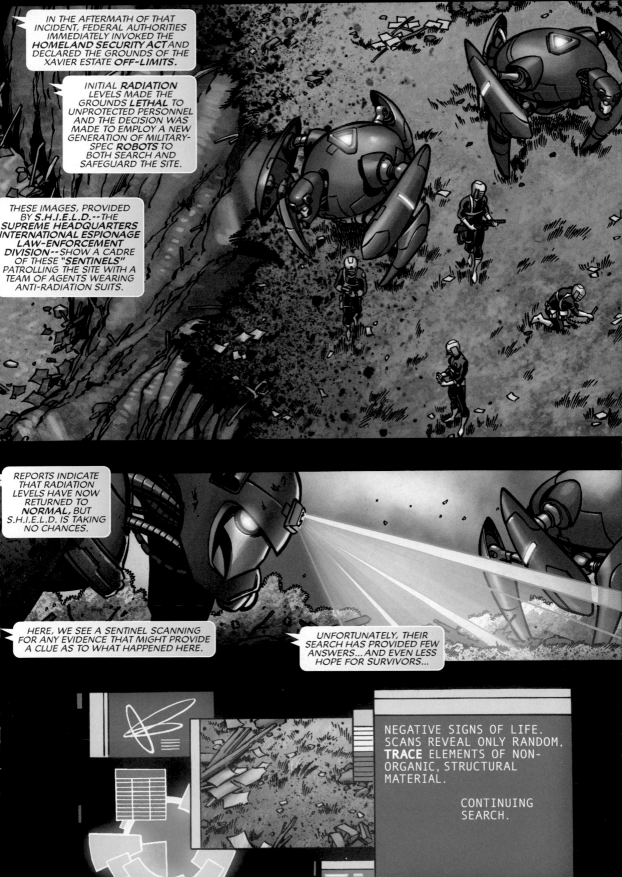

IN THE AFTERMATH OF THAT INCIDENT, FEDERAL AUTHORITIES IMMEDIATELY INVOKED THE *HOMELAND SECURITY ACT* AND DECLARED THE GROUNDS OF THE XAVIER ESTATE *OFF-LIMITS.*

INITIAL *RADIATION* LEVELS MADE THE GROUNDS *LETHAL* TO UNPROTECTED PERSONNEL AND THE DECISION WAS MADE TO EMPLOY A NEW GENERATION OF MILITARY-SPEC *ROBOTS* TO BOTH SEARCH AND SAFEGUARD THE SITE.

THESE IMAGES, PROVIDED BY *S.H.I.E.L.D.*--THE *SUPREME HEADQUARTERS INTERNATIONAL ESPIONAGE LAW-ENFORCEMENT DIVISION*--SHOW A CADRE OF THESE *"SENTINELS"* PATROLLING THE SITE WITH A TEAM OF AGENTS WEARING ANTI-RADIATION SUITS.

REPORTS INDICATE THAT RADIATION LEVELS HAVE NOW RETURNED TO *NORMAL,* BUT *S.H.I.E.L.D.* IS TAKING NO CHANCES.

HERE, WE SEE A SENTINEL SCANNING FOR ANY EVIDENCE THAT MIGHT PROVIDE A CLUE AS TO WHAT HAPPENED HERE.

UNFORTUNATELY, THEIR SEARCH HAS PROVIDED FEW ANSWERS... AND EVEN LESS HOPE FOR SURVIVORS...

NEGATIVE SIGNS OF LIFE. SCANS REVEAL ONLY RANDOM, *TRACE* ELEMENTS OF NON-ORGANIC, STRUCTURAL MATERIAL.

CONTINUING SEARCH.

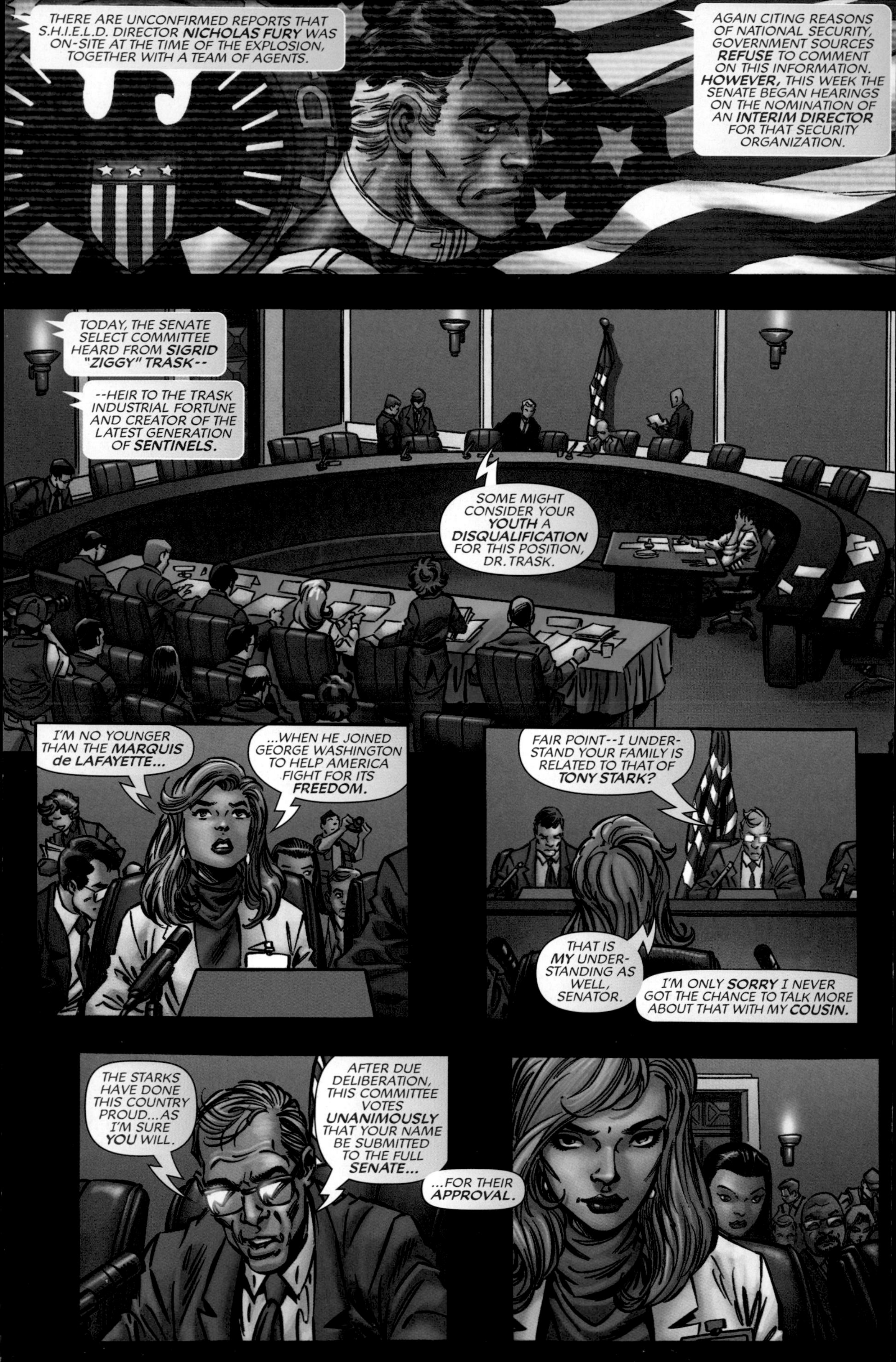
THERE ARE UNCONFIRMED REPORTS THAT S.H.I.E.L.D. DIRECTOR NICHOLAS FURY WAS ON-SITE AT THE TIME OF THE EXPLOSION, TOGETHER WITH A TEAM OF AGENTS.
AGAIN CITING REASONS OF NATIONAL SECURITY, GOVERNMENT SOURCES REFUSE TO COMMENT ON THIS INFORMATION. HOWEVER, THIS WEEK THE SENATE BEGAN HEARINGS ON THE NOMINATION OF AN INTERIM DIRECTOR FOR THAT SECURITY ORGANIZATION.
TODAY, THE SENATE SELECT COMMITTEE HEARD FROM SIGRID "ZIGGY" TRASK--
--HEIR TO THE TRASK INDUSTRIAL FORTUNE AND CREATOR OF THE LATEST GENERATION OF SENTINELS.
SOME MIGHT CONSIDER YOUR YOUTH A DISQUALIFICATION FOR THIS POSITION, DR. TRASK.
I'M NO YOUNGER THAN THE MARQUIS de LAFAYETTE...
...WHEN HE JOINED GEORGE WASHINGTON TO HELP AMERICA FIGHT FOR ITS FREEDOM.
FAIR POINT--I UNDERSTAND YOUR FAMILY IS RELATED TO THAT OF TONY STARK?
THAT IS MY UNDERSTANDING AS WELL, SENATOR.
I'M ONLY SORRY I NEVER GOT THE CHANCE TO TALK MORE ABOUT THAT WITH MY COUSIN.
THE STARKS HAVE DONE THIS COUNTRY PROUD...AS I'M SURE YOU WILL.
AFTER DUE DELIBERATION, THIS COMMITTEE VOTES UNANIMOUSLY THAT YOUR NAME BE SUBMITTED TO THE FULL SENATE...
...FOR THEIR APPROVAL.

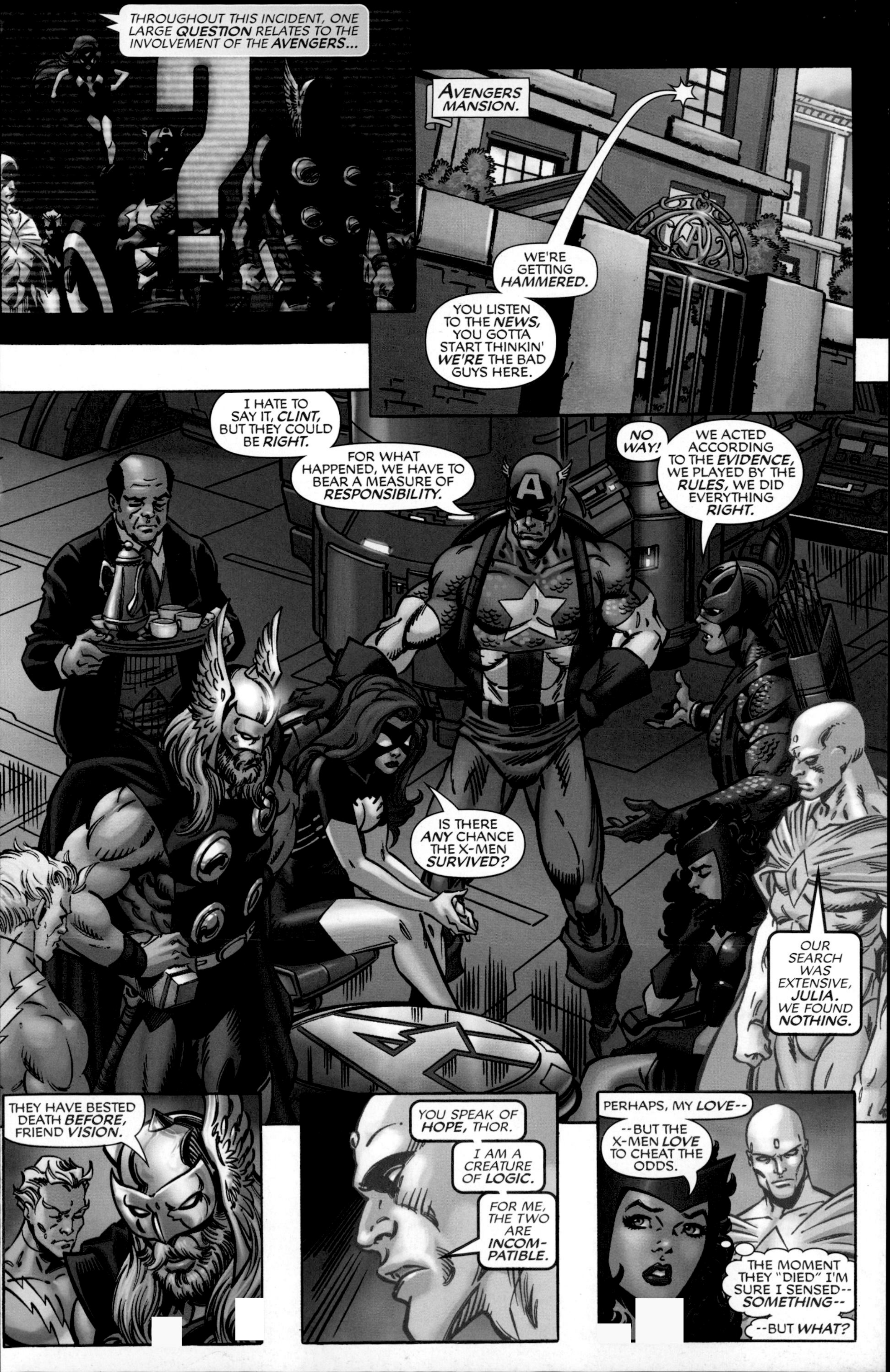
THROUGHOUT THIS INCIDENT, ONE LARGE QUESTION RELATES TO THE INVOLVEMENT OF THE AVENGERS...
AVENGERS MANSION.
WE'RE GETTING HAMMERED.
YOU LISTEN TO THE NEWS, YOU GOTTA START THINKIN' WE'RE THE BAD GUYS HERE.
I HATE TO SAY IT, CLINT, BUT THEY COULD BE RIGHT.
FOR WHAT HAPPENED, WE HAVE TO BEAR A MEASURE OF RESPONSIBILITY.
NO WAY!
WE ACTED ACCORDING TO THE EVIDENCE, WE PLAYED BY THE RULES, WE DID EVERYTHING RIGHT.
IS THERE ANY CHANCE THE X-MEN SURVIVED?
OUR SEARCH WAS EXTENSIVE, JULIA. WE FOUND NOTHING.
THEY HAVE BESTED DEATH BEFORE, FRIEND VISION.
YOU SPEAK OF HOPE, THOR.
I AM A CREATURE OF LOGIC.
FOR ME, THE TWO ARE INCOMPATIBLE.
PERHAPS, MY LOVE--
--BUT THE X-MEN LOVE TO CHEAT THE ODDS.
THE MOMENT THEY "DIED" I'M SURE I SENSED-- SOMETHING--
--BUT WHAT?

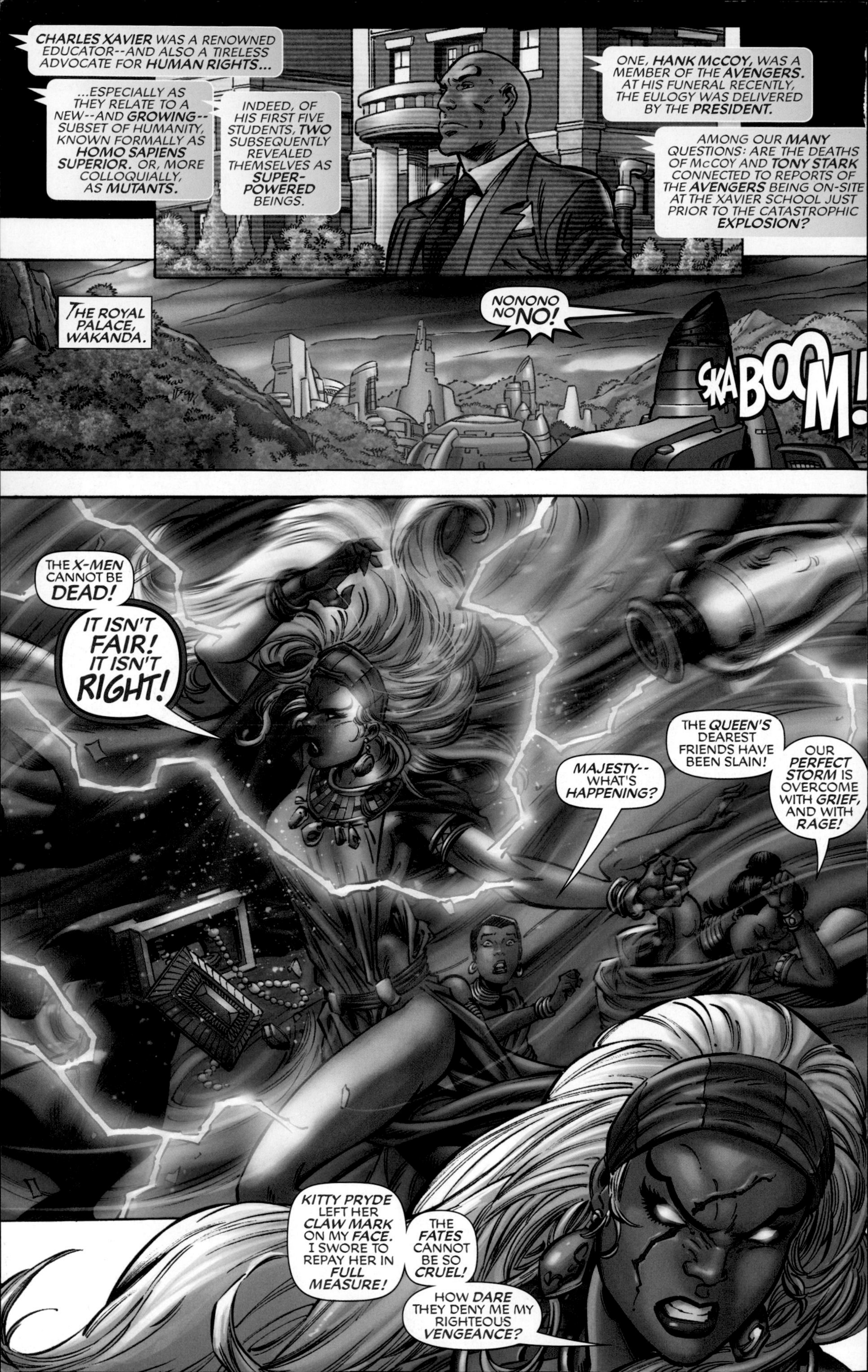
CHARLES XAVIER WAS A RENOWNED EDUCATOR--AND ALSO A TIRELESS ADVOCATE FOR HUMAN RIGHTS...
...ESPECIALLY AS THEY RELATE TO A NEW--AND GROWING--SUBSET OF HUMANITY, KNOWN FORMALLY AS HOMO SAPIENS SUPERIOR. OR, MORE COLLOQUIALLY, AS MUTANTS.
INDEED, OF HIS FIRST FIVE STUDENTS, TWO SUBSEQUENTLY REVEALED THEMSELVES AS SUPER-POWERED BEINGS.
ONE, HANK McCOY, WAS A MEMBER OF THE AVENGERS. AT HIS FUNERAL RECENTLY, THE EULOGY WAS DELIVERED BY THE PRESIDENT.
AMONG OUR MANY QUESTIONS: ARE THE DEATHS OF McCOY AND TONY STARK CONNECTED TO REPORTS OF THE AVENGERS BEING ON-SITE AT THE XAVIER SCHOOL JUST PRIOR TO THE CATASTROPHIC EXPLOSION?
THE ROYAL PALACE, WAKANDA.
NONONO NO NO!
SKABOOM!
THE X-MEN CANNOT BE DEAD!
IT ISN'T FAIR! IT ISN'T RIGHT!
MAJESTY-- WHAT'S HAPPENING?
THE QUEEN'S DEAREST FRIENDS HAVE BEEN SLAIN!
OUR PERFECT STORM IS OVERCOME WITH GRIEF, AND WITH RAGE!
KITTY PRYDE LEFT HER CLAW MARK ON MY FACE. I SWORE TO REPAY HER IN FULL MEASURE!
THE FATES CANNOT BE SO CRUEL!
HOW DARE THEY DENY ME MY RIGHTEOUS VENGEANCE?

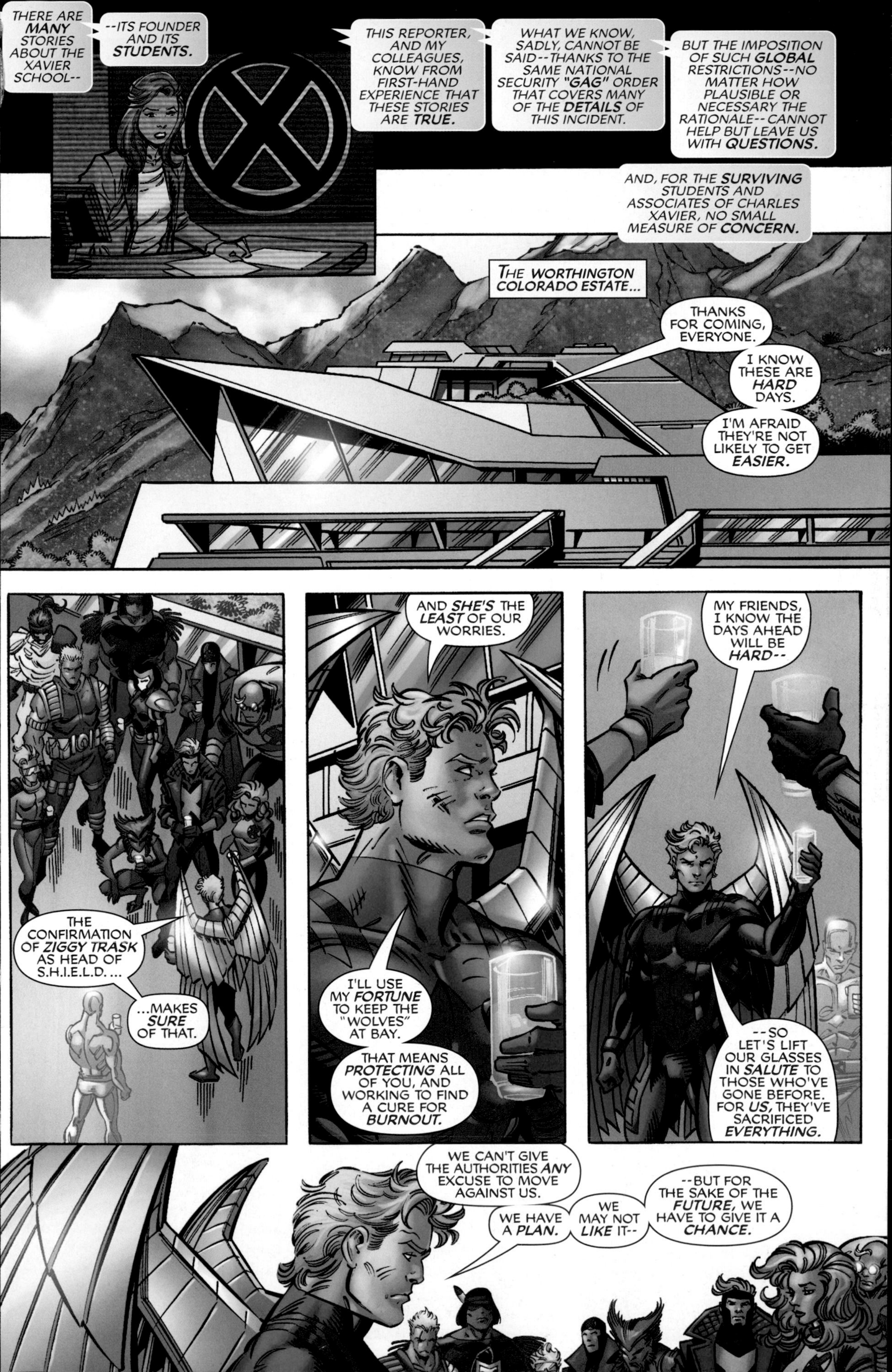

THERE ARE MANY STORIES ABOUT THE XAVIER SCHOOL--
--ITS FOUNDER AND ITS STUDENTS.
THIS REPORTER, AND MY COLLEAGUES, KNOW FROM FIRST-HAND EXPERIENCE THAT THESE STORIES ARE TRUE.
WHAT WE KNOW, SADLY, CANNOT BE SAID--THANKS TO THE SAME NATIONAL SECURITY "GAG" ORDER THAT COVERS MANY OF THE DETAILS OF THIS INCIDENT.
BUT THE IMPOSITION OF SUCH GLOBAL RESTRICTIONS--NO MATTER HOW PLAUSIBLE OR NECESSARY THE RATIONALE--CANNOT HELP BUT LEAVE US WITH QUESTIONS.
AND, FOR THE SURVIVING STUDENTS AND ASSOCIATES OF CHARLES XAVIER, NO SMALL MEASURE OF CONCERN.
THE WORTHINGTON COLORADO ESTATE...
THANKS FOR COMING, EVERYONE.
I KNOW THESE ARE HARD DAYS.
I'M AFRAID THEY'RE NOT LIKELY TO GET EASIER.
THE CONFIRMATION OF ZIGGY TRASK AS HEAD OF S.H.I.E.L.D. ...
...MAKES SURE OF THAT.
AND SHE'S THE LEAST OF OUR WORRIES.
I'LL USE MY FORTUNE TO KEEP THE "WOLVES" AT BAY.
THAT MEANS PROTECTING ALL OF YOU, AND WORKING TO FIND A CURE FOR BURNOUT.
MY FRIENDS, I KNOW THE DAYS AHEAD WILL BE HARD--
--SO LET'S LIFT OUR GLASSES IN SALUTE TO THOSE WHO'VE GONE BEFORE. FOR US, THEY'VE SACRIFICED EVERYTHING.
WE CAN'T GIVE THE AUTHORITIES ANY EXCUSE TO MOVE AGAINST US.
WE HAVE A PLAN.
WE MAY NOT LIKE IT--
--BUT FOR THE SAKE OF THE FUTURE, WE HAVE TO GIVE IT A CHANCE.

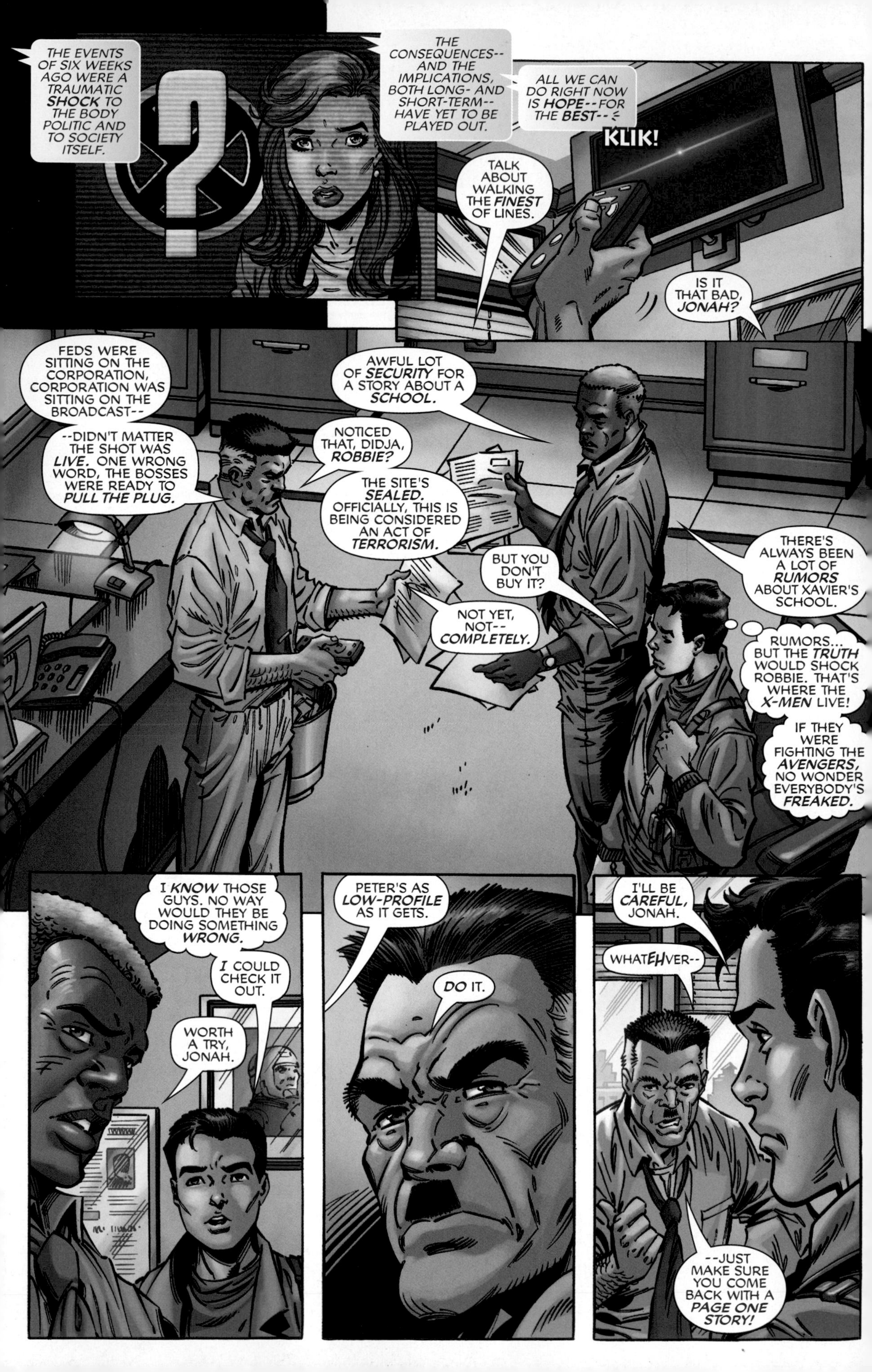
THE EVENTS OF SIX WEEKS AGO WERE A TRAUMATIC SHOCK TO THE BODY POLITIC AND TO SOCIETY ITSELF.
THE CONSEQUENCES-- AND THE IMPLICATIONS, BOTH LONG- AND SHORT-TERM-- HAVE YET TO BE PLAYED OUT.
ALL WE CAN DO RIGHT NOW IS HOPE--FOR THE BEST--
KLIK!
TALK ABOUT WALKING THE FINEST OF LINES.
IS IT THAT BAD, JONAH?
FEDS WERE SITTING ON THE CORPORATION, CORPORATION WAS SITTING ON THE BROADCAST--
--DIDN'T MATTER THE SHOT WAS LIVE. ONE WRONG WORD, THE BOSSES WERE READY TO PULL THE PLUG.
AWFUL LOT OF SECURITY FOR A STORY ABOUT A SCHOOL.
NOTICED THAT, DIDJA, ROBBIE?
THE SITE'S SEALED. OFFICIALLY, THIS IS BEING CONSIDERED AN ACT OF TERRORISM.
BUT YOU DON'T BUY IT?
NOT YET, NOT-- COMPLETELY.
THERE'S ALWAYS BEEN A LOT OF RUMORS ABOUT XAVIER'S SCHOOL.
RUMORS... BUT THE TRUTH WOULD SHOCK ROBBIE. THAT'S WHERE THE X-MEN LIVE!
IF THEY WERE FIGHTING THE AVENGERS, NO WONDER EVERYBODY'S FREAKED.
I KNOW THOSE GUYS. NO WAY WOULD THEY BE DOING SOMETHING WRONG.
I COULD CHECK IT OUT.
WORTH A TRY, JONAH.
PETER'S AS LOW-PROFILE AS IT GETS.
DO IT.
I'LL BE CAREFUL, JONAH.
WHATEHVER--
--JUST MAKE SURE YOU COME BACK WITH A PAGE ONE STORY!

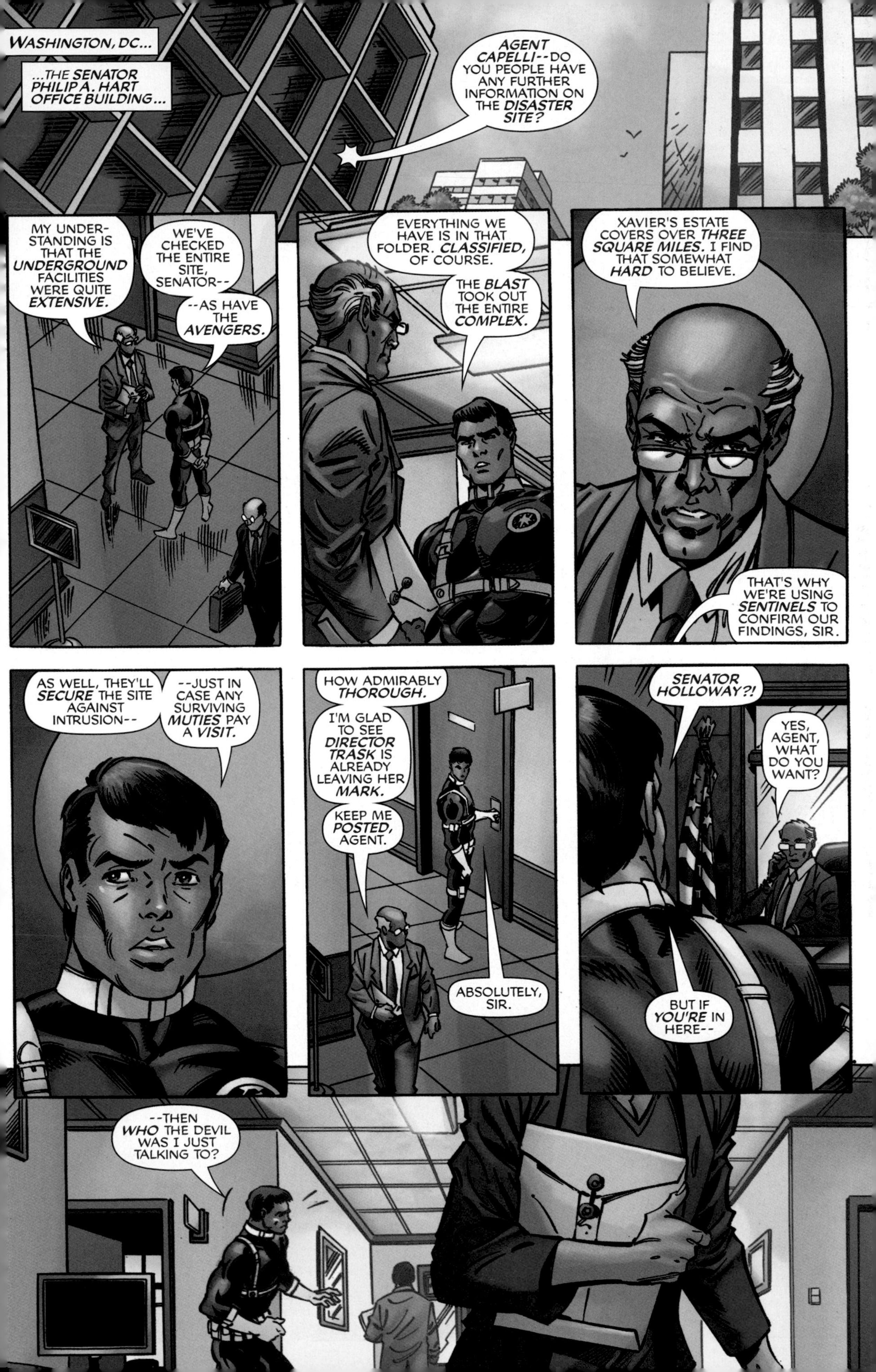
WASHINGTON, DC...
...THE SENATOR PHILIP A. HART OFFICE BUILDING...
AGENT CAPELLI--DO YOU PEOPLE HAVE ANY FURTHER INFORMATION ON THE DISASTER SITE?
MY UNDERSTANDING IS THAT THE UNDERGROUND FACILITIES WERE QUITE EXTENSIVE.
WE'VE CHECKED THE ENTIRE SITE, SENATOR--
--AS HAVE THE AVENGERS.
EVERYTHING WE HAVE IS IN THAT FOLDER. CLASSIFIED, OF COURSE.
THE BLAST TOOK OUT THE ENTIRE COMPLEX.
XAVIER'S ESTATE COVERS OVER THREE SQUARE MILES. I FIND THAT SOMEWHAT HARD TO BELIEVE.
THAT'S WHY WE'RE USING SENTINELS TO CONFIRM OUR FINDINGS, SIR.
AS WELL, THEY'LL SECURE THE SITE AGAINST INTRUSION--
--JUST IN CASE ANY SURVIVING MUTIES PAY A VISIT.
HOW ADMIRABLY THOROUGH.
I'M GLAD TO SEE DIRECTOR TRASK IS ALREADY LEAVING HER MARK.
KEEP ME POSTED, AGENT.
ABSOLUTELY, SIR.
SENATOR HOLLOWAY?!
YES, AGENT, WHAT DO YOU WANT?
BUT IF YOU'RE IN HERE--
--THEN WHO THE DEVIL WAS I JUST TALKING TO?

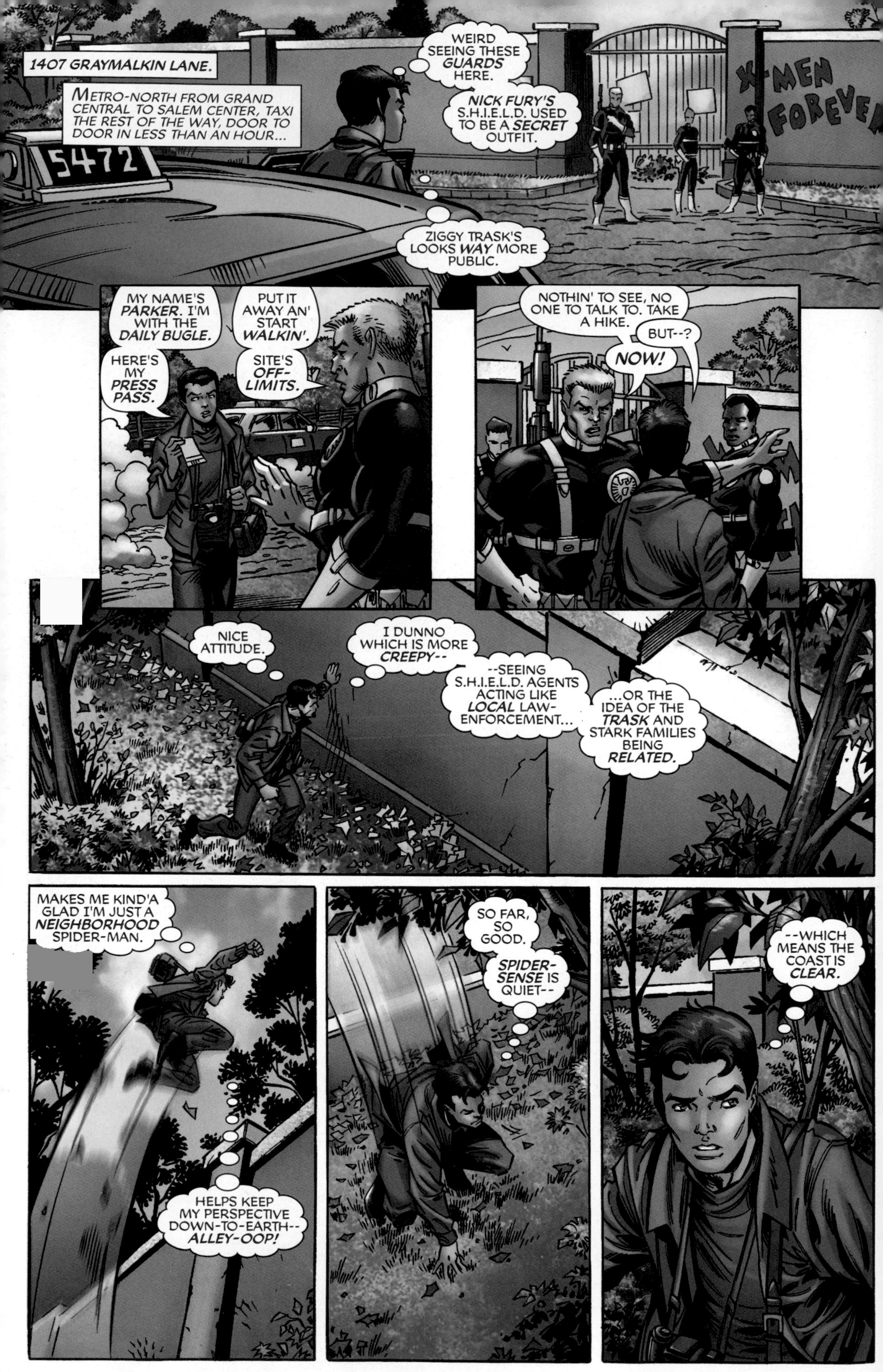
1407 GRAYMALKIN LANE.
METRO-NORTH FROM GRAND CENTRAL TO SALEM CENTER, TAXI THE REST OF THE WAY, DOOR TO DOOR IN LESS THAN AN HOUR...
5472
WEIRD SEEING THESE GUARDS HERE.
NICK FURY'S S.H.I.E.L.D. USED TO BE A SECRET OUTFIT.
X-MEN FOREVE
ZIGGY TRASK'S LOOKS WAY MORE PUBLIC.
MY NAME'S PARKER. I'M WITH THE DAILY BUGLE.
HERE'S MY PRESS PASS.
PUT IT AWAY AN' START WALKIN'.
SITE'S OFF-LIMITS.
NOTHIN' TO SEE, NO ONE TO TALK TO. TAKE A HIKE.
BUT--?
NOW!
NICE ATTITUDE.
I DUNNO WHICH IS MORE CREEPY--
--SEEING S.H.I.E.L.D. AGENTS ACTING LIKE LOCAL LAW-ENFORCEMENT...
...OR THE IDEA OF THE TRASK AND STARK FAMILIES BEING RELATED.
MAKES ME KIND'A GLAD I'M JUST A NEIGHBORHOOD SPIDER-MAN.
HELPS KEEP MY PERSPECTIVE DOWN-TO-EARTH-- ALLEY-OOP!
SO FAR, SO GOOD.
SPIDER-SENSE IS QUIET--
--WHICH MEANS THE COAST IS CLEAR.

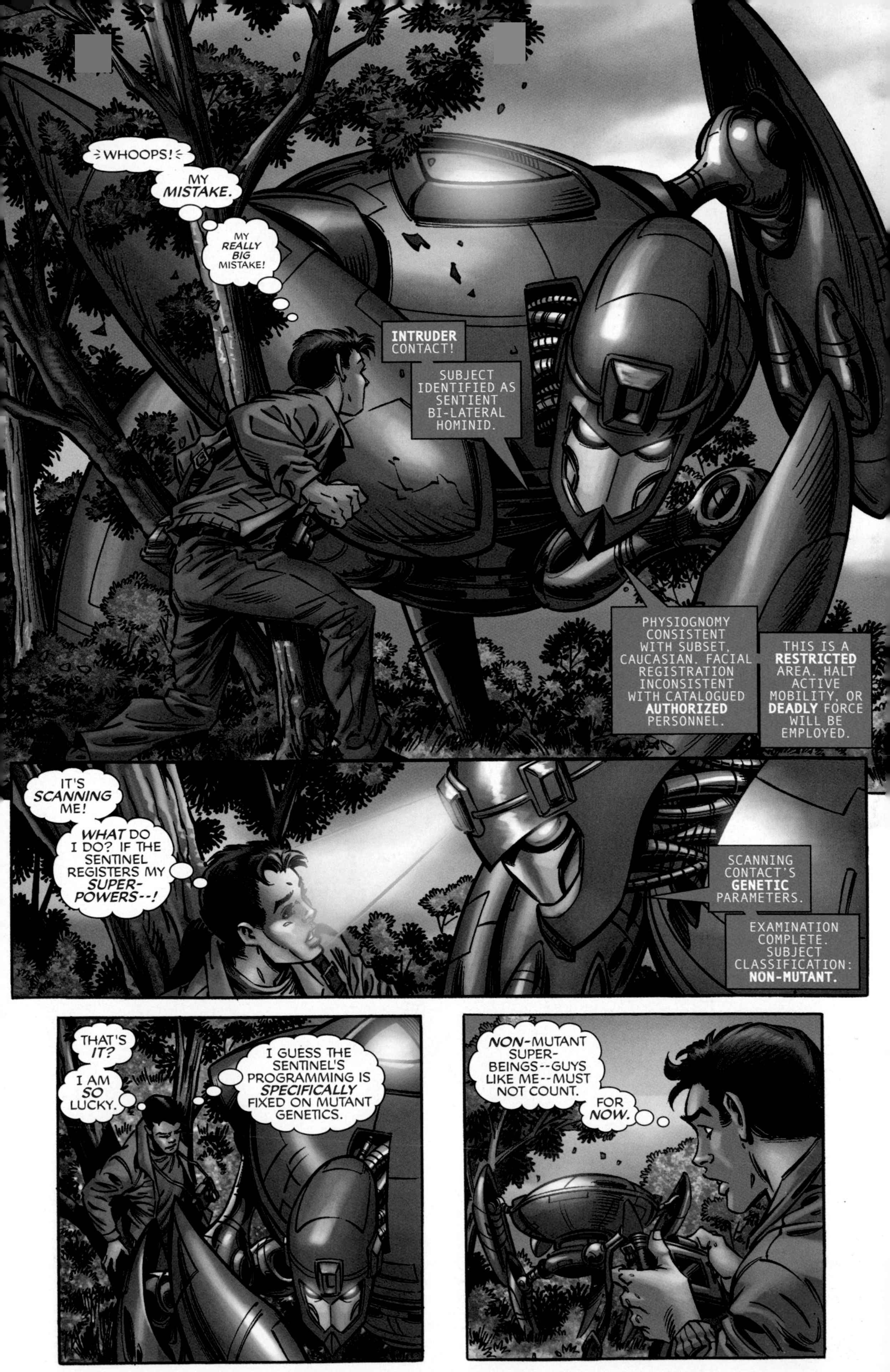
WHOOPS!
MY MISTAKE.
MY REALLY BIG MISTAKE!
INTRUDER CONTACT!
SUBJECT IDENTIFIED AS SENTIENT BI-LATERAL HOMINID.
PHYSIOGNOMY CONSISTENT WITH SUBSET, CAUCASIAN. FACIAL REGISTRATION INCONSISTENT WITH CATALOGUED AUTHORIZED PERSONNEL.
THIS IS A RESTRICTED AREA. HALT ACTIVE MOBILITY, OR DEADLY FORCE WILL BE EMPLOYED.
IT'S SCANNING ME!
WHAT DO I DO? IF THE SENTINEL REGISTERS MY SUPER-POWERS--!
SCANNING CONTACT'S GENETIC PARAMETERS.
EXAMINATION COMPLETE. SUBJECT CLASSIFICATION: NON-MUTANT.
THAT'S IT?
I AM SO LUCKY.
I GUESS THE SENTINEL'S PROGRAMMING IS SPECIFICALLY FIXED ON MUTANT GENETICS.
NON-MUTANT SUPER-BEINGS--GUYS LIKE ME--MUST NOT COUNT.
FOR NOW.

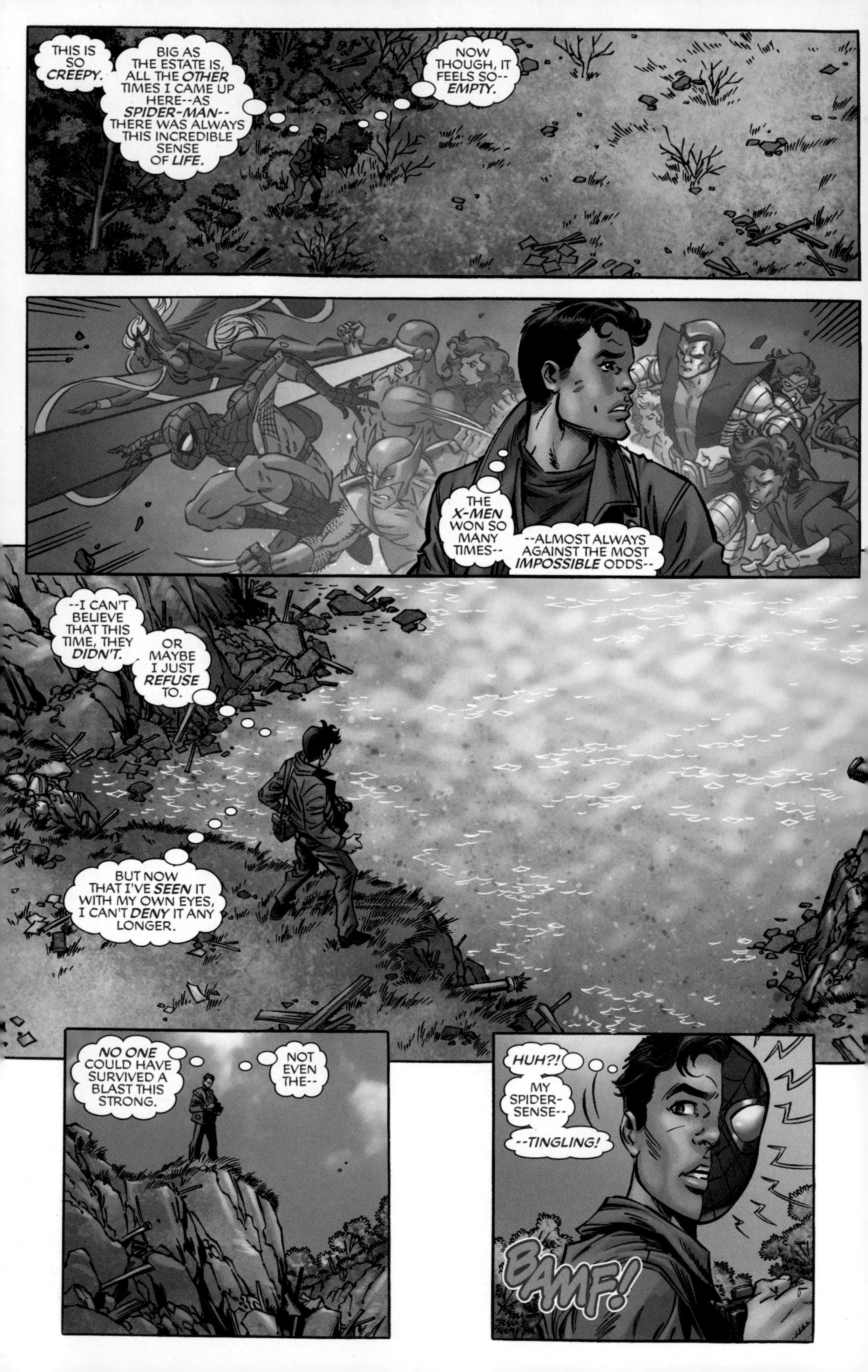
THIS IS SO *CREEPY.*
BIG AS THE ESTATE IS, ALL THE *OTHER* TIMES I CAME UP HERE--AS *SPIDER-MAN--* THERE WAS ALWAYS THIS INCREDIBLE SENSE OF *LIFE.*
NOW THOUGH, IT FEELS SO-- *EMPTY.*
THE *X-MEN* WON SO MANY TIMES--
--ALMOST ALWAYS AGAINST THE MOST *IMPOSSIBLE* ODDS--
--I CAN'T BELIEVE THAT THIS TIME, THEY *DIDN'T.*
OR MAYBE I JUST *REFUSE* TO.
BUT NOW THAT I'VE *SEEN* IT WITH MY OWN EYES, I CAN'T *DENY* IT ANY LONGER.
NO ONE COULD HAVE SURVIVED A BLAST THIS STRONG.
NOT EVEN THE--
HUH?!
MY SPIDER-SENSE--
--TINGLING!
BAMF!

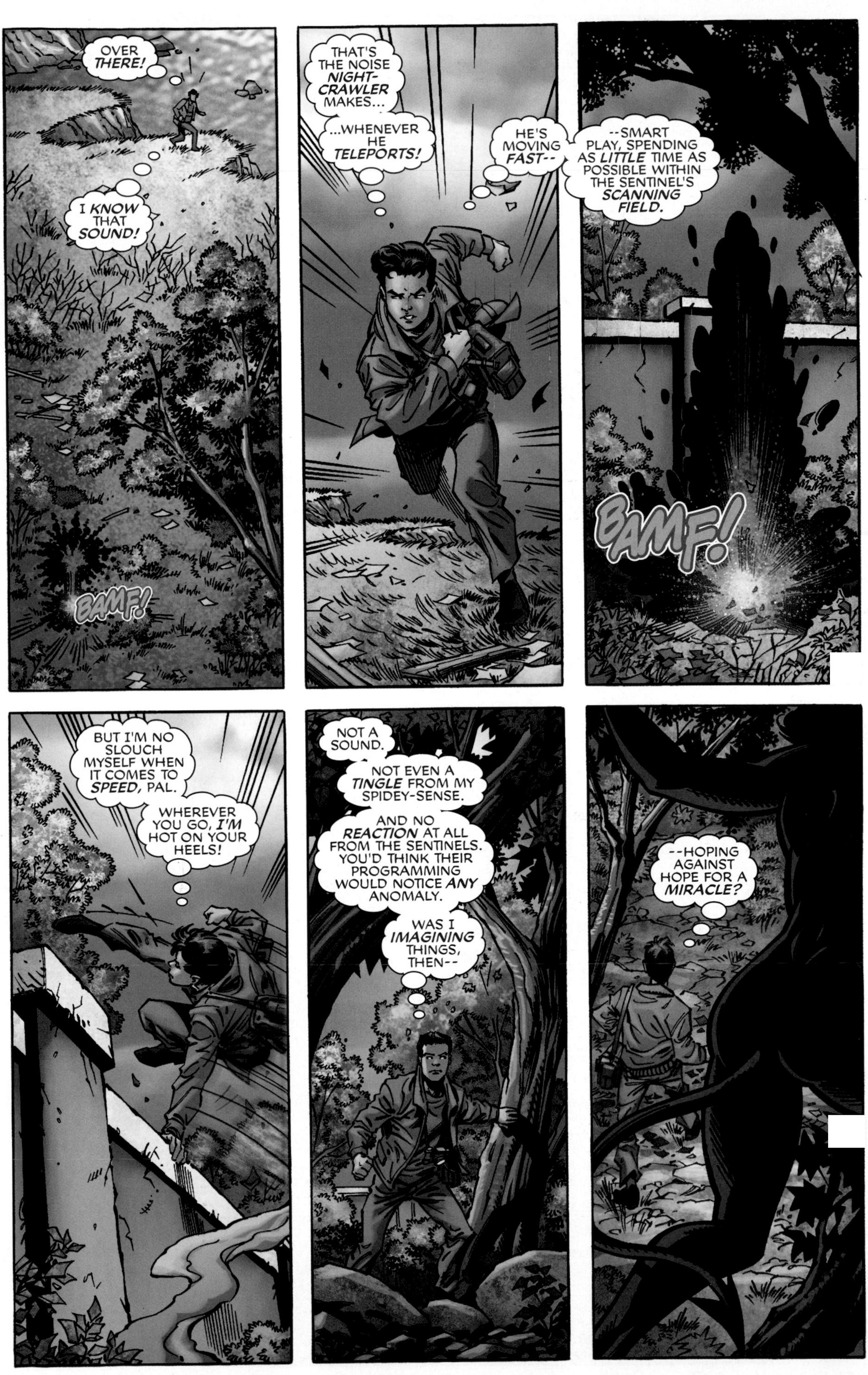
OVER THERE!
I KNOW THAT SOUND!
BAMF!
THAT'S THE NOISE NIGHT-CRAWLER MAKES...
...WHENEVER HE TELEPORTS!
HE'S MOVING FAST--
--SMART PLAY, SPENDING AS LITTLE TIME AS POSSIBLE WITHIN THE SENTINEL'S SCANNING FIELD.
BAMF!
BUT I'M NO SLOUCH MYSELF WHEN IT COMES TO SPEED, PAL.
WHEREVER YOU GO, I'M HOT ON YOUR HEELS!
NOT A SOUND.
NOT EVEN A TINGLE FROM MY SPIDEY-SENSE.
AND NO REACTION AT ALL FROM THE SENTINELS. YOU'D THINK THEIR PROGRAMMING WOULD NOTICE ANY ANOMALY.
WAS I IMAGINING THINGS, THEN--
--HOPING AGAINST HOPE FOR A MIRACLE?

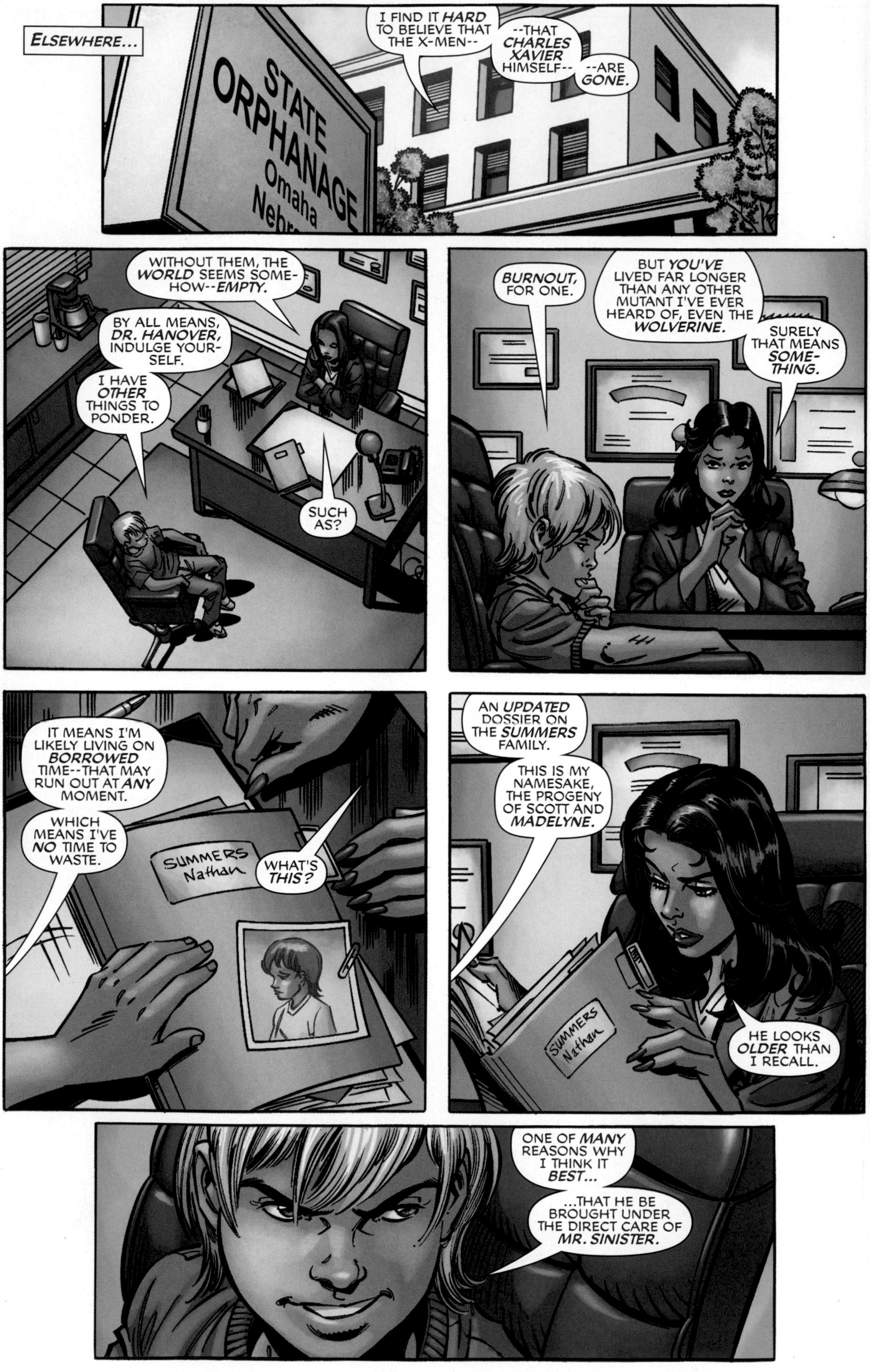
ELSEWHERE...
STATE ORPHANAGE Omaha Nebr
I FIND IT HARD TO BELIEVE THAT THE X-MEN--
--THAT CHARLES XAVIER HIMSELF--
--ARE GONE.
WITHOUT THEM, THE WORLD SEEMS SOME-HOW--EMPTY.
BY ALL MEANS, DR. HANOVER, INDULGE YOURSELF.
I HAVE OTHER THINGS TO PONDER.
SUCH AS?
BURNOUT, FOR ONE.
BUT YOU'VE LIVED FAR LONGER THAN ANY OTHER MUTANT I'VE EVER HEARD OF, EVEN THE WOLVERINE.
SURELY THAT MEANS SOME-THING.
IT MEANS I'M LIKELY LIVING ON BORROWED TIME--THAT MAY RUN OUT AT ANY MOMENT.
WHICH MEANS I'VE NO TIME TO WASTE.
SUMMERS Nathan
WHAT'S THIS?
AN UPDATED DOSSIER ON THE SUMMERS FAMILY.
THIS IS MY NAMESAKE, THE PROGENY OF SCOTT AND MADELYNE.
SUMMERS Nathan
HE LOOKS OLDER THAN I RECALL.
ONE OF MANY REASONS WHY I THINK IT BEST...
...THAT HE BE BROUGHT UNDER THE DIRECT CARE OF MR. SINISTER.

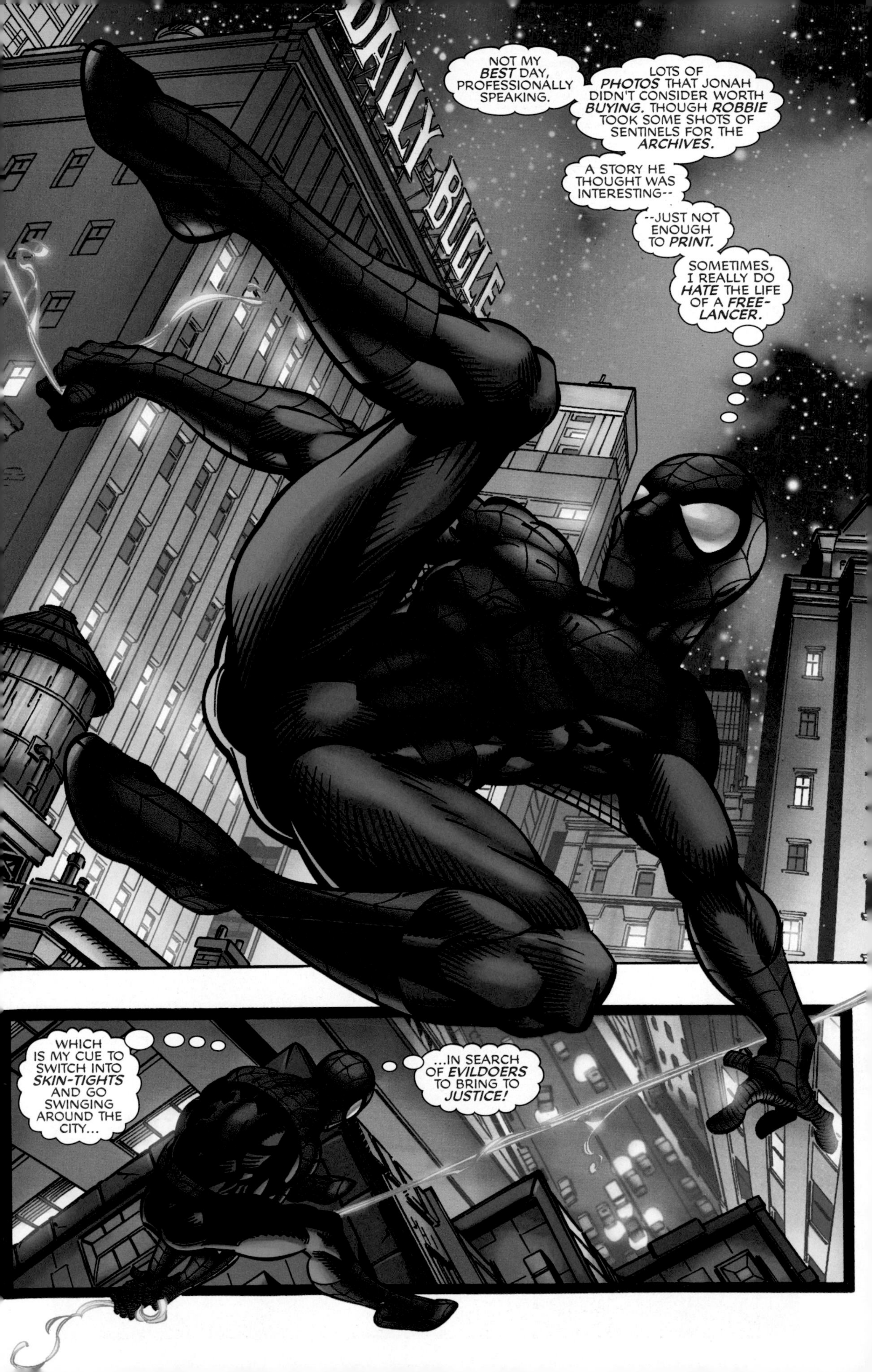
NOT MY BEST DAY, PROFESSIONALLY SPEAKING.
LOTS OF PHOTOS THAT JONAH DIDN'T CONSIDER WORTH BUYING. THOUGH ROBBIE TOOK SOME SHOTS OF SENTINELS FOR THE ARCHIVES.
A STORY HE THOUGHT WAS INTERESTING--
--JUST NOT ENOUGH TO PRINT.
SOMETIMES, I REALLY DO HATE THE LIFE OF A FREE-LANCER.
DAILY BUGLE
WHICH IS MY CUE TO SWITCH INTO SKIN-TIGHTS AND GO SWINGING AROUND THE CITY...
...IN SEARCH OF EVILDOERS TO BRING TO JUSTICE!

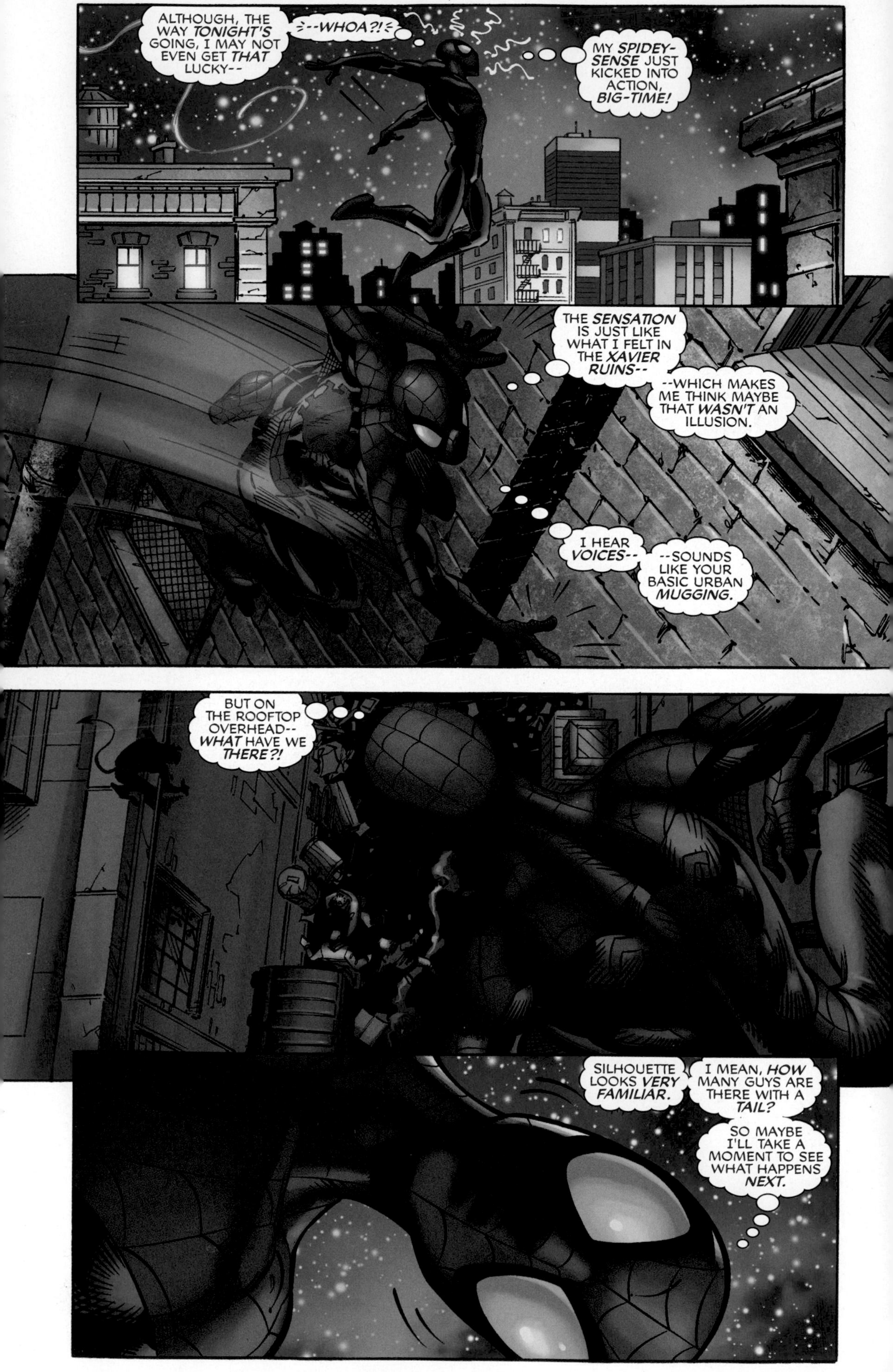
ALTHOUGH, THE WAY TONIGHT'S GOING, I MAY NOT EVEN GET THAT LUCKY--
--WHOA?!
MY SPIDEY-SENSE JUST KICKED INTO ACTION, BIG-TIME!
THE SENSATION IS JUST LIKE WHAT I FELT IN THE XAVIER RUINS--
--WHICH MAKES ME THINK MAYBE THAT WASN'T AN ILLUSION.
I HEAR VOICES--
--SOUNDS LIKE YOUR BASIC URBAN MUGGING.
BUT ON THE ROOFTOP OVERHEAD-- WHAT HAVE WE THERE?!
SILHOUETTE LOOKS VERY FAMILIAR.
I MEAN, HOW MANY GUYS ARE THERE WITH A TAIL?
SO MAYBE I'LL TAKE A MOMENT TO SEE WHAT HAPPENS NEXT.

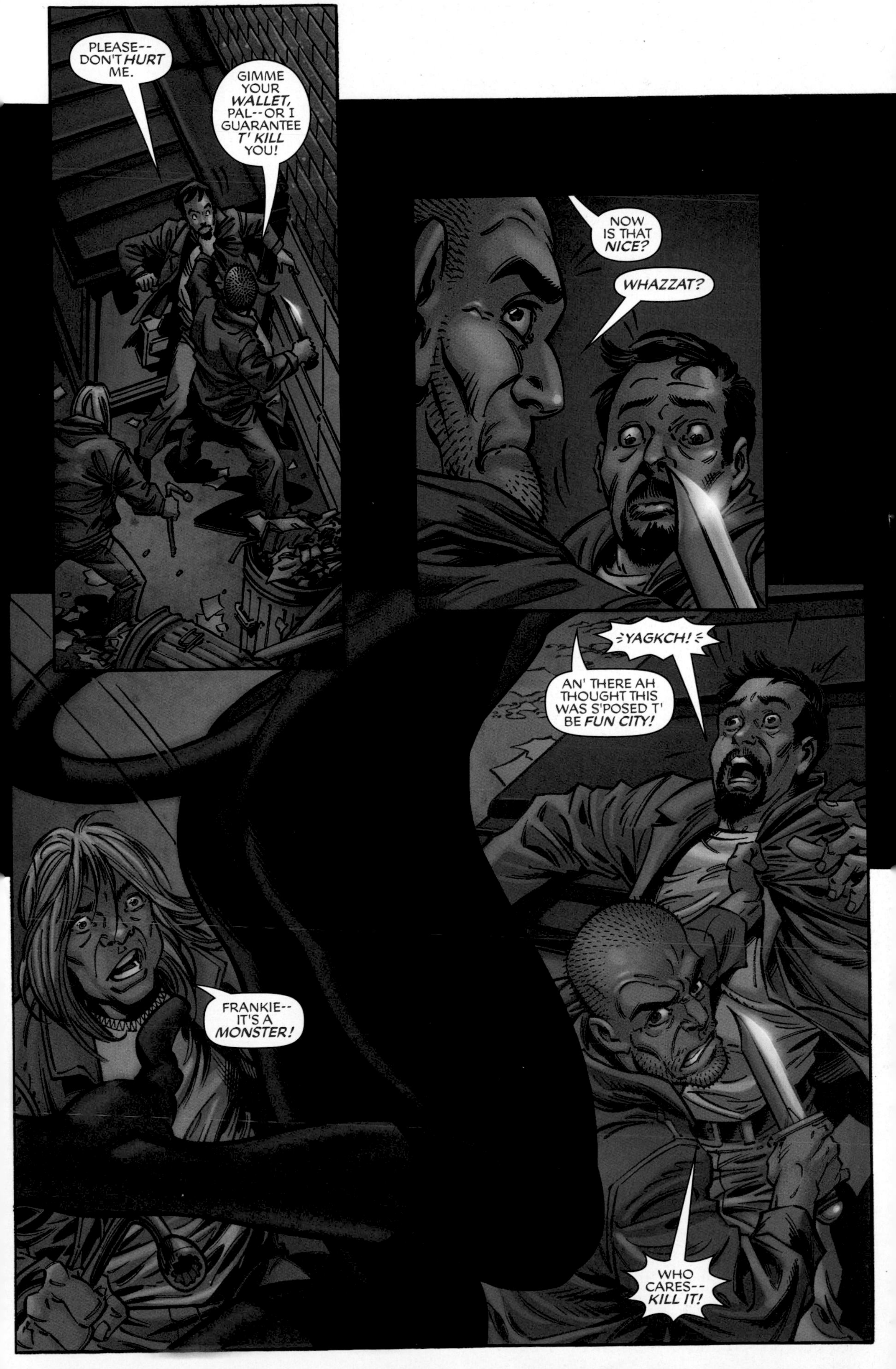
PLEASE-- DON'T HURT ME.
GIMME YOUR WALLET, PAL--OR I GUARANTEE T' KILL YOU!
NOW IS THAT NICE?
WHAZZAT?
AN' THERE AH THOUGHT THIS WAS S'POSED T' BE FUN CITY!
YAGKCH!
FRANKIE-- IT'S A MONSTER!
WHO CARES-- KILL IT!

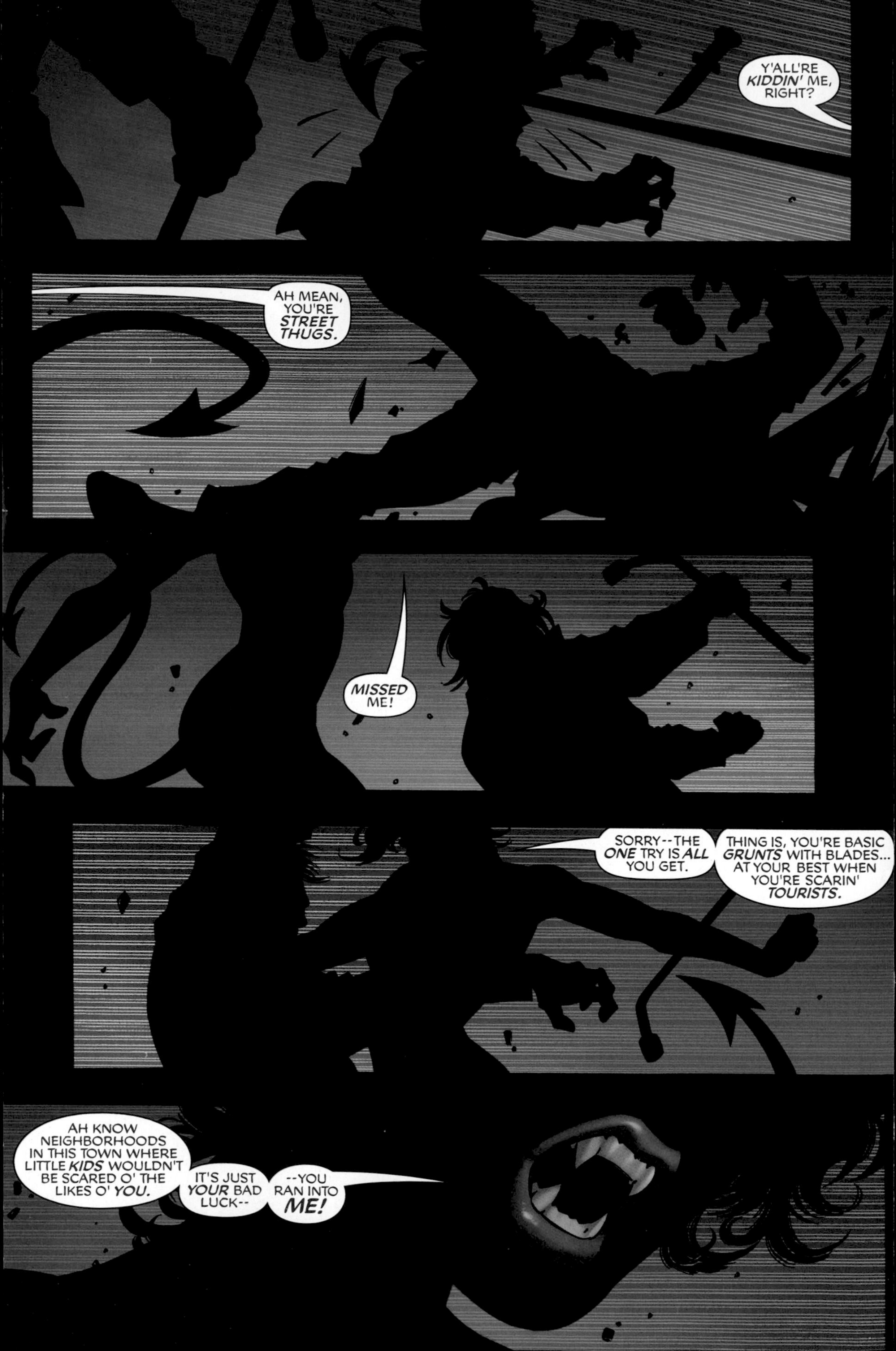
Y'ALL'RE KIDDIN' ME, RIGHT?
AH MEAN, YOU'RE STREET THUGS.
MISSED ME!
SORRY--THE ONE TRY IS ALL YOU GET.
THING IS, YOU'RE BASIC GRUNTS WITH BLADES... AT YOUR BEST WHEN YOU'RE SCARIN' TOURISTS.
AH KNOW NEIGHBORHOODS IN THIS TOWN WHERE LITTLE KIDS WOULDN'T BE SCARED O' THE LIKES O' YOU.
IT'S JUST YOUR BAD LUCK--
--YOU RAN INTO ME!

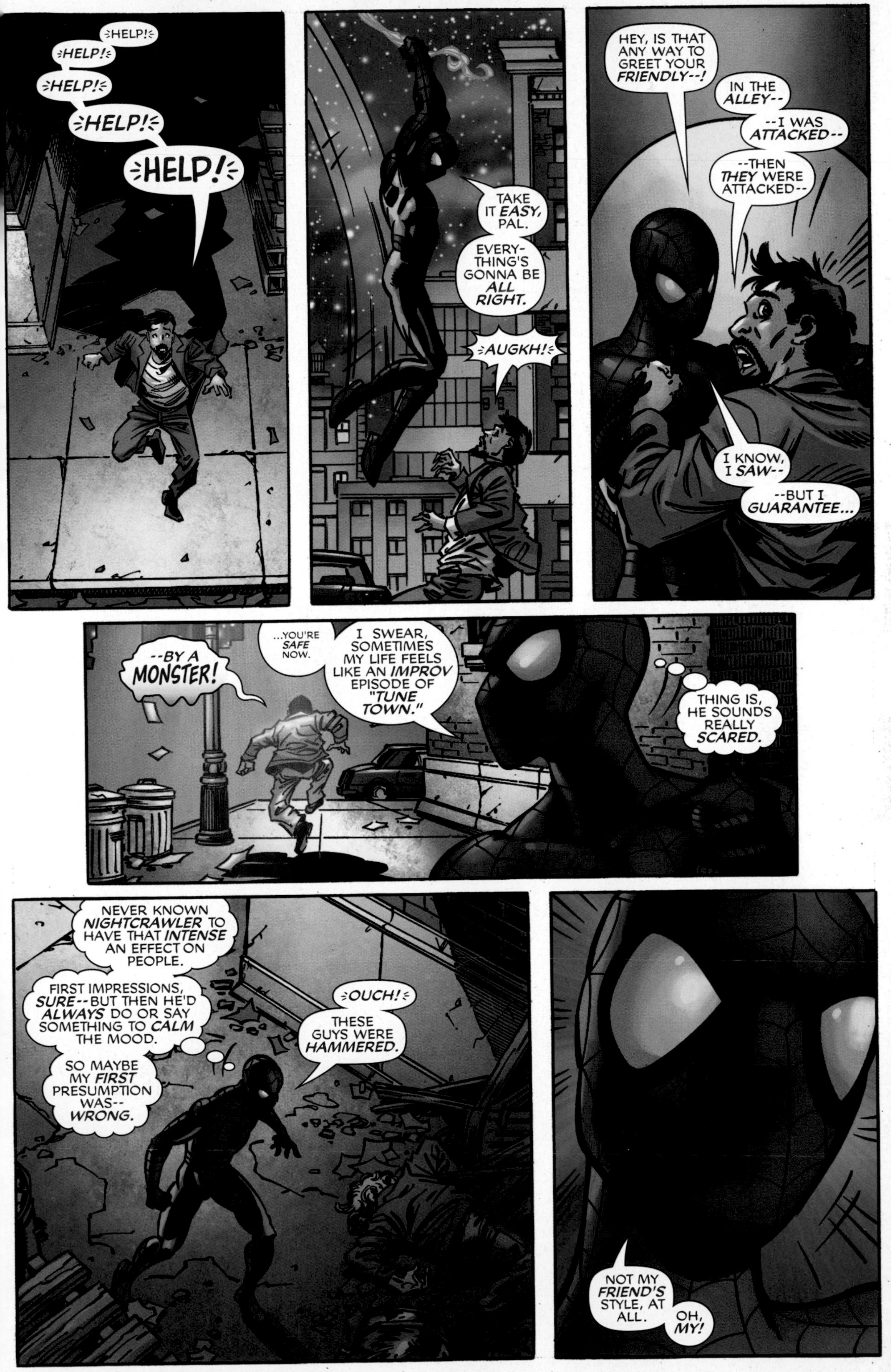
HELP!
HELP!
HELP!
HELP!
HELP!
TAKE IT EASY, PAL.
EVERY-THING'S GONNA BE ALL RIGHT.
AUGKH!
HEY, IS THAT ANY WAY TO GREET YOUR FRIENDLY--!
IN THE ALLEY--
--I WAS ATTACKED--
--THEN THEY WERE ATTACKED--
I KNOW, I SAW--
--BUT I GUARANTEE...
--BY A MONSTER!
...YOU'RE SAFE NOW.
I SWEAR, SOMETIMES MY LIFE FEELS LIKE AN IMPROV EPISODE OF "TUNE TOWN."
THING IS, HE SOUNDS REALLY SCARED.
NEVER KNOWN NIGHTCRAWLER TO HAVE THAT INTENSE AN EFFECT ON PEOPLE.
FIRST IMPRESSIONS, SURE--BUT THEN HE'D ALWAYS DO OR SAY SOMETHING TO CALM THE MOOD.
SO MAYBE MY FIRST PRESUMPTION WAS--WRONG.
OUCH!
THESE GUYS WERE HAMMERED.
NOT MY FRIEND'S STYLE, AT ALL.
OH, MY!

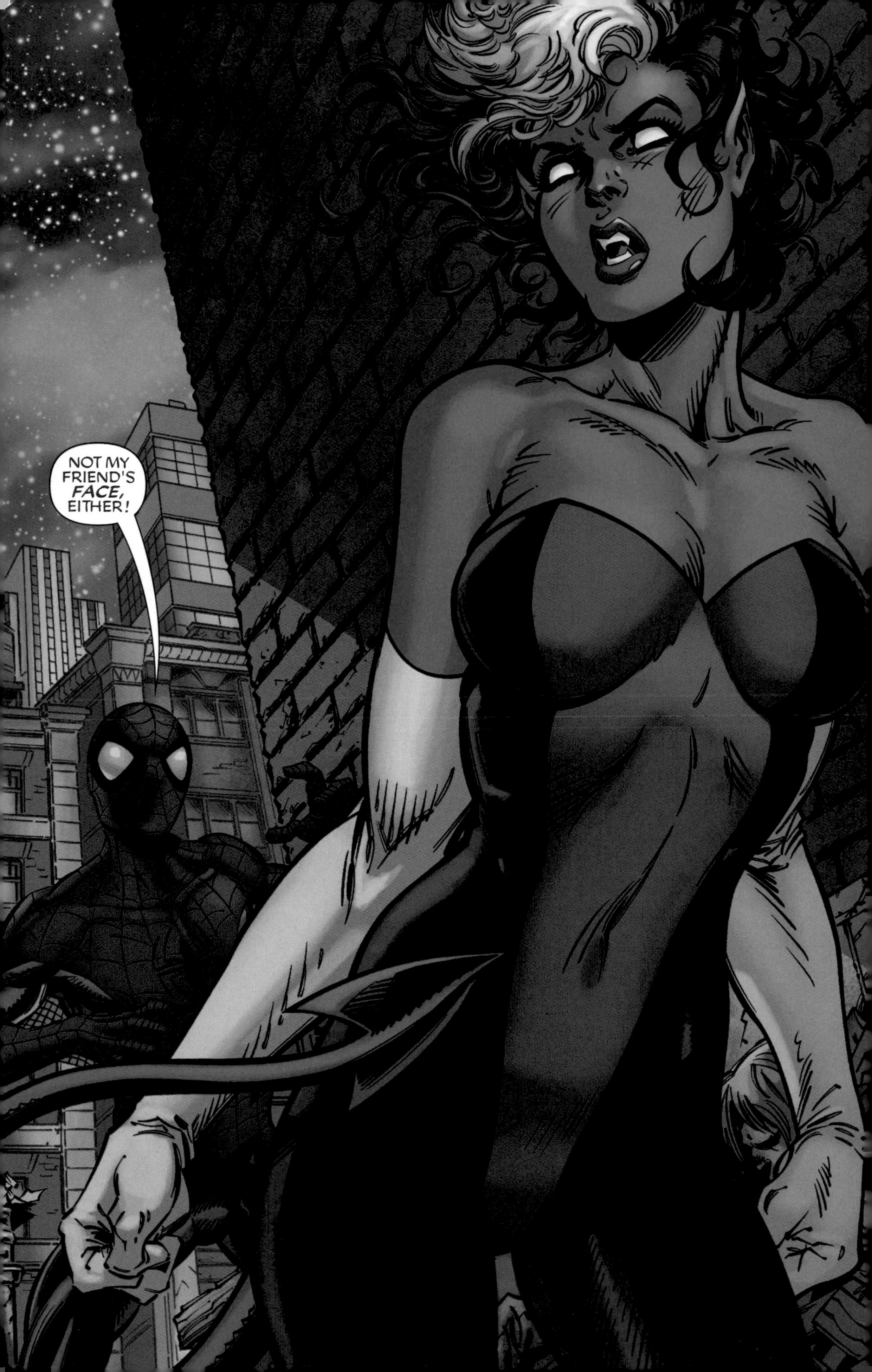
NOT MY FRIEND'S *FACE,* EITHER!

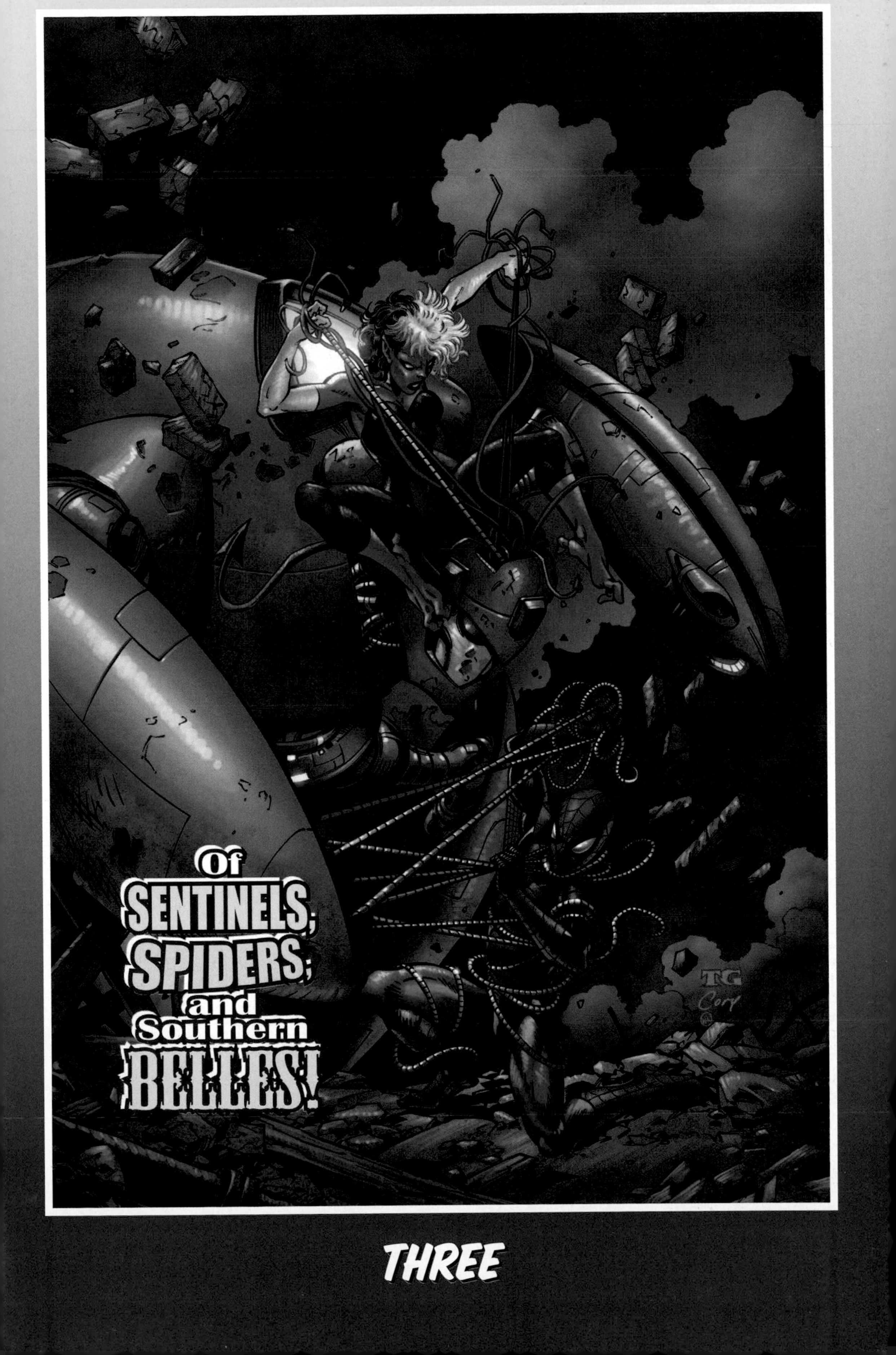
Of
SENTINELS,
SPIDERS,
and
Southern
BELLES!

THREE

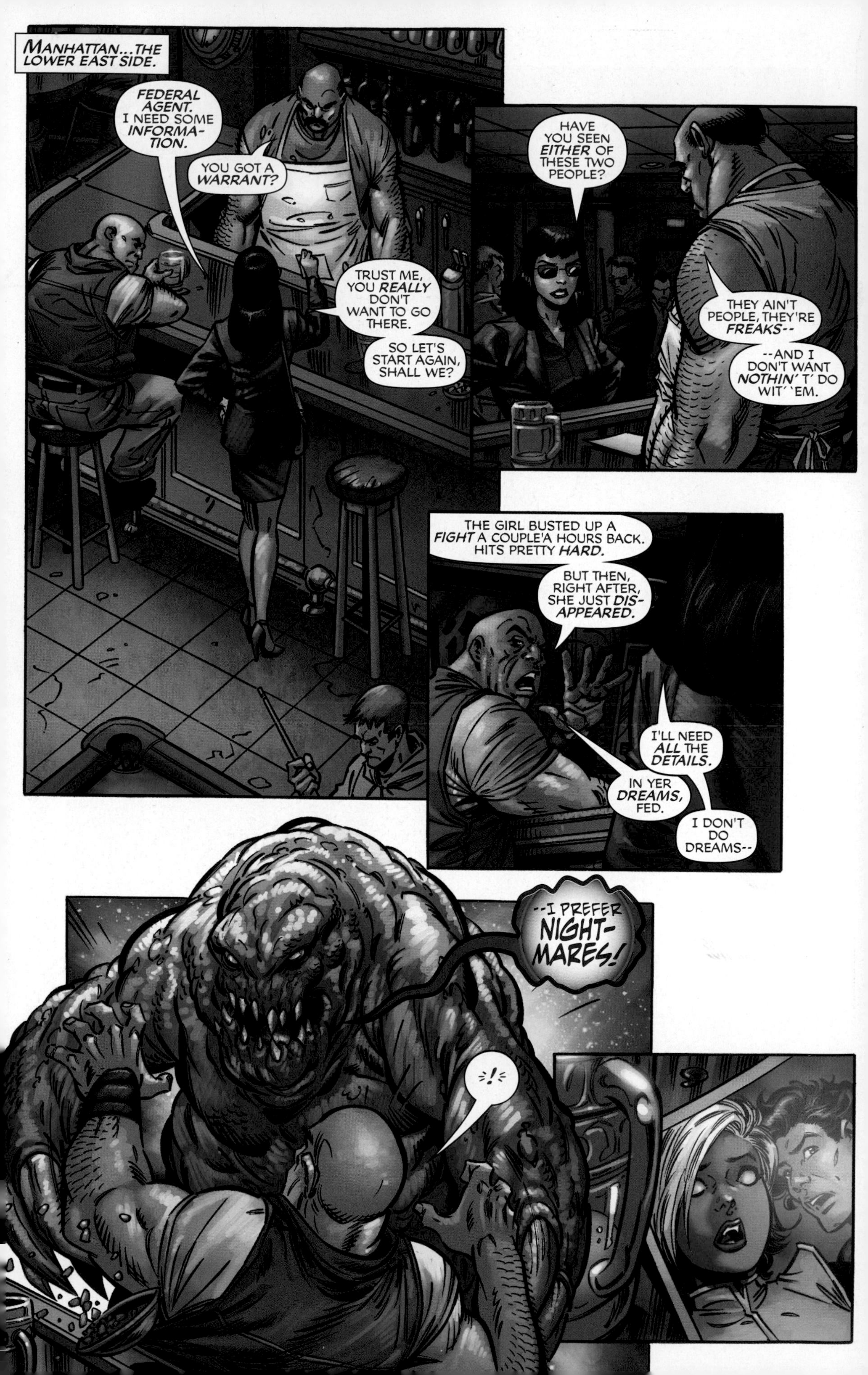
MANHATTAN...THE LOWER EAST SIDE.
FEDERAL AGENT. I NEED SOME INFORMA-TION.
YOU GOT A WARRANT?
TRUST ME, YOU REALLY DON'T WANT TO GO THERE.
SO LET'S START AGAIN, SHALL WE?
HAVE YOU SEEN EITHER OF THESE TWO PEOPLE?
THEY AIN'T PEOPLE, THEY'RE FREAKS--
--AND I DON'T WANT NOTHIN' T' DO WIT' 'EM.
THE GIRL BUSTED UP A FIGHT A COUPLE'A HOURS BACK. HITS PRETTY HARD.
BUT THEN, RIGHT AFTER, SHE JUST DIS-APPEARED.
I'LL NEED ALL THE DETAILS.
IN YER DREAMS, FED.
I DON'T DO DREAMS--
--I PREFER NIGHT-MARES!
!

AT THE SAME MOMENT, ELSEWHERE IN MANHATTAN...
I'M-- SPIDER-MAN.
OCCASIONALLY AMAZING. SOMETIMES SPECTACULAR. RIGHT NOW, A LITTLE BIT CONFUSED.
I KNOW THIS IS KIND OF A CRAZY QUESTION--
--BUT ARE YOU RELATED TO A GUY CALLED NIGHT-CRAWLER?
HE AND I, WE'RE FRIENDS.
AND IT'S JUST, WELL, I MEAN-- YOU LOOK JUST LIKE HIM.

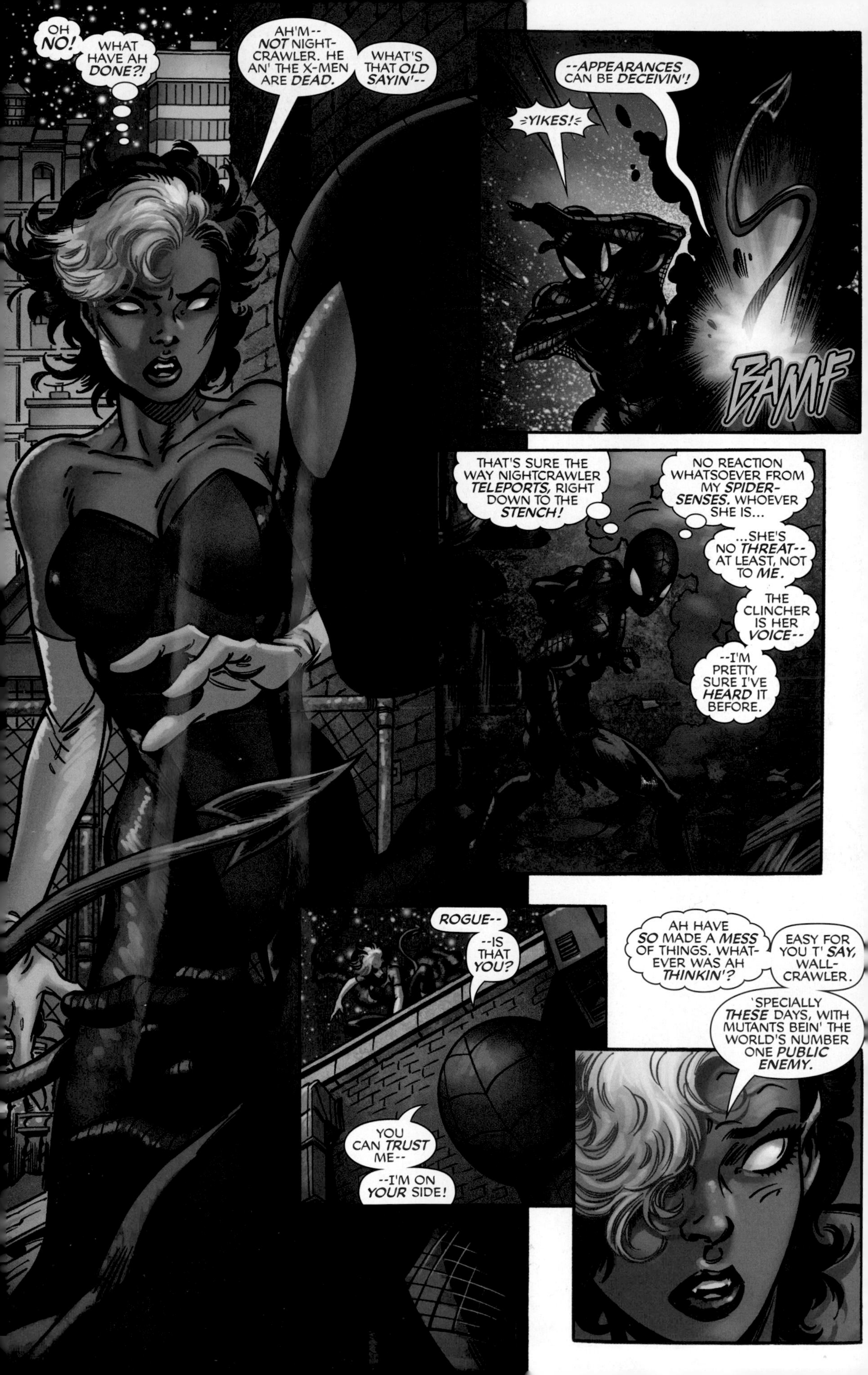

OH NO! WHAT HAVE AH DONE?!
AH'M--NOT NIGHT-CRAWLER. HE AN' THE X-MEN ARE DEAD.
WHAT'S THAT OLD SAYIN'--
--APPEARANCES CAN BE DECEIVIN'!
=YIKES!=
BAMF
THAT'S SURE THE WAY NIGHTCRAWLER TELEPORTS, RIGHT DOWN TO THE STENCH!
NO REACTION WHATSOEVER FROM MY SPIDER-SENSES. WHOEVER SHE IS...
...SHE'S NO THREAT--AT LEAST, NOT TO ME.
THE CLINCHER IS HER VOICE--
--I'M PRETTY SURE I'VE HEARD IT BEFORE.
ROGUE--
--IS THAT YOU?
YOU CAN TRUST ME--
--I'M ON YOUR SIDE!
AH HAVE SO MADE A MESS OF THINGS. WHAT-EVER WAS AH THINKIN'?
EASY FOR YOU T' SAY, WALL-CRAWLER.
'SPECIALLY THESE DAYS, WITH MUTANTS BEIN' THE WORLD'S NUMBER ONE PUBLIC ENEMY.

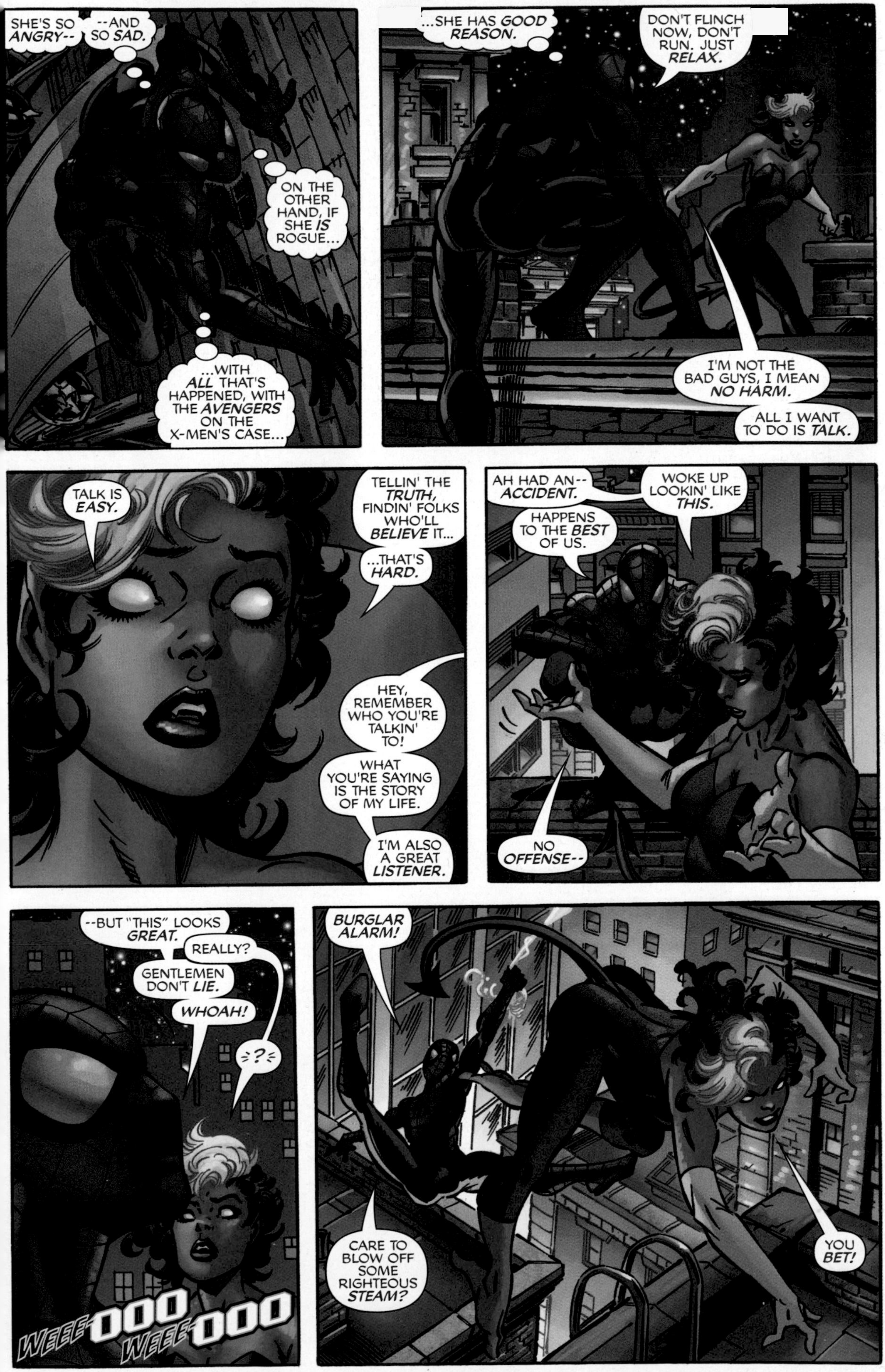

SHE'S SO ANGRY--
--AND SO SAD.
ON THE OTHER HAND, IF SHE IS ROGUE...
...WITH ALL THAT'S HAPPENED, WITH THE AVENGERS ON THE X-MEN'S CASE...
...SHE HAS GOOD REASON.
DON'T FLINCH NOW, DON'T RUN. JUST RELAX.
I'M NOT THE BAD GUYS, I MEAN NO HARM.
ALL I WANT TO DO IS TALK.
TALK IS EASY.
TELLIN' THE TRUTH, FINDIN' FOLKS WHO'LL BELIEVE IT...
...THAT'S HARD.
HEY, REMEMBER WHO YOU'RE TALKIN' TO!
WHAT YOU'RE SAYING IS THE STORY OF MY LIFE.
I'M ALSO A GREAT LISTENER.
AH HAD AN-- ACCIDENT.
WOKE UP LOOKIN' LIKE THIS.
HAPPENS TO THE BEST OF US.
NO OFFENSE--
--BUT "THIS" LOOKS GREAT.
REALLY?
GENTLEMEN DON'T LIE.
WHOAH!
?
WEEE-OOO WEEE-OOO
BURGLAR ALARM!
CARE TO BLOW OFF SOME RIGHTEOUS STEAM?
YOU BET!

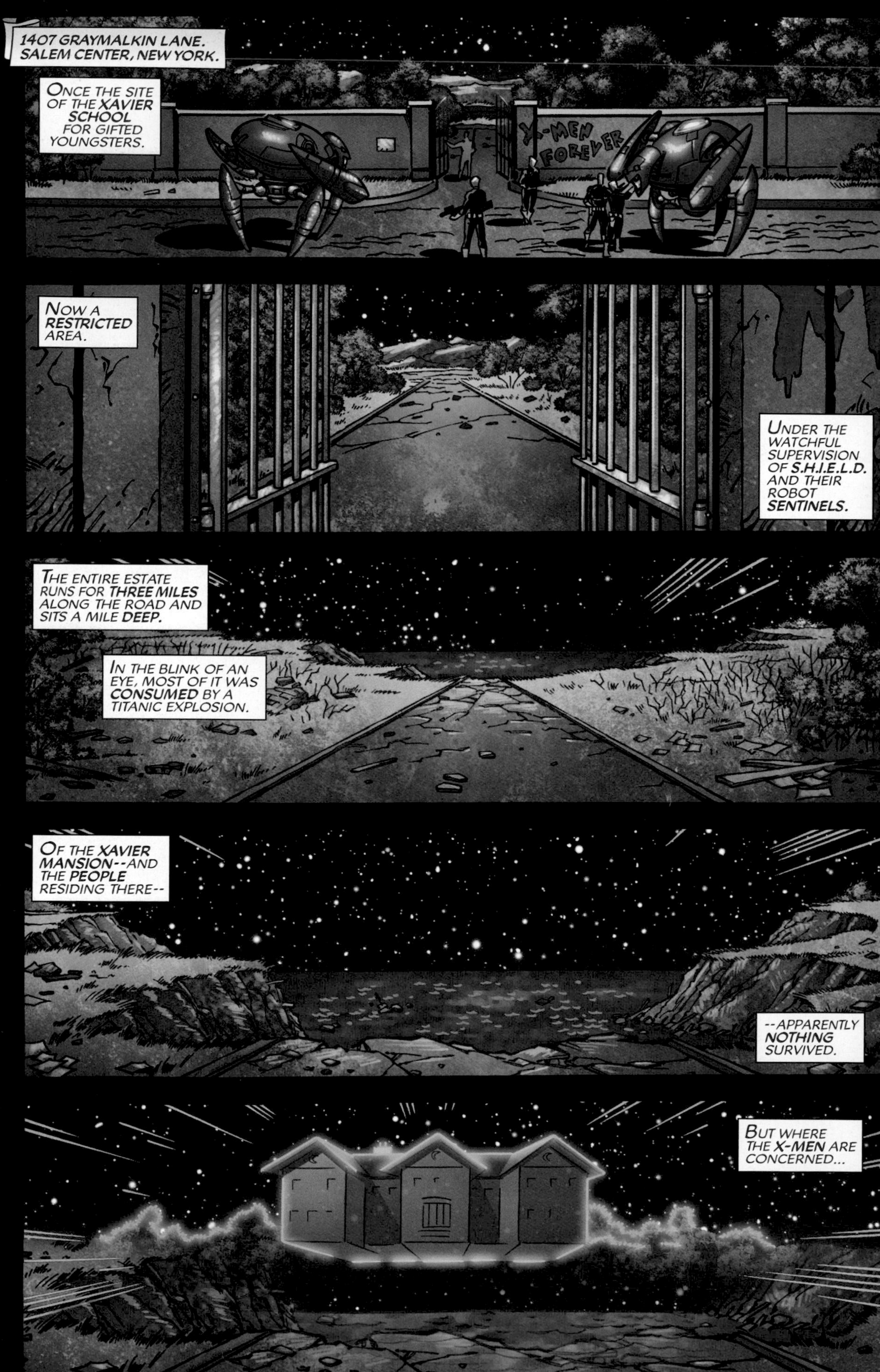
1407 GRAYMALKIN LANE. SALEM CENTER, NEW YORK.
ONCE THE SITE OF THE XAVIER SCHOOL FOR GIFTED YOUNGSTERS.
X-MEN FOREVER
NOW A RESTRICTED AREA.
UNDER THE WATCHFUL SUPERVISION OF S.H.I.E.L.D. AND THEIR ROBOT SENTINELS.
THE ENTIRE ESTATE RUNS FOR THREE MILES ALONG THE ROAD AND SITS A MILE DEEP.
IN THE BLINK OF AN EYE, MOST OF IT WAS CONSUMED BY A TITANIC EXPLOSION.
OF THE XAVIER MANSION--AND THE PEOPLE RESIDING THERE--
--APPARENTLY NOTHING SURVIVED.
BUT WHERE THE X-MEN ARE CONCERNED...

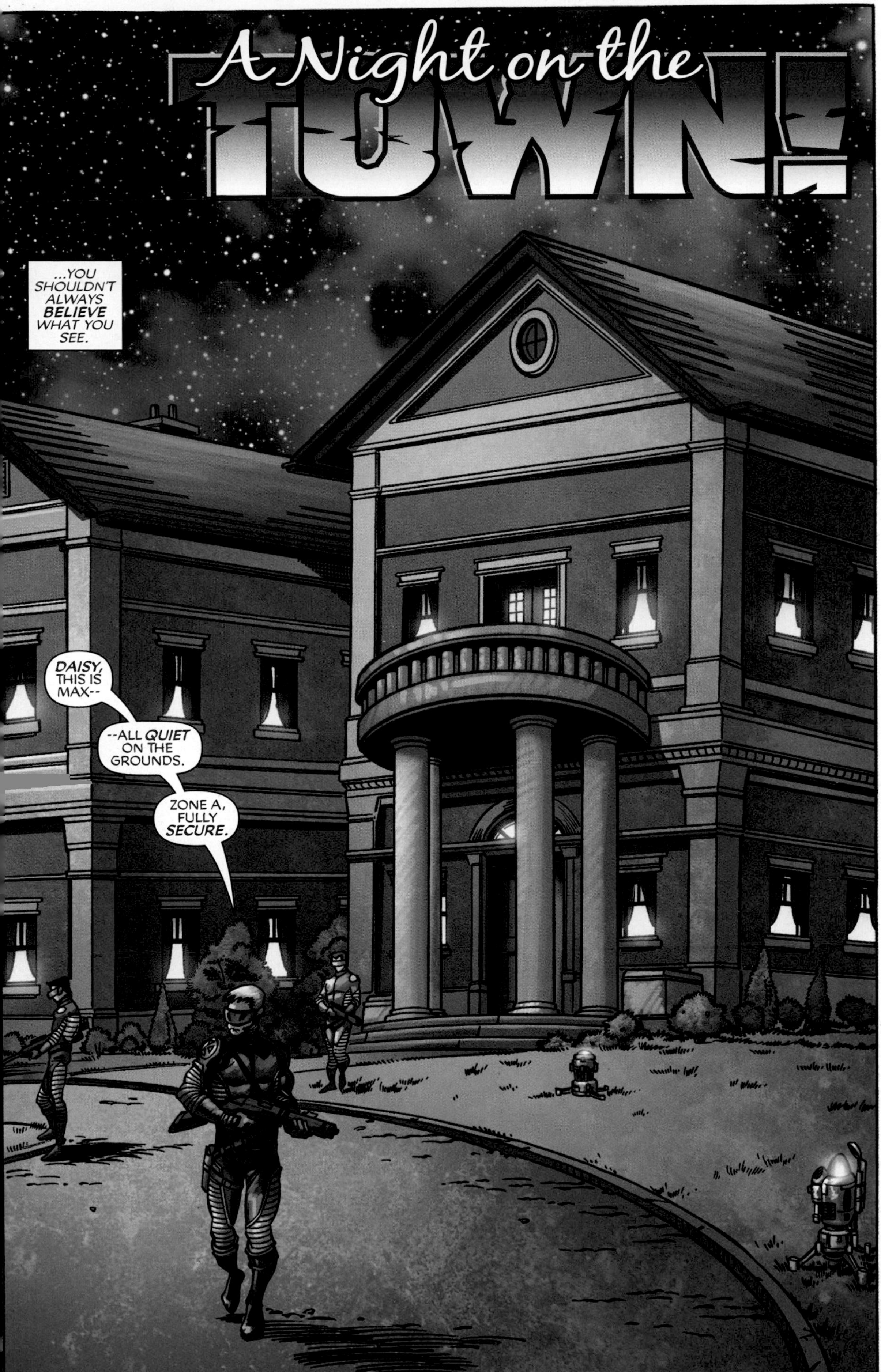
A Night on the
TOWN!
...YOU SHOULDN'T ALWAYS BELIEVE WHAT YOU SEE.
DAISY, THIS IS MAX--
--ALL QUIET ON THE GROUNDS.
ZONE A, FULLY SECURE.

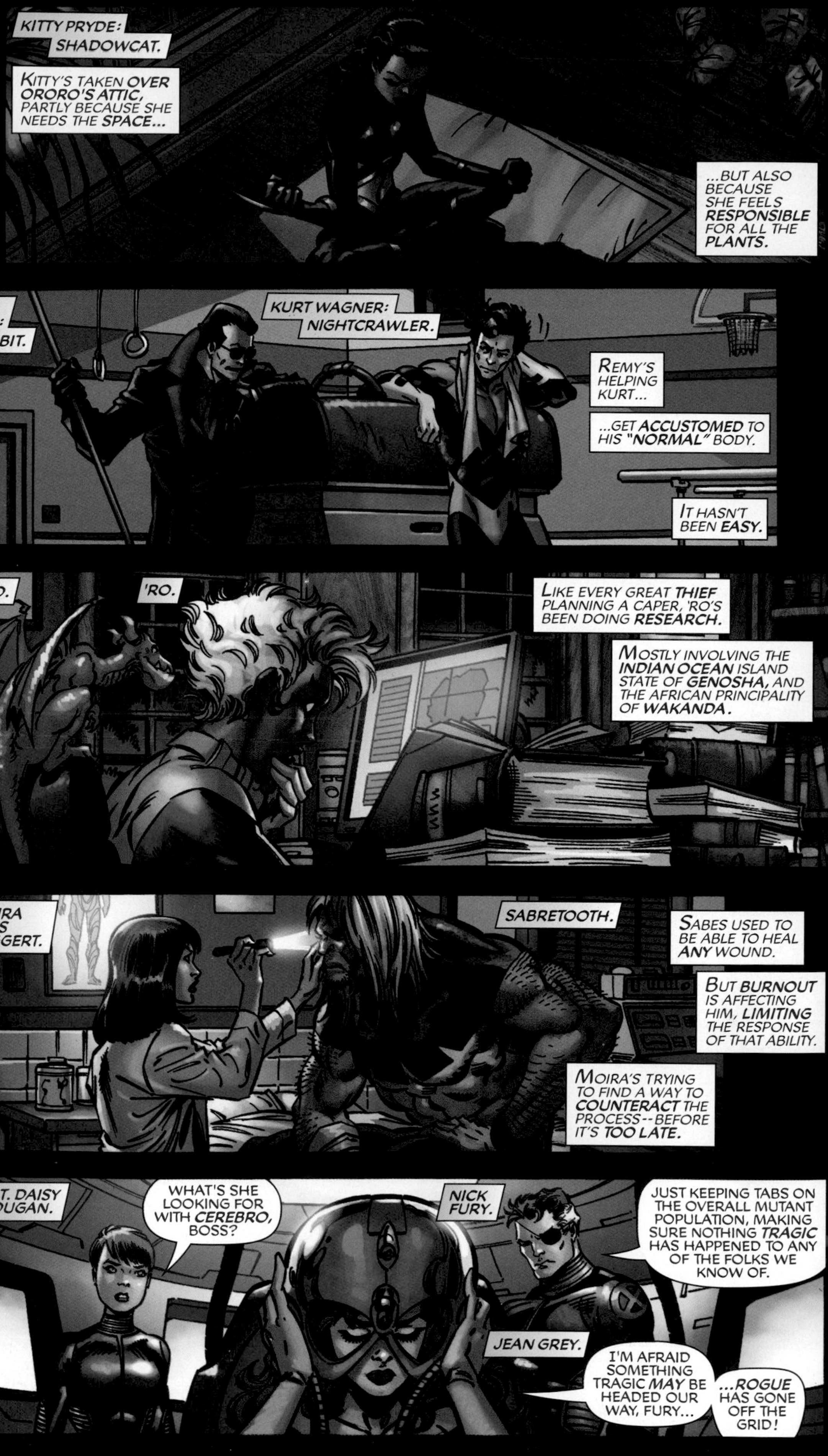
KITTY PRYDE: SHADOWCAT.
KITTY'S TAKEN OVER ORORO'S ATTIC, PARTLY BECAUSE SHE NEEDS THE SPACE...
...BUT ALSO BECAUSE SHE FEELS RESPONSIBLE FOR ALL THE PLANTS.
REMY PICARD: GAMBIT.
KURT WAGNER: NIGHTCRAWLER.
REMY'S HELPING KURT...
...GET ACCUSTOMED TO HIS "NORMAL" BODY.
IT HASN'T BEEN EASY.
LOCKHEED.
'RO.
LIKE EVERY GREAT THIEF PLANNING A CAPER, 'RO'S BEEN DOING RESEARCH.
MOSTLY INVOLVING THE INDIAN OCEAN ISLAND STATE OF GENOSHA, AND THE AFRICAN PRINCIPALITY OF WAKANDA.
DR. MOIRA KINROSS MacTAGGERT.
SABRETOOTH.
SABES USED TO BE ABLE TO HEAL ANY WOUND.
BUT BURNOUT IS AFFECTING HIM, LIMITING THE RESPONSE OF THAT ABILITY.
MOIRA'S TRYING TO FIND A WAY TO COUNTERACT THE PROCESS--BEFORE IT'S TOO LATE.
LT. DAISY DUGAN.
WHAT'S SHE LOOKING FOR WITH CEREBRO, BOSS?
NICK FURY.
JUST KEEPING TABS ON THE OVERALL MUTANT POPULATION, MAKING SURE NOTHING TRAGIC HAS HAPPENED TO ANY OF THE FOLKS WE KNOW OF.
JEAN GREY.
I'M AFRAID SOMETHING TRAGIC MAY BE HEADED OUR WAY, FURY...
...ROGUE HAS GONE OFF THE GRID!

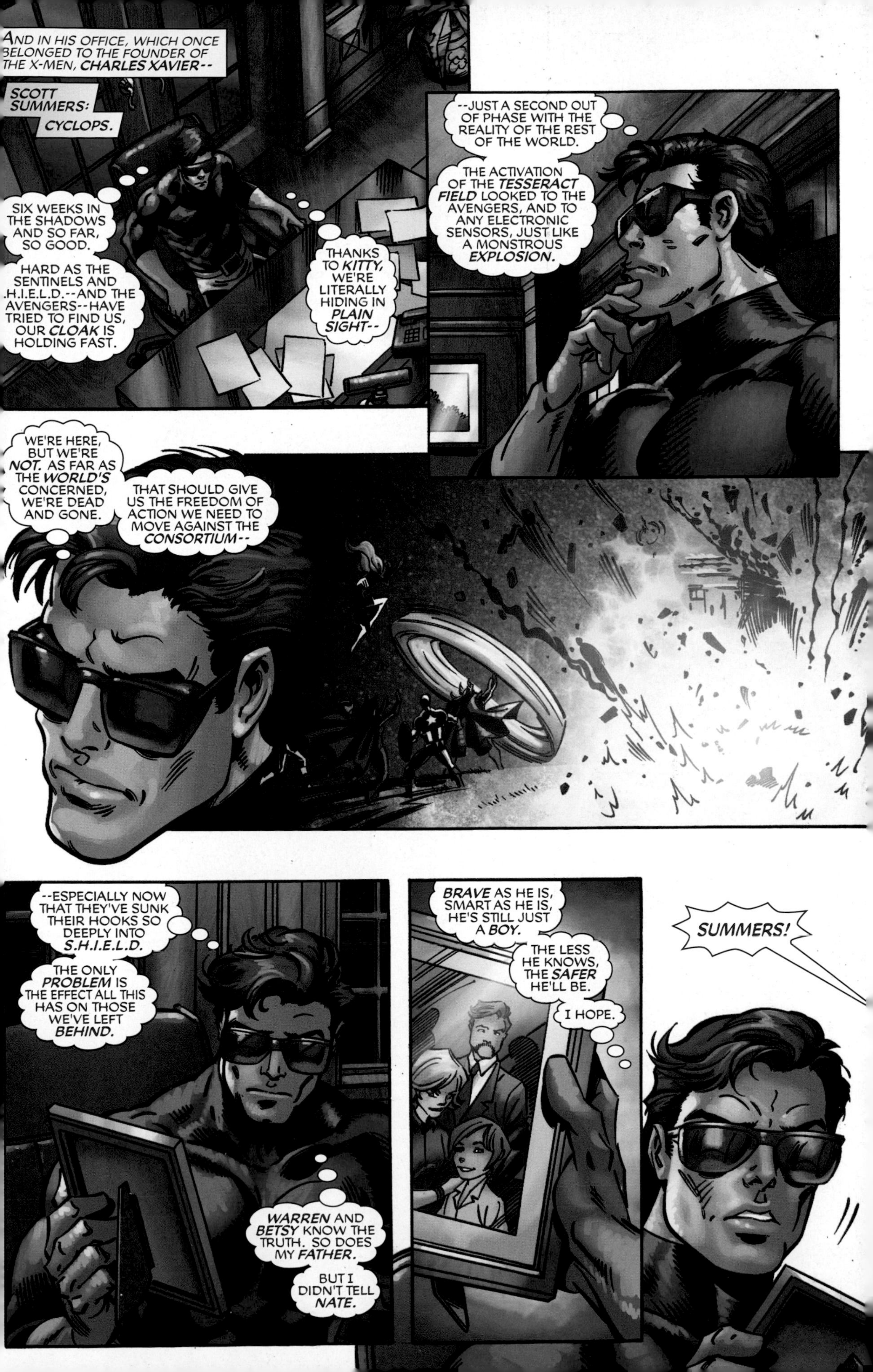
AND IN HIS OFFICE, WHICH ONCE BELONGED TO THE FOUNDER OF THE X-MEN, CHARLES XAVIER--
SCOTT SUMMERS:
CYCLOPS.
SIX WEEKS IN THE SHADOWS AND SO FAR, SO GOOD.
HARD AS THE SENTINELS AND .H.I.E.L.D.--AND THE AVENGERS--HAVE TRIED TO FIND US, OUR CLOAK IS HOLDING FAST.
THANKS TO KITTY, WE'RE LITERALLY HIDING IN PLAIN SIGHT--
--JUST A SECOND OUT OF PHASE WITH THE REALITY OF THE REST OF THE WORLD.
THE ACTIVATION OF THE TESSERACT FIELD LOOKED TO THE AVENGERS, AND TO ANY ELECTRONIC SENSORS, JUST LIKE A MONSTROUS EXPLOSION.
WE'RE HERE, BUT WE'RE NOT. AS FAR AS THE WORLD'S CONCERNED, WE'RE DEAD AND GONE.
THAT SHOULD GIVE US THE FREEDOM OF ACTION WE NEED TO MOVE AGAINST THE CONSORTIUM--
--ESPECIALLY NOW THAT THEY'VE SUNK THEIR HOOKS SO DEEPLY INTO S.H.I.E.L.D.
THE ONLY PROBLEM IS THE EFFECT ALL THIS HAS ON THOSE WE'VE LEFT BEHIND.
WARREN AND BETSY KNOW THE TRUTH. SO DOES MY FATHER.
BUT I DIDN'T TELL NATE.
BRAVE AS HE IS, SMART AS HE IS, HE'S STILL JUST A BOY.
THE LESS HE KNOWS, THE SAFER HE'LL BE.
I HOPE.
SUMMERS!

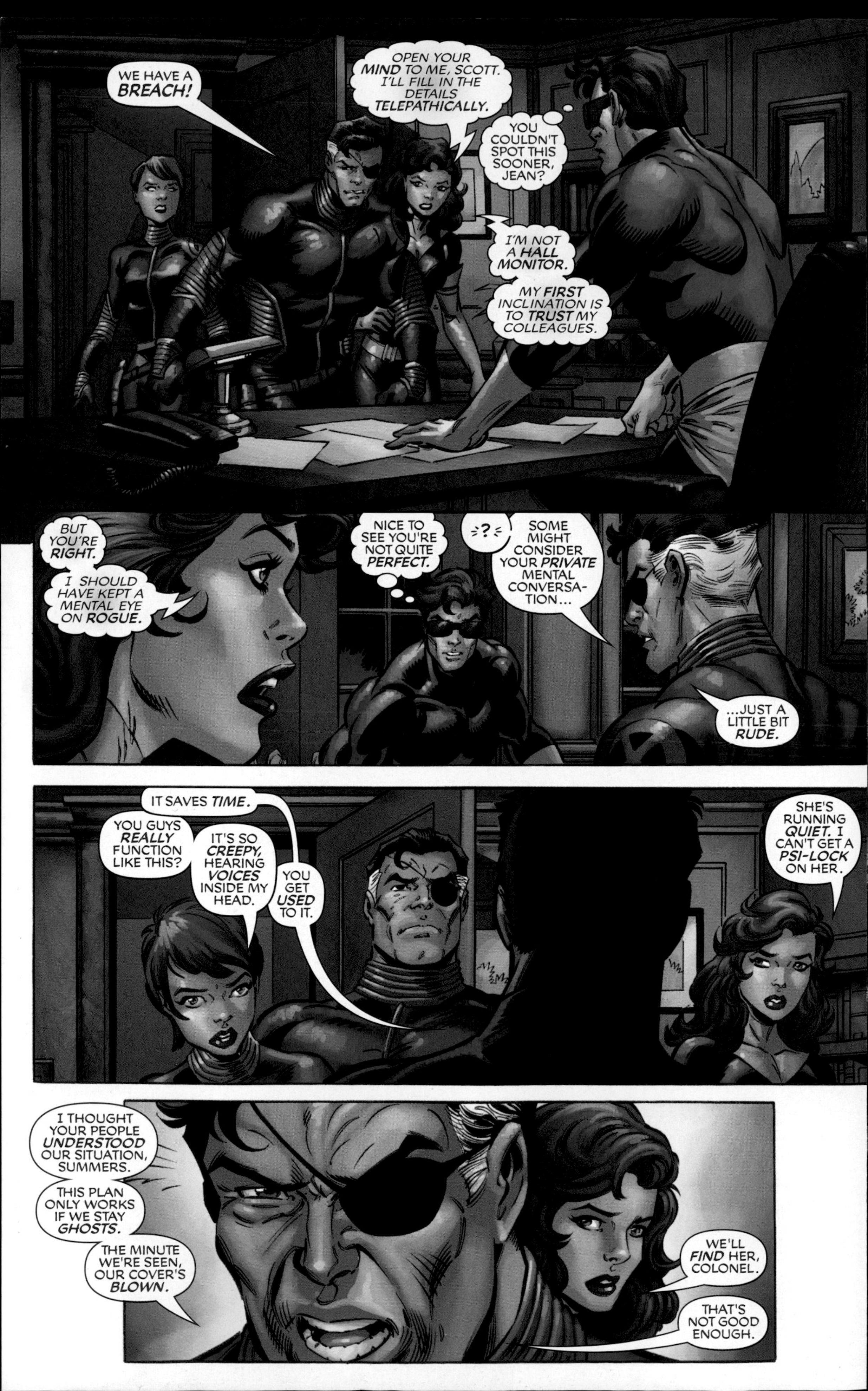
WE HAVE A BREACH!
OPEN YOUR MIND TO ME, SCOTT. I'LL FILL IN THE DETAILS TELEPATHICALLY.
YOU COULDN'T SPOT THIS SOONER, JEAN?
I'M NOT A HALL MONITOR.
MY FIRST INCLINATION IS TO TRUST MY COLLEAGUES.
BUT YOU'RE RIGHT.
I SHOULD HAVE KEPT A MENTAL EYE ON ROGUE.
NICE TO SEE YOU'RE NOT QUITE PERFECT.
?
SOME MIGHT CONSIDER YOUR PRIVATE MENTAL CONVERSA-TION...
...JUST A LITTLE BIT RUDE.
IT SAVES TIME.
YOU GUYS REALLY FUNCTION LIKE THIS?
IT'S SO CREEPY, HEARING VOICES INSIDE MY HEAD.
YOU GET USED TO IT.
SHE'S RUNNING QUIET. I CAN'T GET A PSI-LOCK ON HER.
I THOUGHT YOUR PEOPLE UNDERSTOOD OUR SITUATION, SUMMERS.
THIS PLAN ONLY WORKS IF WE STAY GHOSTS.
THE MINUTE WE'RE SEEN, OUR COVER'S BLOWN.
WE'LL FIND HER, COLONEL.
THAT'S NOT GOOD ENOUGH.

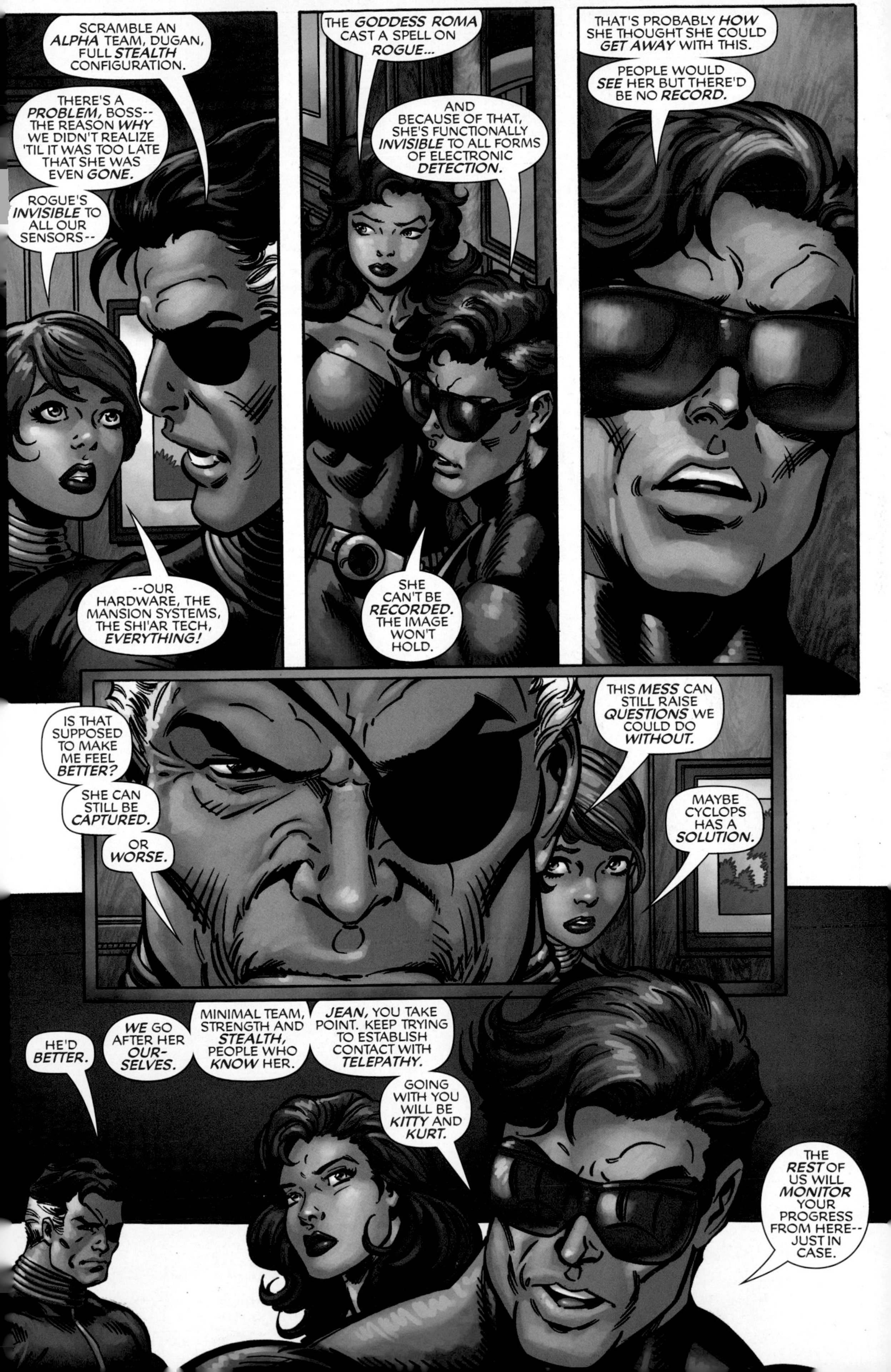
SCRAMBLE AN ALPHA TEAM, DUGAN, FULL STEALTH CONFIGURATION.
THERE'S A PROBLEM, BOSS-- THE REASON WHY WE DIDN'T REALIZE 'TIL IT WAS TOO LATE THAT SHE WAS EVEN GONE.
ROGUE'S INVISIBLE TO ALL OUR SENSORS--
--OUR HARDWARE, THE MANSION SYSTEMS, THE SHI'AR TECH, EVERYTHING!
THE GODDESS ROMA CAST A SPELL ON ROGUE...
AND BECAUSE OF THAT, SHE'S FUNCTIONALLY INVISIBLE TO ALL FORMS OF ELECTRONIC DETECTION.
SHE CAN'T BE RECORDED. THE IMAGE WON'T HOLD.
THAT'S PROBABLY HOW SHE THOUGHT SHE COULD GET AWAY WITH THIS.
PEOPLE WOULD SEE HER BUT THERE'D BE NO RECORD.
IS THAT SUPPOSED TO MAKE ME FEEL BETTER?
SHE CAN STILL BE CAPTURED.
OR WORSE.
THIS MESS CAN STILL RAISE QUESTIONS WE COULD DO WITHOUT.
MAYBE CYCLOPS HAS A SOLUTION.
HE'D BETTER.
WE GO AFTER HER OUR-SELVES.
MINIMAL TEAM, STRENGTH AND STEALTH, PEOPLE WHO KNOW HER.
JEAN, YOU TAKE POINT. KEEP TRYING TO ESTABLISH CONTACT WITH TELEPATHY.
GOING WITH YOU WILL BE KITTY AND KURT.
THE REST OF US WILL MONITOR YOUR PROGRESS FROM HERE-- JUST IN CASE.

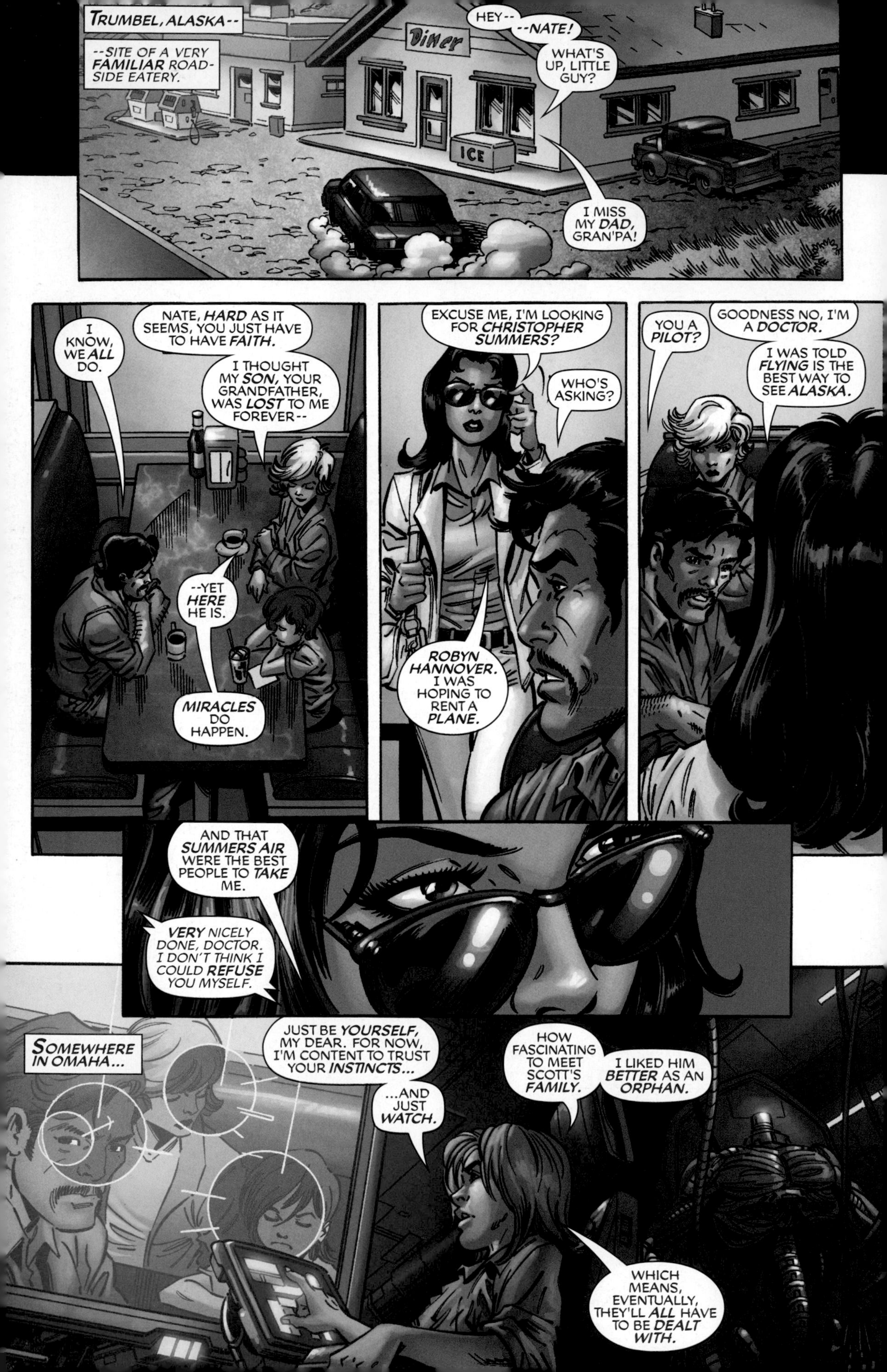
TRUMBEL, ALASKA--
--SITE OF A VERY FAMILIAR ROAD-SIDE EATERY.
Diner
HEY--
--NATE! WHAT'S UP, LITTLE GUY?
ICE
I MISS MY DAD, GRAN'PA!
I KNOW, WE ALL DO.
NATE, HARD AS IT SEEMS, YOU JUST HAVE TO HAVE FAITH.
I THOUGHT MY SON, YOUR GRANDFATHER, WAS LOST TO ME FOREVER--
--YET HERE HE IS.
MIRACLES DO HAPPEN.
EXCUSE ME, I'M LOOKING FOR CHRISTOPHER SUMMERS?
WHO'S ASKING?
ROBYN HANNOVER. I WAS HOPING TO RENT A PLANE.
YOU A PILOT?
GOODNESS NO, I'M A DOCTOR.
I WAS TOLD FLYING IS THE BEST WAY TO SEE ALASKA.
AND THAT SUMMERS AIR WERE THE BEST PEOPLE TO TAKE ME.
VERY NICELY DONE, DOCTOR. I DON'T THINK I COULD REFUSE YOU MYSELF.
SOMEWHERE IN OMAHA...
JUST BE YOURSELF, MY DEAR. FOR NOW, I'M CONTENT TO TRUST YOUR INSTINCTS...
...AND JUST WATCH.
HOW FASCINATING TO MEET SCOTT'S FAMILY.
I LIKED HIM BETTER AS AN ORPHAN.
WHICH MEANS, EVENTUALLY, THEY'LL ALL HAVE TO BE DEALT WITH.

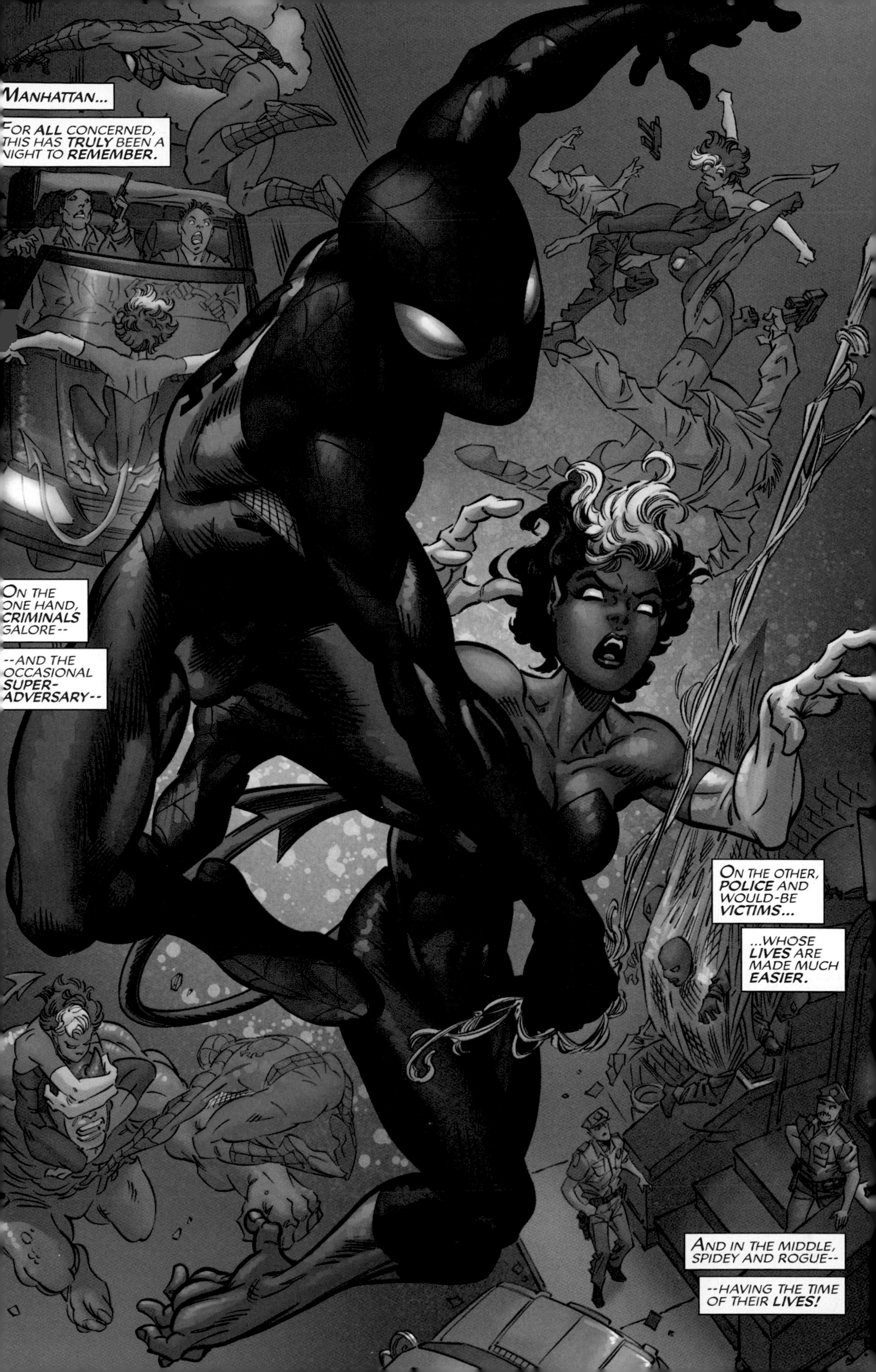
MANHATTAN...
FOR ALL CONCERNED, THIS HAS TRULY BEEN A NIGHT TO REMEMBER.
ON THE ONE HAND, CRIMINALS GALORE--
--AND THE OCCASIONAL SUPER-ADVERSARY--
ON THE OTHER, POLICE AND WOULD-BE VICTIMS...
...WHOSE LIVES ARE MADE MUCH EASIER.
AND IN THE MIDDLE, SPIDEY AND ROGUE--
--HAVING THE TIME OF THEIR LIVES!

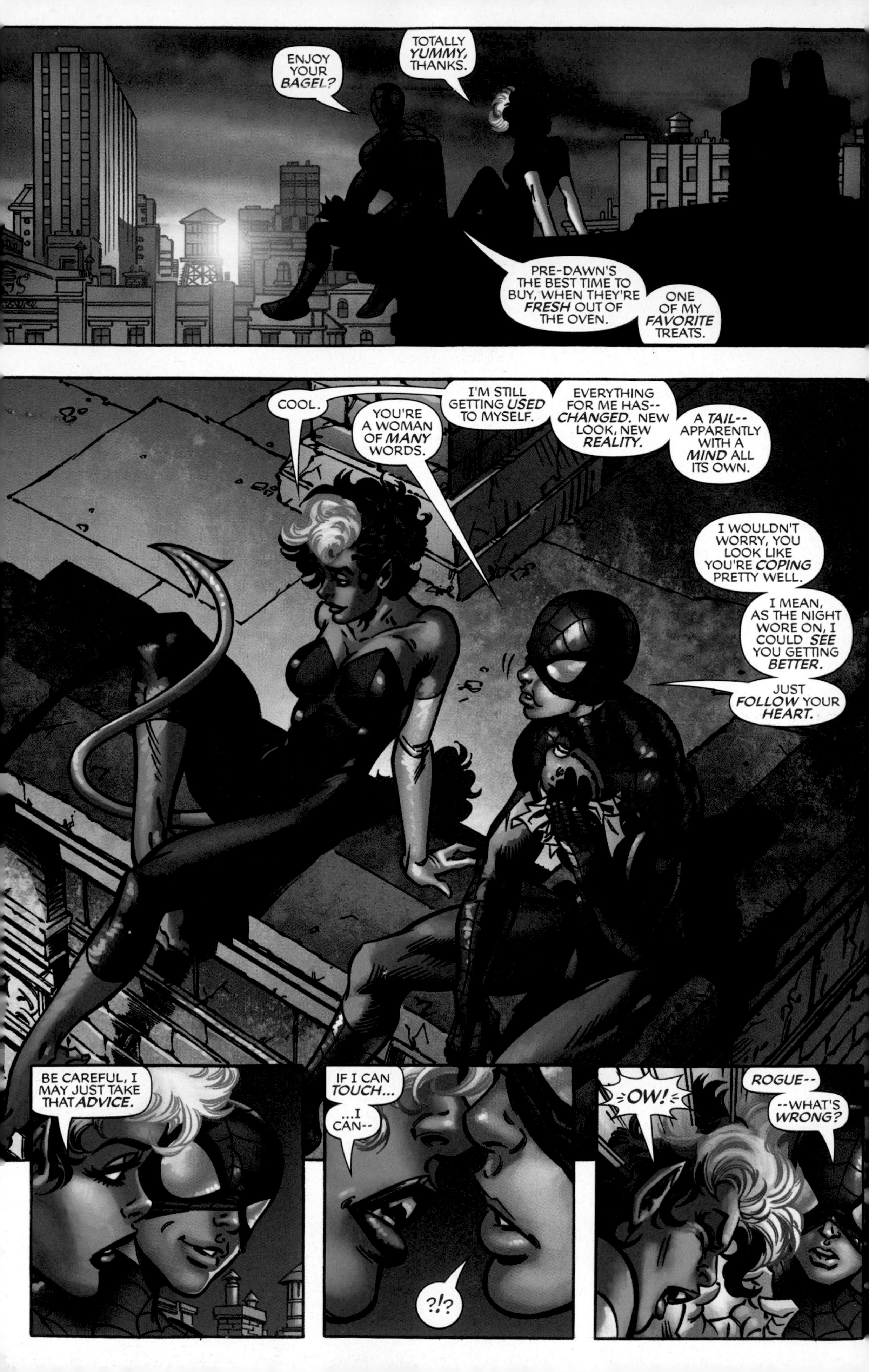
ENJOY YOUR *BAGEL?*
TOTALLY *YUMMY,* THANKS.
PRE-DAWN'S THE BEST TIME TO BUY, WHEN THEY'RE *FRESH* OUT OF THE OVEN.
ONE OF MY *FAVORITE* TREATS.
COOL.
YOU'RE A WOMAN OF *MANY* WORDS.
I'M STILL GETTING *USED* TO MYSELF.
EVERYTHING FOR ME HAS-- *CHANGED.* NEW LOOK, NEW *REALITY.*
A *TAIL*-- APPARENTLY WITH A *MIND* ALL ITS OWN.
I WOULDN'T WORRY, YOU LOOK LIKE YOU'RE *COPING* PRETTY WELL.
I MEAN, AS THE NIGHT WORE ON, I COULD *SEE* YOU GETTING *BETTER.*
JUST *FOLLOW* YOUR *HEART.*
BE CAREFUL, I MAY JUST TAKE THAT *ADVICE.*
IF I CAN *TOUCH...*
...I CAN--
?!?
OW!
ROGUE--
--WHAT'S *WRONG?*

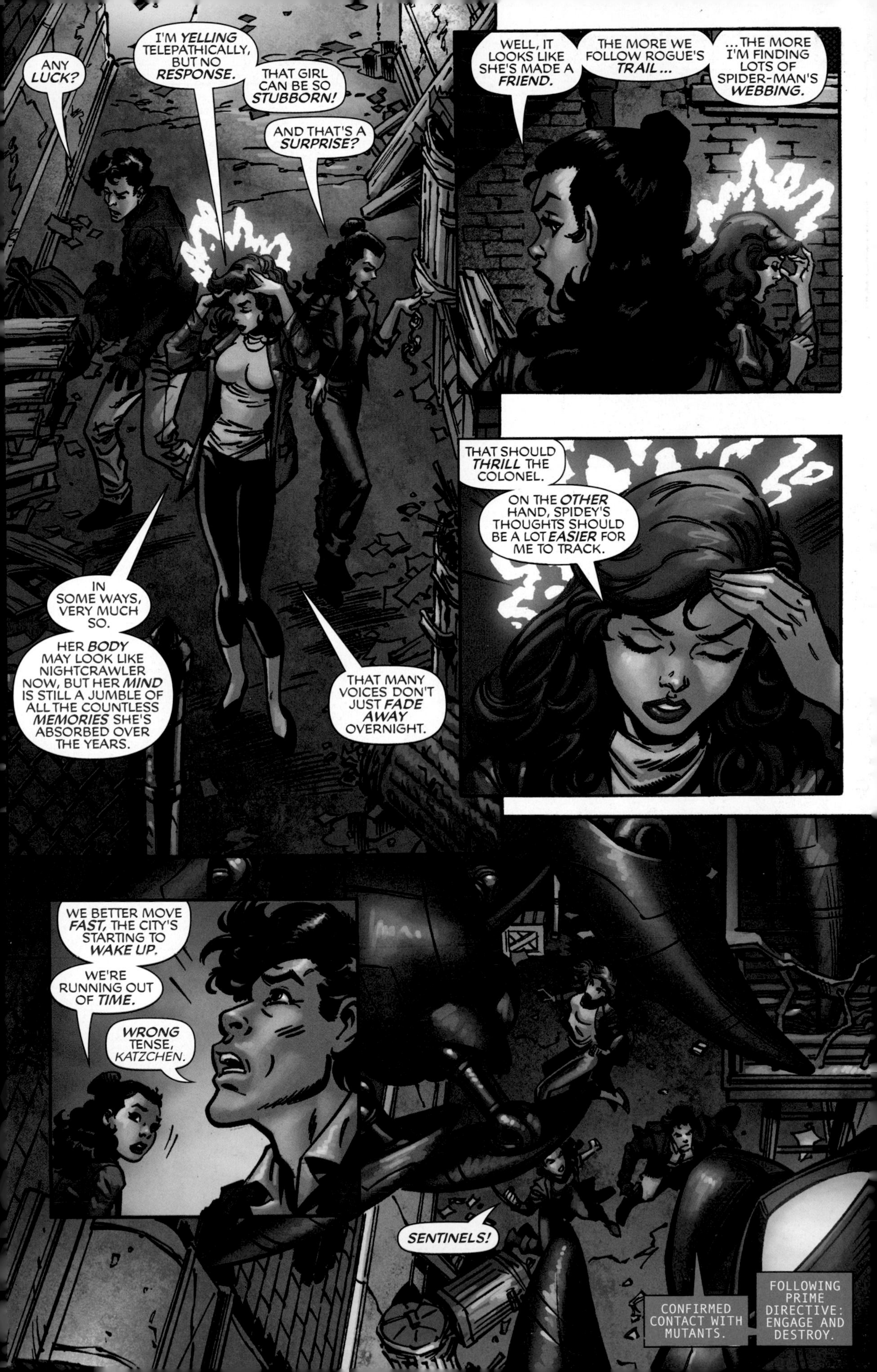
ANY LUCK?
I'M YELLING TELEPATHICALLY, BUT NO RESPONSE.
THAT GIRL CAN BE SO STUBBORN!
AND THAT'S A SURPRISE?
IN SOME WAYS, VERY MUCH SO.
HER BODY MAY LOOK LIKE NIGHTCRAWLER NOW, BUT HER MIND IS STILL A JUMBLE OF ALL THE COUNTLESS MEMORIES SHE'S ABSORBED OVER THE YEARS.
THAT MANY VOICES DON'T JUST FADE AWAY OVERNIGHT.
WELL, IT LOOKS LIKE SHE'S MADE A FRIEND.
THE MORE WE FOLLOW ROGUE'S TRAIL...
...THE MORE I'M FINDING LOTS OF SPIDER-MAN'S WEBBING.
THAT SHOULD THRILL THE COLONEL.
ON THE OTHER HAND, SPIDEY'S THOUGHTS SHOULD BE A LOT EASIER FOR ME TO TRACK.
WE BETTER MOVE FAST, THE CITY'S STARTING TO WAKE UP.
WE'RE RUNNING OUT OF TIME.
WRONG TENSE, KATZCHEN.
SENTINELS!
CONFIRMED CONTACT WITH MUTANTS.
FOLLOWING PRIME DIRECTIVE: ENGAGE AND DESTROY.

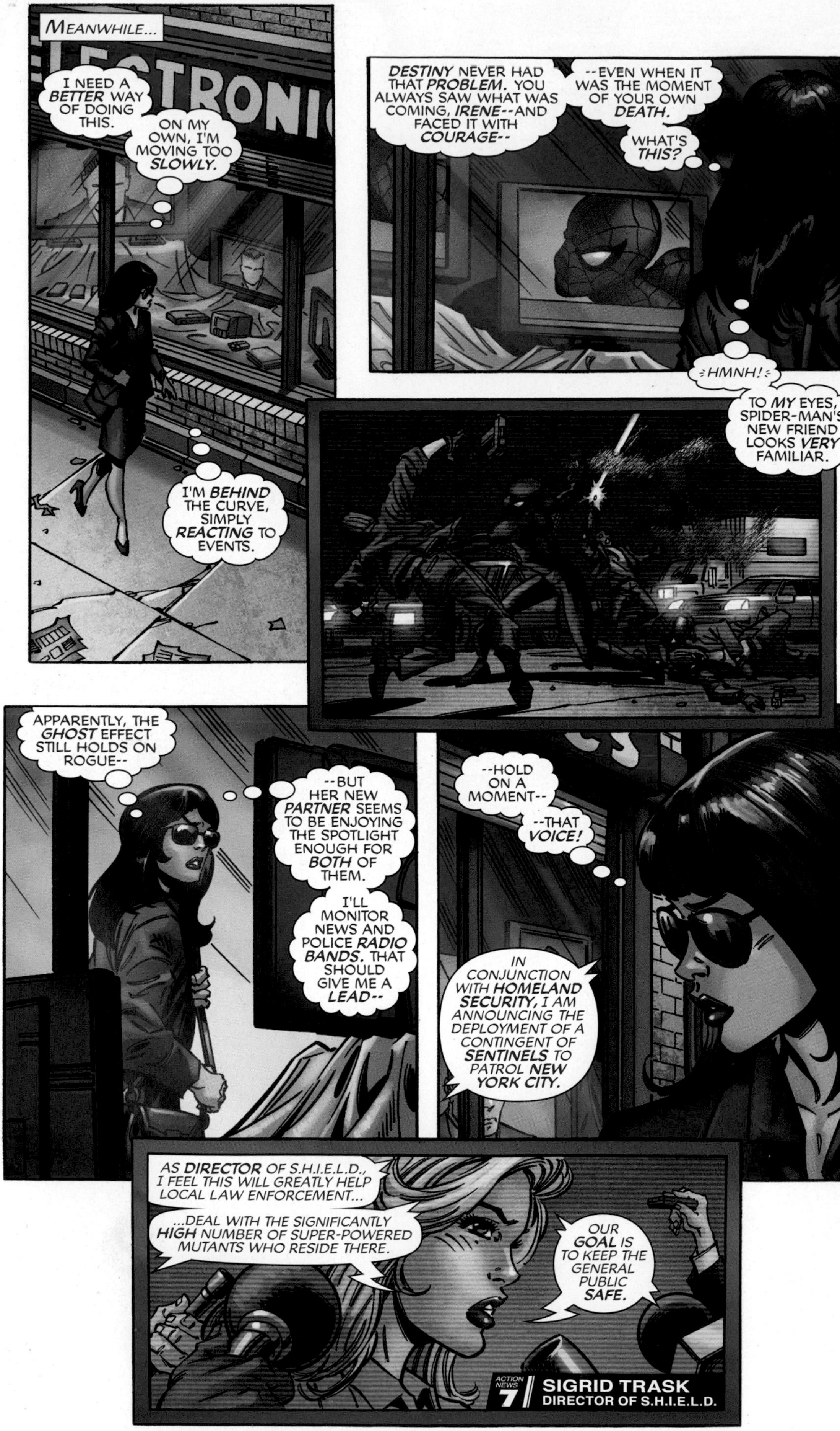
MEANWHILE...
ELECTRONIC
I NEED A BETTER WAY OF DOING THIS.
ON MY OWN, I'M MOVING TOO SLOWLY.
I'M BEHIND THE CURVE, SIMPLY REACTING TO EVENTS.
DESTINY NEVER HAD THAT PROBLEM. YOU ALWAYS SAW WHAT WAS COMING, IRENE--AND FACED IT WITH COURAGE--
--EVEN WHEN IT WAS THE MOMENT OF YOUR OWN DEATH.
WHAT'S THIS?
HMNH!
TO MY EYES, SPIDER-MAN'S NEW FRIEND LOOKS VERY FAMILIAR.
APPARENTLY, THE GHOST EFFECT STILL HOLDS ON ROGUE--
--BUT HER NEW PARTNER SEEMS TO BE ENJOYING THE SPOTLIGHT ENOUGH FOR BOTH OF THEM.
I'LL MONITOR NEWS AND POLICE RADIO BANDS. THAT SHOULD GIVE ME A LEAD--
--HOLD ON A MOMENT--
--THAT VOICE!
IN CONJUNCTION WITH HOMELAND SECURITY, I AM ANNOUNCING THE DEPLOYMENT OF A CONTINGENT OF SENTINELS TO PATROL NEW YORK CITY.
AS DIRECTOR OF S.H.I.E.L.D., I FEEL THIS WILL GREATLY HELP LOCAL LAW ENFORCEMENT...
...DEAL WITH THE SIGNIFICANTLY HIGH NUMBER OF SUPER-POWERED MUTANTS WHO RESIDE THERE.
OUR GOAL IS TO KEEP THE GENERAL PUBLIC SAFE.
ACTION NEWS 7
SIGRID TRASK
DIRECTOR OF S.H.I.E.L.D.

I DIDN'T EXPECT TO SEE THEM ON *PATROL* IN THE CITY.

ZIGGY TRASK ISN'T WASTING ANY TIME FULFILLING HER *AGENDA.*

LET'S HOPE WE CAN *BEAT* THEM.

PROGNOSIS: MINIMAL.

CHOOM!

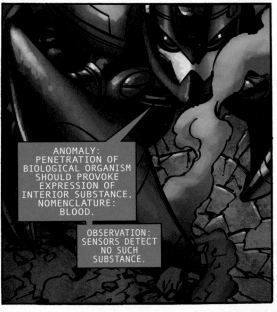

ANOMALY: PENETRATION OF BIOLOGICAL ORGANISM SHOULD PROVOKE EXPRESSION OF INTERIOR SUBSTANCE, NOMENCLATURE: BLOOD.

OBSERVATION: SENSORS DETECT NO SUCH SUBSTANCE.

THAT'S BECAUSE YOU DIDN'T *CUT* ME, ROBOT.

PITY--FOR *YOU*--THE SAME CAN'T BE SAID IN *REVERSE.*

SLANG!

MY NEW POWERS ONLY WORK ON FLESH AND BLOOD-- NOT *METAL* AND OIL!

NO WAY TO *FIGHT BACK.*

ALL I CAN DO FOR NOW IS *DUCK--*

ZARK!

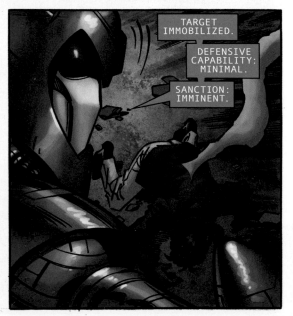

TARGET IMMOBILIZED.

DEFENSIVE CAPABILITY: MINIMAL.

SANCTION: IMMINENT.

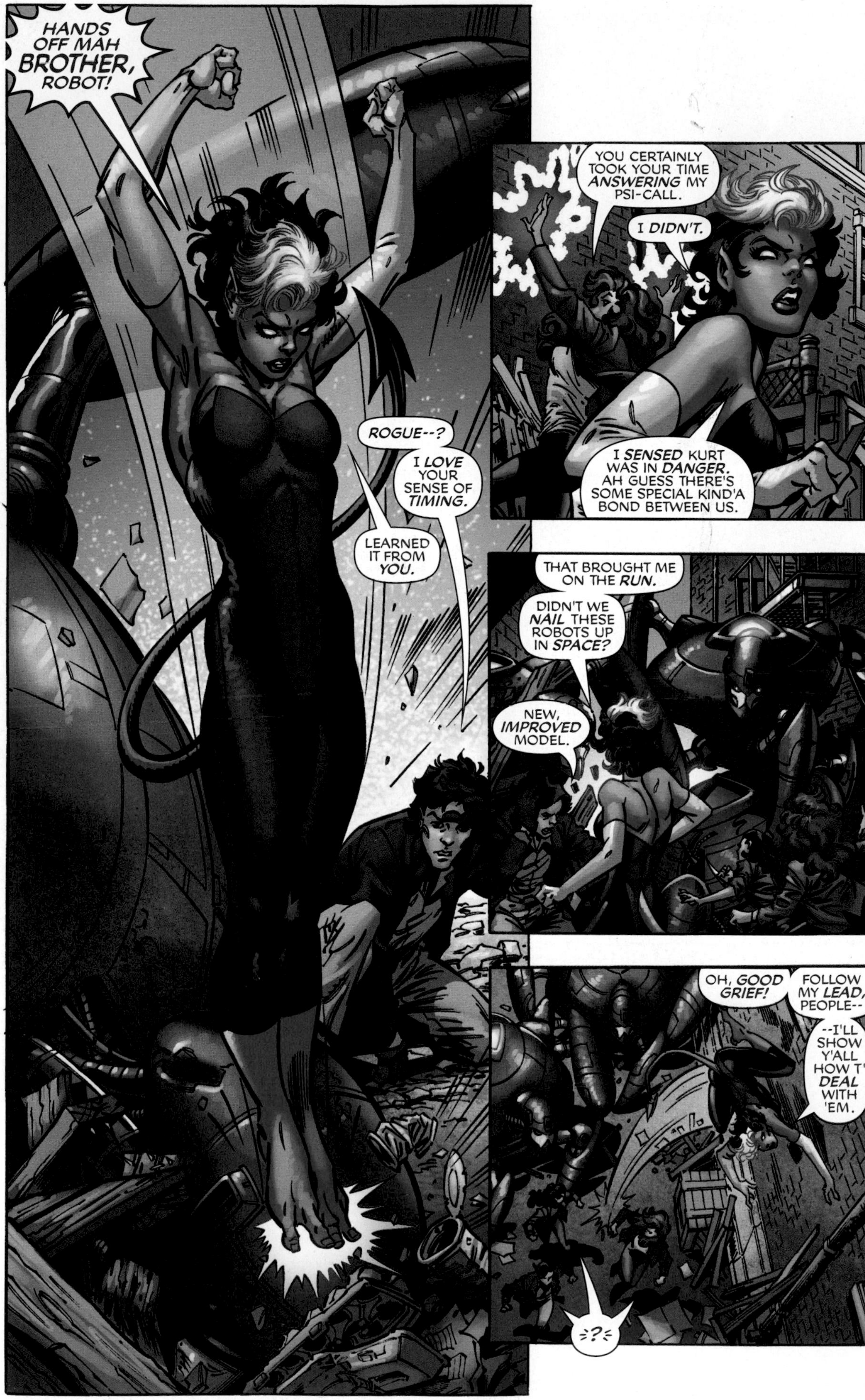
HANDS OFF MAH BROTHER, ROBOT!
ROGUE--?
I LOVE YOUR SENSE OF TIMING.
LEARNED IT FROM YOU.
YOU CERTAINLY TOOK YOUR TIME ANSWERING MY PSI-CALL.
I DIDN'T.
I SENSED KURT WAS IN DANGER. AH GUESS THERE'S SOME SPECIAL KIND'A BOND BETWEEN US.
THAT BROUGHT ME ON THE RUN.
DIDN'T WE NAIL THESE ROBOTS UP IN SPACE?
NEW, IMPROVED MODEL.
OH, GOOD GRIEF!
FOLLOW MY LEAD, PEOPLE--
--I'LL SHOW Y'ALL HOW T' DEAL WITH 'EM.
!?

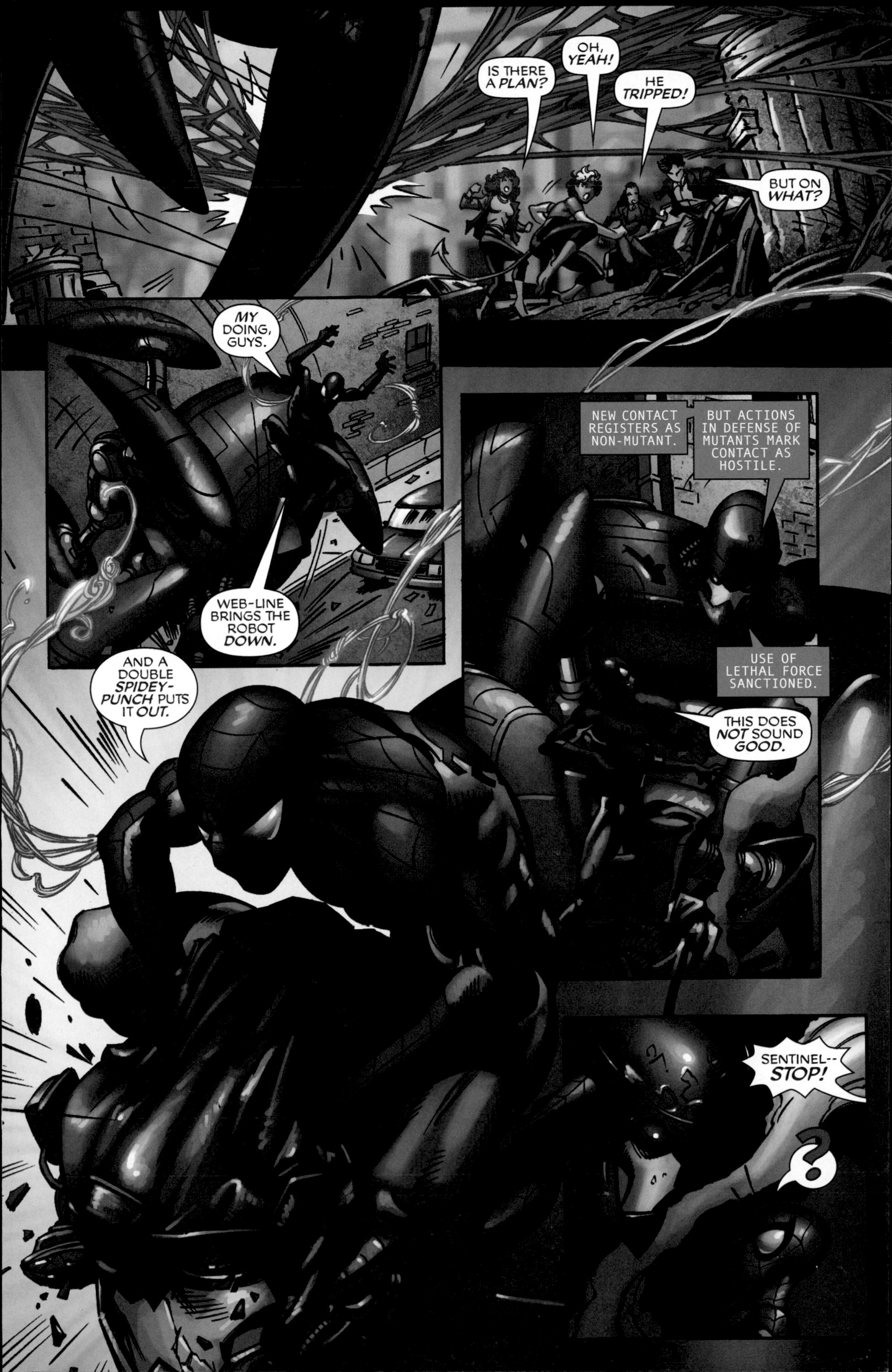
IS THERE A PLAN?
OH, YEAH!
HE TRIPPED!
BUT ON WHAT?
MY DOING, GUYS.
WEB-LINE BRINGS THE ROBOT DOWN.
AND A DOUBLE SPIDEY-PUNCH PUTS IT OUT.
NEW CONTACT REGISTERS AS NON-MUTANT.
BUT ACTIONS IN DEFENSE OF MUTANTS MARK CONTACT AS HOSTILE.
USE OF LETHAL FORCE SANCTIONED.
THIS DOES NOT SOUND GOOD.
SENTINEL-- STOP!

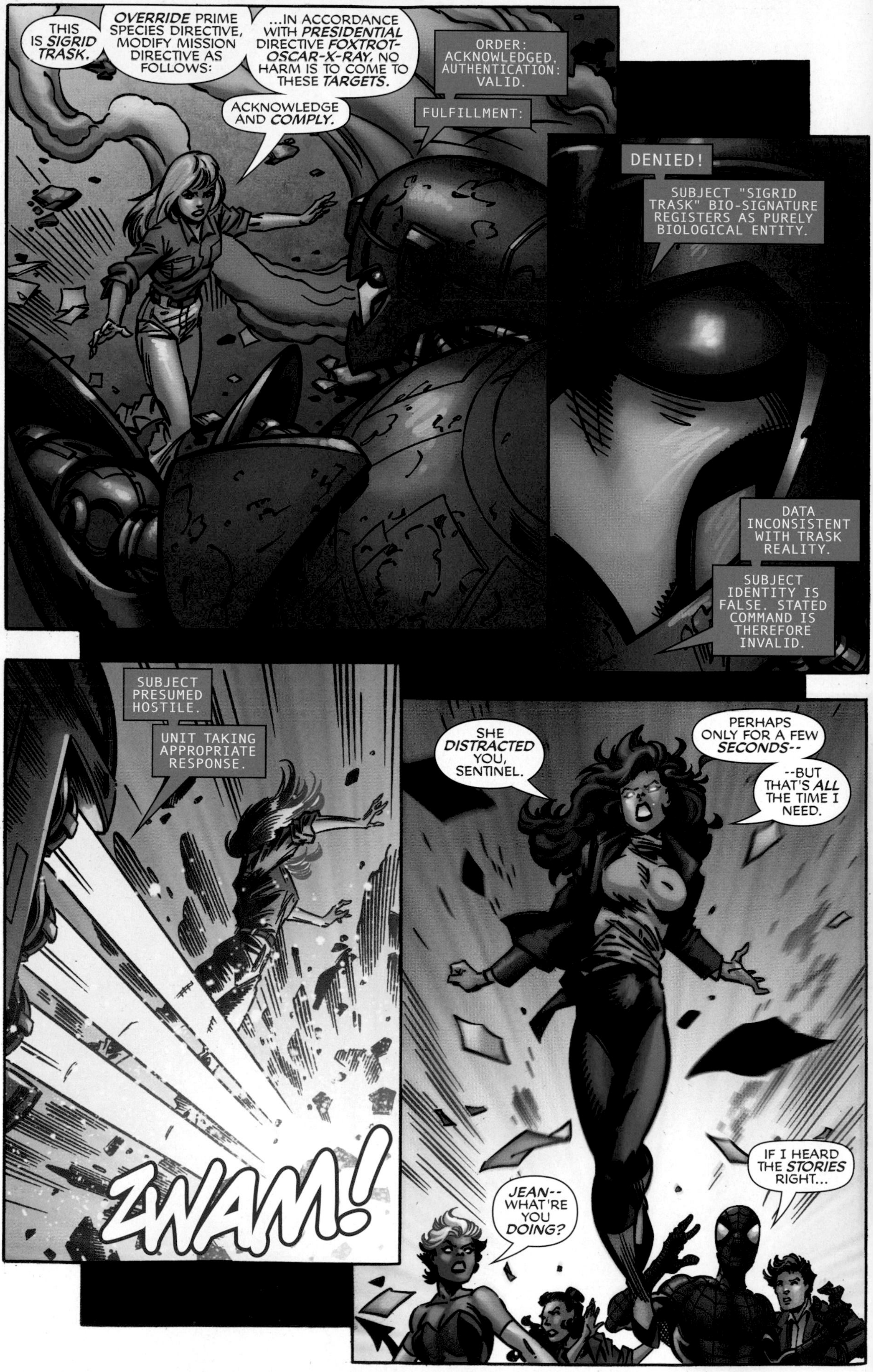
THIS IS SIGRID TRASK.
OVERRIDE PRIME SPECIES DIRECTIVE, MODIFY MISSION DIRECTIVE AS FOLLOWS:
...IN ACCORDANCE WITH PRESIDENTIAL DIRECTIVE FOXTROT-OSCAR-X-RAY, NO HARM IS TO COME TO THESE TARGETS.
ACKNOWLEDGE AND COMPLY.
ORDER: ACKNOWLEDGED. AUTHENTICATION: VALID.
FULFILLMENT:
DENIED!
SUBJECT "SIGRID TRASK" BIO-SIGNATURE REGISTERS AS PURELY BIOLOGICAL ENTITY.
DATA INCONSISTENT WITH TRASK REALITY.
SUBJECT IDENTITY IS FALSE. STATED COMMAND IS THEREFORE INVALID.
SUBJECT PRESUMED HOSTILE.
UNIT TAKING APPROPRIATE RESPONSE.
ZWAM!
SHE DISTRACTED YOU, SENTINEL.
PERHAPS ONLY FOR A FEW SECONDS--
--BUT THAT'S ALL THE TIME I NEED.
JEAN--WHAT'RE YOU DOING?
IF I HEARD THE STORIES RIGHT...

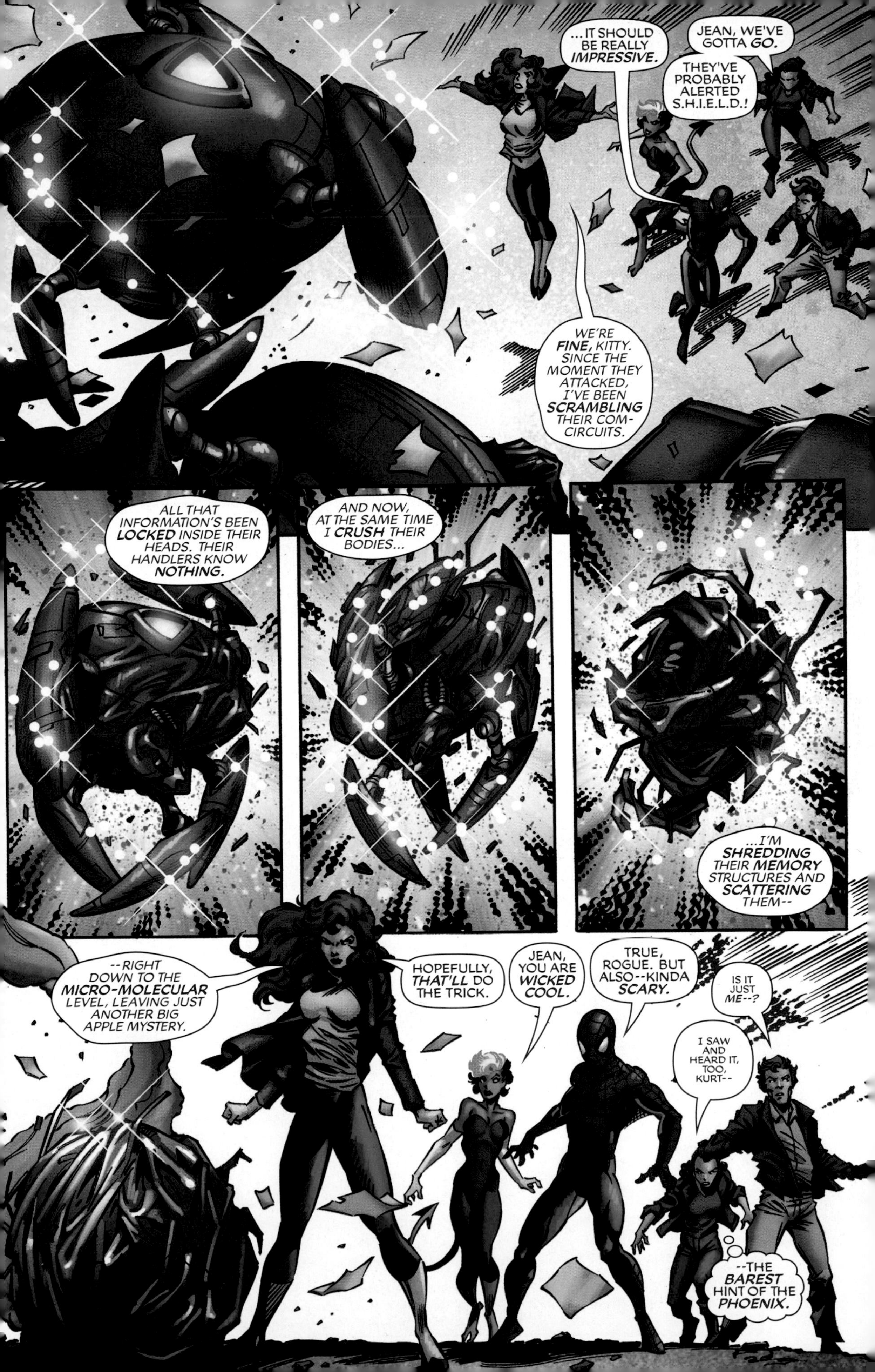
...IT SHOULD BE REALLY IMPRESSIVE.
JEAN, WE'VE GOTTA GO.
THEY'VE PROBABLY ALERTED S.H.I.E.L.D.!
WE'RE FINE, KITTY. SINCE THE MOMENT THEY ATTACKED, I'VE BEEN SCRAMBLING THEIR COM-CIRCUITS.
ALL THAT INFORMATION'S BEEN LOCKED INSIDE THEIR HEADS. THEIR HANDLERS KNOW NOTHING.
AND NOW, AT THE SAME TIME I CRUSH THEIR BODIES...
...I'M SHREDDING THEIR MEMORY STRUCTURES AND SCATTERING THEM--
--RIGHT DOWN TO THE MICRO-MOLECULAR LEVEL, LEAVING JUST ANOTHER BIG APPLE MYSTERY.
HOPEFULLY, THAT'LL DO THE TRICK.
JEAN, YOU ARE WICKED COOL.
TRUE, ROGUE. BUT ALSO--KINDA SCARY.
IS IT JUST ME--?
I SAW AND HEARD IT, TOO, KURT--
--THE BAREST HINT OF THE PHOENIX.

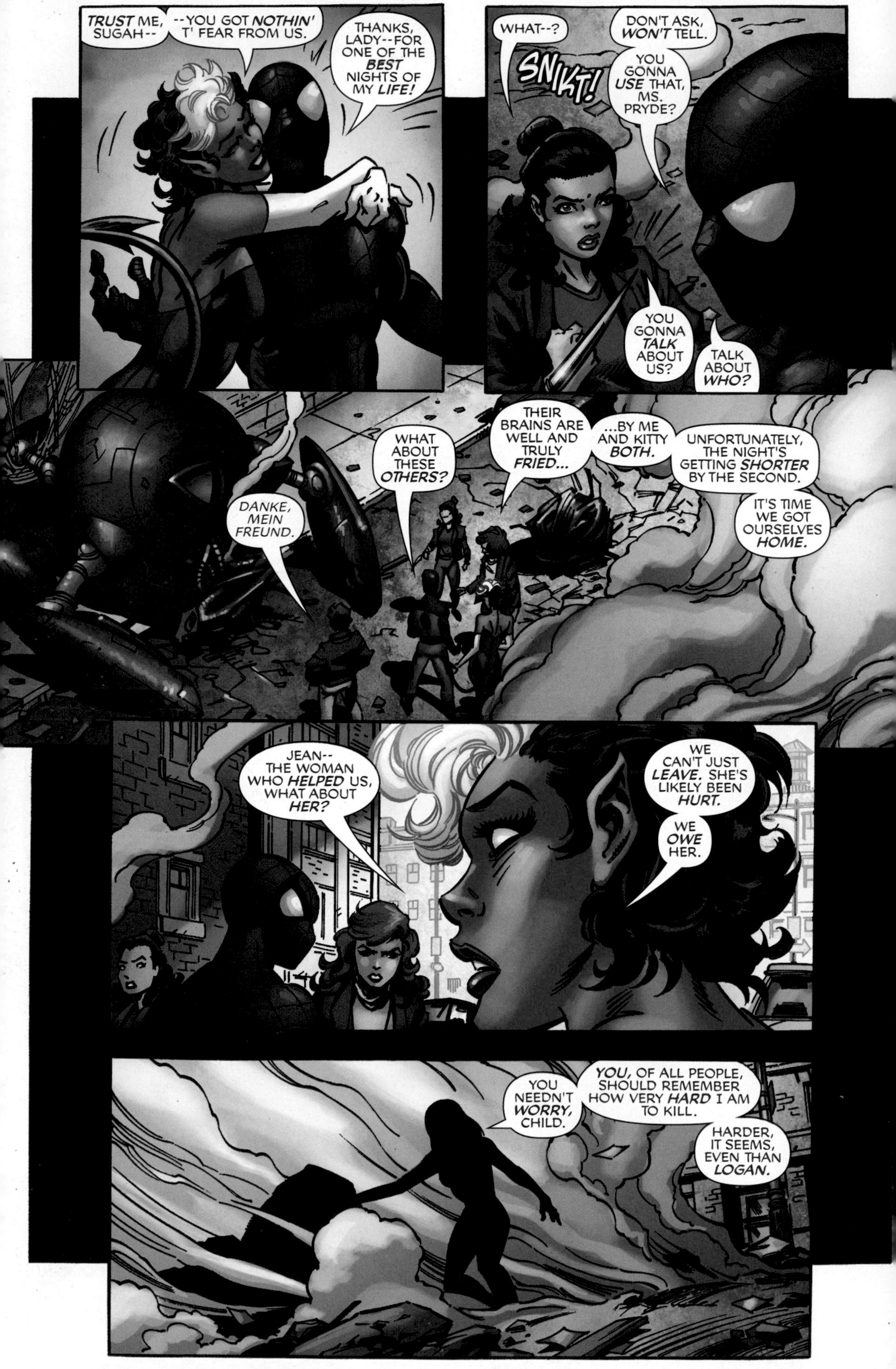
TRUST ME, SUGAH--
--YOU GOT NOTHIN' T' FEAR FROM US.
THANKS, LADY--FOR ONE OF THE BEST NIGHTS OF MY LIFE!
WHAT--?
SNIKT!
DON'T ASK, WON'T TELL.
YOU GONNA USE THAT, MS. PRYDE?
YOU GONNA TALK ABOUT US?
TALK ABOUT WHO?
DANKE, MEIN FREUND.
WHAT ABOUT THESE OTHERS?
THEIR BRAINS ARE WELL AND TRULY FRIED...
...BY ME AND KITTY BOTH.
UNFORTUNATELY, THE NIGHT'S GETTING SHORTER BY THE SECOND.
IT'S TIME WE GOT OURSELVES HOME.
JEAN-- THE WOMAN WHO HELPED US, WHAT ABOUT HER?
WE CAN'T JUST LEAVE. SHE'S LIKELY BEEN HURT.
WE OWE HER.
YOU NEEDN'T WORRY, CHILD.
YOU, OF ALL PEOPLE, SHOULD REMEMBER HOW VERY HARD I AM TO KILL.
HARDER, IT SEEMS, EVEN THAN LOGAN.

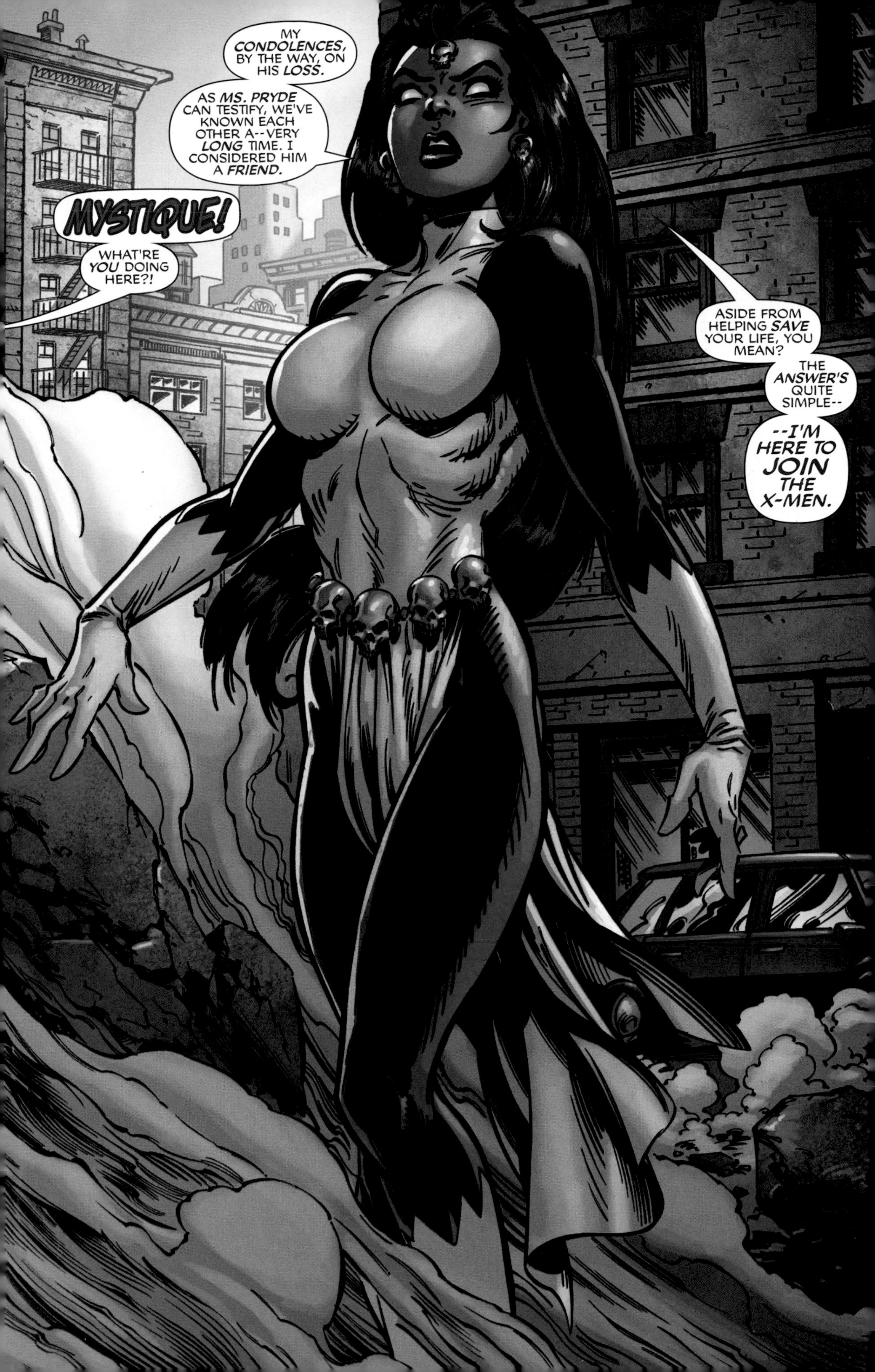
MY CONDOLENCES, BY THE WAY, ON HIS LOSS.
AS MS. PRYDE CAN TESTIFY, WE'VE KNOWN EACH OTHER A--VERY LONG TIME. I CONSIDERED HIM A FRIEND.
MYSTIQUE!
WHAT'RE YOU DOING HERE?!
ASIDE FROM HELPING SAVE YOUR LIFE, YOU MEAN?
THE ANSWER'S QUITE SIMPLE--
--I'M HERE TO JOIN THE X-MEN.

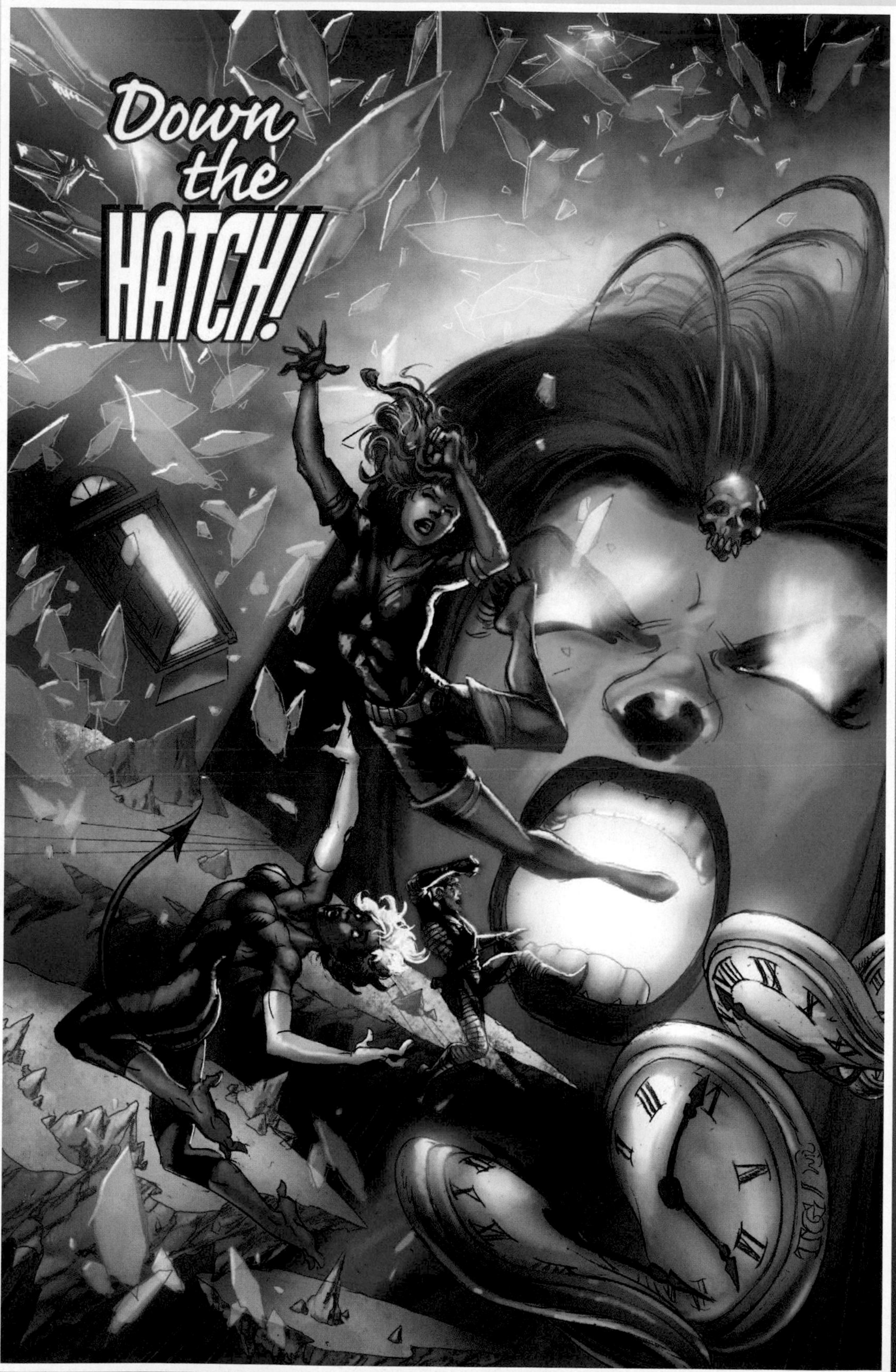
Down the HATCH!

FOUR

THE SITE OF THE XAVIER SCHOOL FOR GIFTED YOUNGSTERS--

--OR RATHER, WHAT'S LEFT OF IT.

LIEUTENANT DAISY DUGAN--

--THIRD IN HER CLASS AT WEST POINT.

PERSONAL AIDE TO NICK FURY.

A SOLDIER WHO ISN'T AFRAID OF DANGER.

ROMANCE, THOUGH--

Just so Stories

--THAT'S A WHOLE DIFFERENT STORY.

I MUST BE CRAZY.

THINKING THERE CAN BE ANYTHING BETWEEN ME AND SABRE-TOOTH.

HE'S A KILLER.

THEN AGAIN, SO AM I.

IS THAT WHAT ATTRACTS ME--AND SCARES ME--

--THAT WE'RE SO MUCH ALIKE?

HEY, DOC, SABES. HOW'S IT GOING--

‡GASP‡

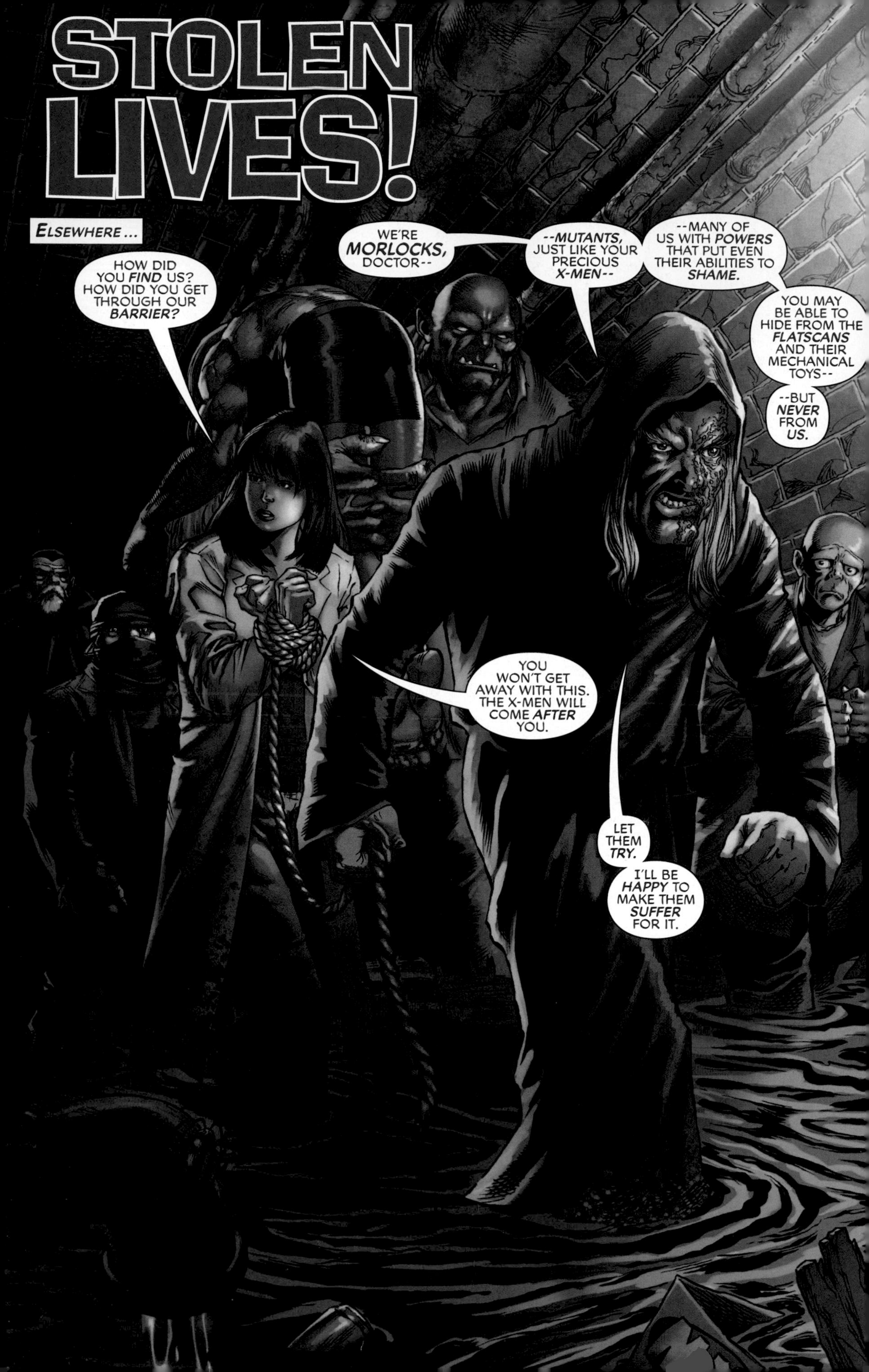
STOLEN LIVES!
ELSEWHERE...
HOW DID YOU FIND US? HOW DID YOU GET THROUGH OUR BARRIER?
WE'RE MORLOCKS, DOCTOR--
--MUTANTS, JUST LIKE YOUR PRECIOUS X-MEN--
--MANY OF US WITH POWERS THAT PUT EVEN THEIR ABILITIES TO SHAME.
YOU MAY BE ABLE TO HIDE FROM THE FLATSCANS AND THEIR MECHANICAL TOYS--
--BUT NEVER FROM US.
YOU WON'T GET AWAY WITH THIS. THE X-MEN WILL COME AFTER YOU.
LET THEM TRY.
I'LL BE HAPPY TO MAKE THEM SUFFER FOR IT.

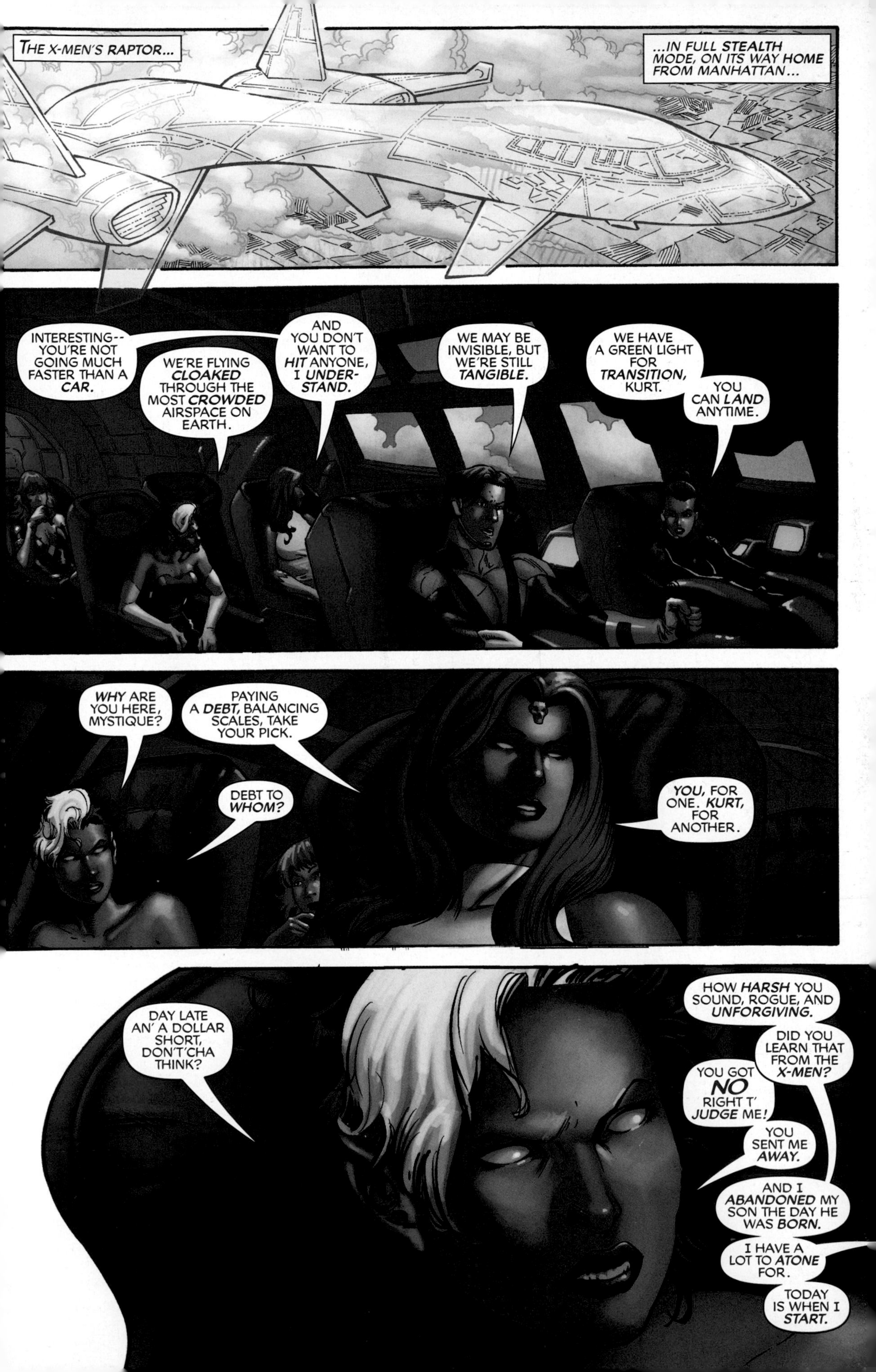
THE X-MEN'S RAPTOR...
...IN FULL STEALTH MODE, ON ITS WAY HOME FROM MANHATTAN...
INTERESTING-- YOU'RE NOT GOING MUCH FASTER THAN A CAR.
AND YOU DON'T WANT TO HIT ANYONE, I UNDERSTAND.
WE'RE FLYING CLOAKED THROUGH THE MOST CROWDED AIRSPACE ON EARTH.
WE MAY BE INVISIBLE, BUT WE'RE STILL TANGIBLE.
WE HAVE A GREEN LIGHT FOR TRANSITION, KURT.
YOU CAN LAND ANYTIME.
WHY ARE YOU HERE, MYSTIQUE?
PAYING A DEBT, BALANCING SCALES, TAKE YOUR PICK.
DEBT TO WHOM?
YOU, FOR ONE. KURT, FOR ANOTHER.
DAY LATE AN' A DOLLAR SHORT, DON'T'CHA THINK?
HOW HARSH YOU SOUND, ROGUE, AND UNFORGIVING.
DID YOU LEARN THAT FROM THE X-MEN?
YOU GOT NO RIGHT T' JUDGE ME!
YOU SENT ME AWAY.
AND I ABANDONED MY SON THE DAY HE WAS BORN.
I HAVE A LOT TO ATONE FOR.
TODAY IS WHEN I START.

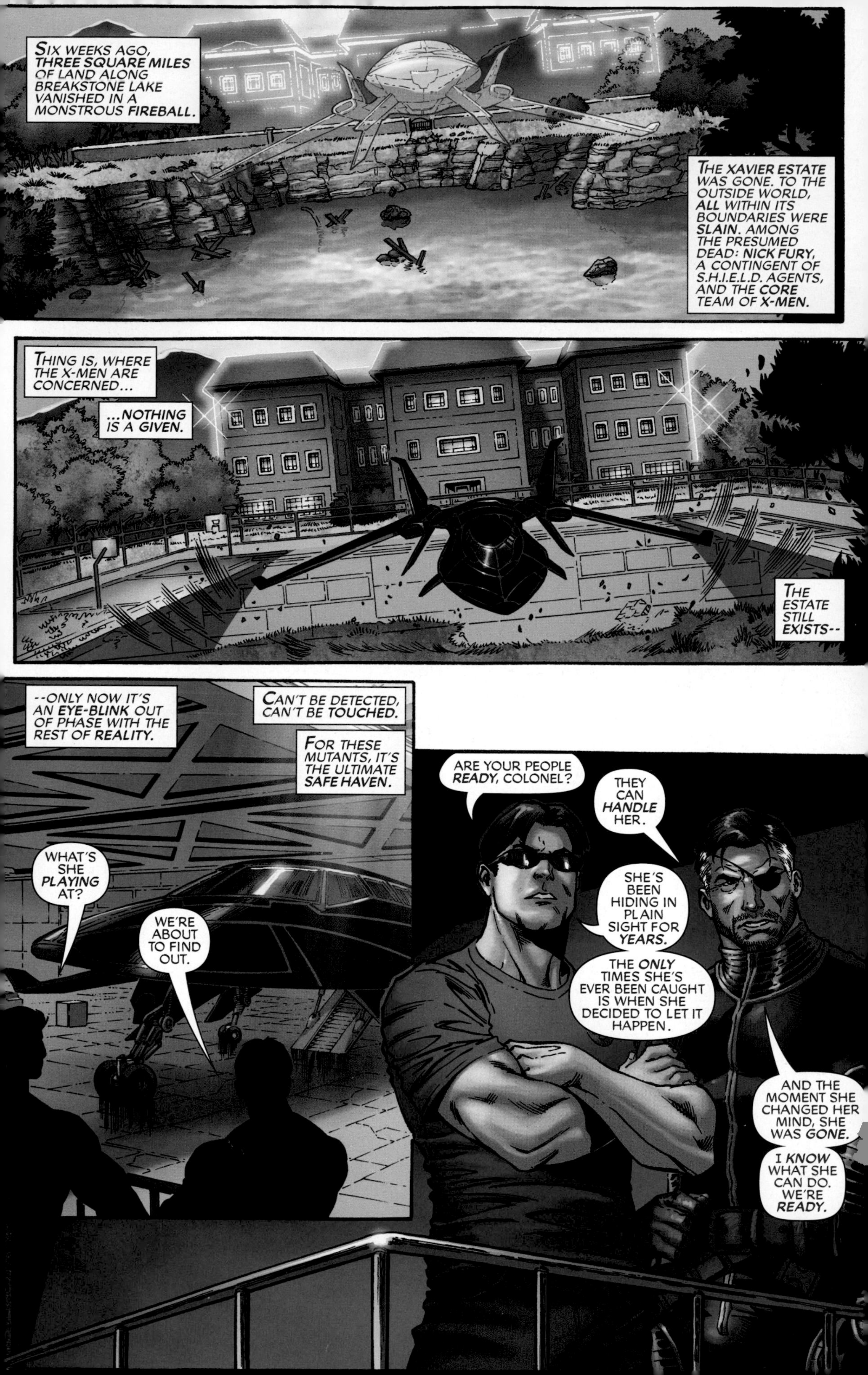

SIX WEEKS AGO, THREE SQUARE MILES OF LAND ALONG BREAKSTONE LAKE VANISHED IN A MONSTROUS FIREBALL.
THE XAVIER ESTATE WAS GONE. TO THE OUTSIDE WORLD, ALL WITHIN ITS BOUNDARIES WERE SLAIN. AMONG THE PRESUMED DEAD: NICK FURY, A CONTINGENT OF S.H.I.E.L.D. AGENTS, AND THE CORE TEAM OF X-MEN.
THING IS, WHERE THE X-MEN ARE CONCERNED...
...NOTHING IS A GIVEN.
THE ESTATE STILL EXISTS--
--ONLY NOW IT'S AN EYE-BLINK OUT OF PHASE WITH THE REST OF REALITY.
CAN'T BE DETECTED, CAN'T BE TOUCHED.
FOR THESE MUTANTS, IT'S THE ULTIMATE SAFE HAVEN.
WHAT'S SHE PLAYING AT?
WE'RE ABOUT TO FIND OUT.
ARE YOUR PEOPLE READY, COLONEL?
THEY CAN HANDLE HER.
SHE'S BEEN HIDING IN PLAIN SIGHT FOR YEARS.
THE ONLY TIMES SHE'S EVER BEEN CAUGHT IS WHEN SHE DECIDED TO LET IT HAPPEN.
AND THE MOMENT SHE CHANGED HER MIND, SHE WAS GONE.
I KNOW WHAT SHE CAN DO. WE'RE READY.

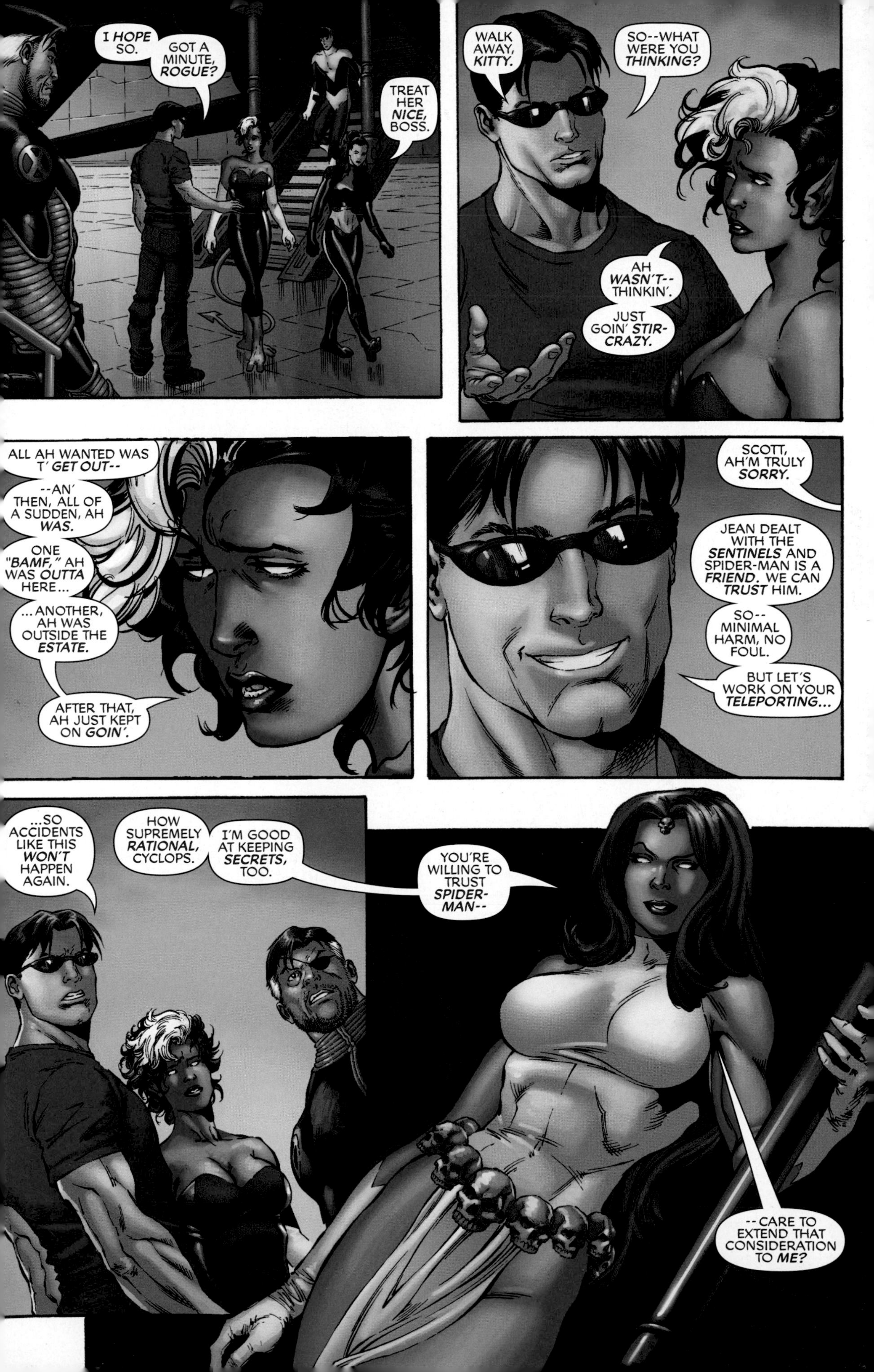
I HOPE SO.
GOT A MINUTE, ROGUE?
TREAT HER NICE, BOSS.
WALK AWAY, KITTY.
SO--WHAT WERE YOU THINKING?
AH WASN'T-- THINKIN'.
JUST GOIN' STIR-CRAZY.
ALL AH WANTED WAS T' GET OUT--
--AN' THEN, ALL OF A SUDDEN, AH WAS.
ONE "BAMF," AH WAS OUTTA HERE...
...ANOTHER, AH WAS OUTSIDE THE ESTATE.
AFTER THAT, AH JUST KEPT ON GOIN'.
SCOTT, AH'M TRULY SORRY.
JEAN DEALT WITH THE SENTINELS AND SPIDER-MAN IS A FRIEND. WE CAN TRUST HIM.
SO-- MINIMAL HARM, NO FOUL.
BUT LET'S WORK ON YOUR TELEPORTING...
...SO ACCIDENTS LIKE THIS WON'T HAPPEN AGAIN.
HOW SUPREMELY RATIONAL, CYCLOPS.
I'M GOOD AT KEEPING SECRETS, TOO.
YOU'RE WILLING TO TRUST SPIDER-MAN--
--CARE TO EXTEND THAT CONSIDERATION TO ME?

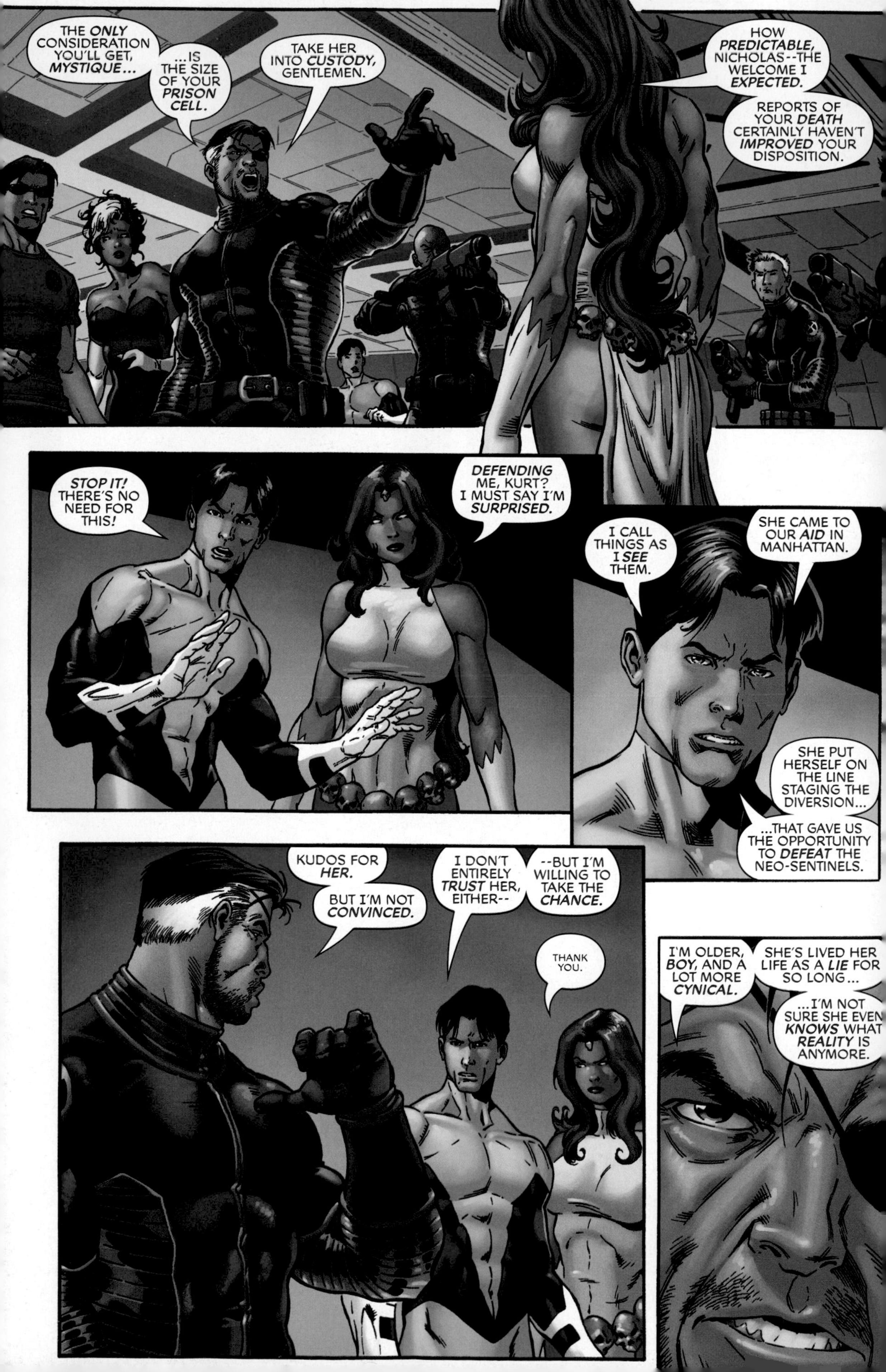
THE ONLY CONSIDERATION YOU'LL GET, MYSTIQUE...
...IS THE SIZE OF YOUR PRISON CELL.
TAKE HER INTO CUSTODY, GENTLEMEN.
HOW PREDICTABLE, NICHOLAS--THE WELCOME I EXPECTED.
REPORTS OF YOUR DEATH CERTAINLY HAVEN'T IMPROVED YOUR DISPOSITION.
STOP IT! THERE'S NO NEED FOR THIS!
DEFENDING ME, KURT? I MUST SAY I'M SURPRISED.
I CALL THINGS AS I SEE THEM.
SHE CAME TO OUR AID IN MANHATTAN.
SHE PUT HERSELF ON THE LINE STAGING THE DIVERSION...
...THAT GAVE US THE OPPORTUNITY TO DEFEAT THE NEO-SENTINELS.
KUDOS FOR HER.
BUT I'M NOT CONVINCED.
I DON'T ENTIRELY TRUST HER, EITHER--
--BUT I'M WILLING TO TAKE THE CHANCE.
THANK YOU.
I'M OLDER, BOY, AND A LOT MORE CYNICAL.
SHE'S LIVED HER LIFE AS A LIE FOR SO LONG...
...I'M NOT SURE SHE EVEN KNOWS WHAT REALITY IS ANYMORE.

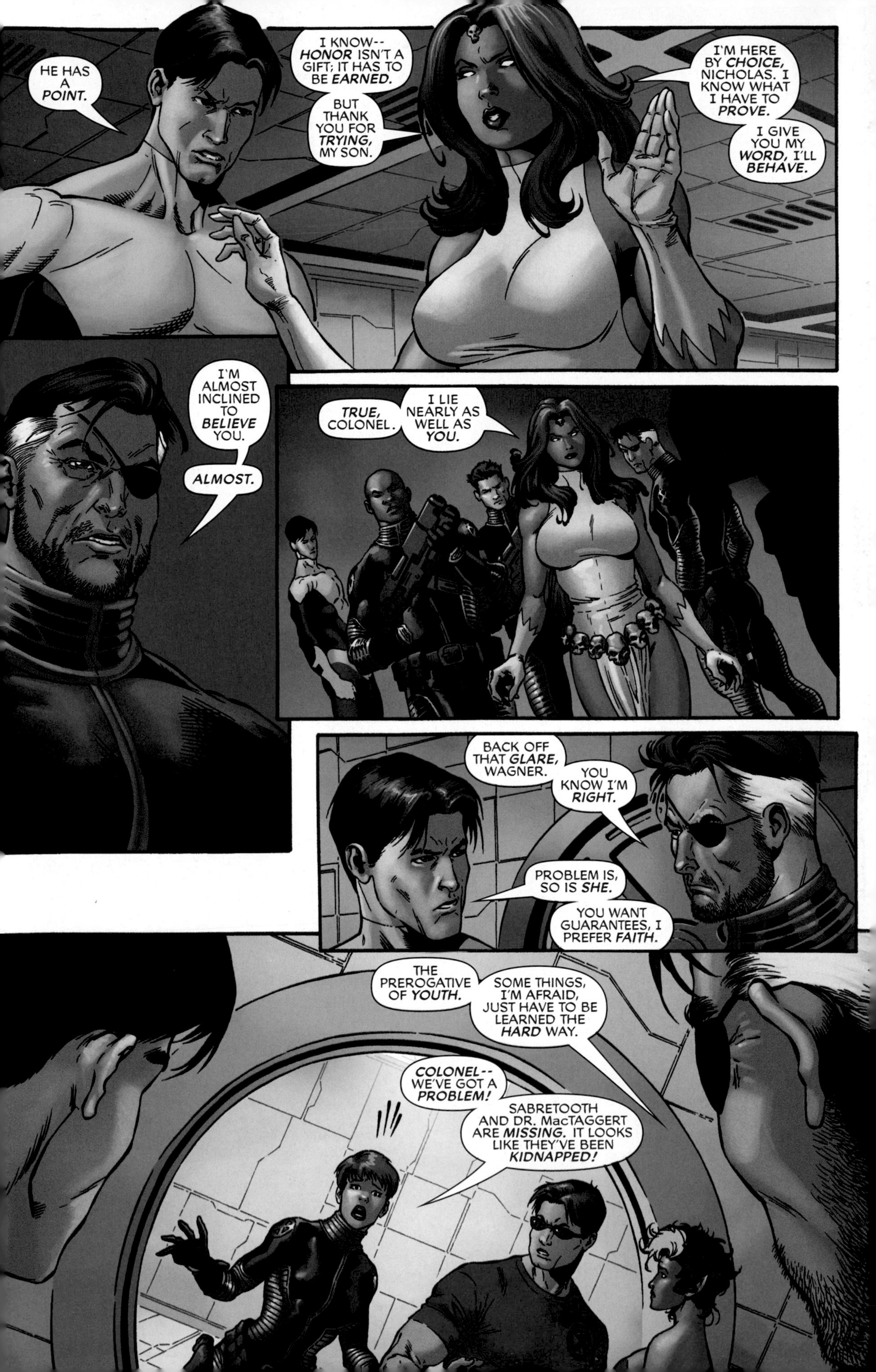
HE HAS A POINT.
I KNOW-- HONOR ISN'T A GIFT; IT HAS TO BE EARNED.
BUT THANK YOU FOR TRYING, MY SON.
I'M HERE BY CHOICE, NICHOLAS. I KNOW WHAT I HAVE TO PROVE.
I GIVE YOU MY WORD, I'LL BEHAVE.
I'M ALMOST INCLINED TO BELIEVE YOU.
ALMOST.
TRUE, COLONEL.
I LIE NEARLY AS WELL AS YOU.
BACK OFF THAT GLARE, WAGNER.
YOU KNOW I'M RIGHT.
PROBLEM IS, SO IS SHE.
YOU WANT GUARANTEES, I PREFER FAITH.
THE PREROGATIVE OF YOUTH.
SOME THINGS, I'M AFRAID, JUST HAVE TO BE LEARNED THE HARD WAY.
COLONEL-- WE'VE GOT A PROBLEM!
SABRETOOTH AND DR. MacTAGGERT ARE MISSING. IT LOOKS LIKE THEY'VE BEEN KIDNAPPED!

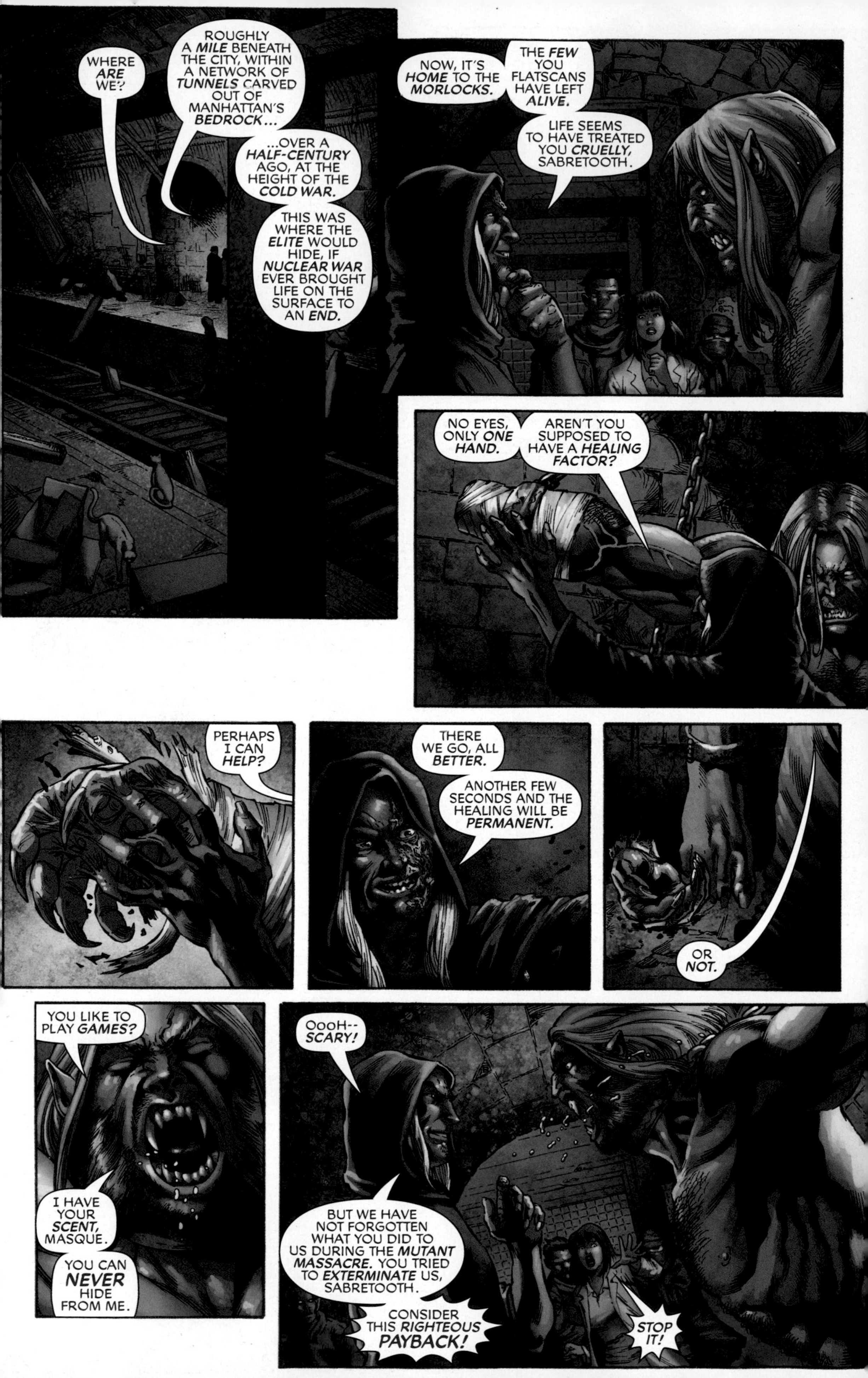
WHERE ARE WE?
ROUGHLY A MILE BENEATH THE CITY, WITHIN A NETWORK OF TUNNELS CARVED OUT OF MANHATTAN'S BEDROCK...
...OVER A HALF-CENTURY AGO, AT THE HEIGHT OF THE COLD WAR.
THIS WAS WHERE THE ELITE WOULD HIDE, IF NUCLEAR WAR EVER BROUGHT LIFE ON THE SURFACE TO AN END.
NOW, IT'S HOME TO THE MORLOCKS.
THE FEW YOU FLATSCANS HAVE LEFT ALIVE.
LIFE SEEMS TO HAVE TREATED YOU CRUELLY, SABRETOOTH.
NO EYES, ONLY ONE HAND.
AREN'T YOU SUPPOSED TO HAVE A HEALING FACTOR?
PERHAPS I CAN HELP?
THERE WE GO, ALL BETTER.
ANOTHER FEW SECONDS AND THE HEALING WILL BE PERMANENT.
OR NOT.
YOU LIKE TO PLAY GAMES?
I HAVE YOUR SCENT, MASQUE.
YOU CAN NEVER HIDE FROM ME.
OooH-- SCARY!
BUT WE HAVE NOT FORGOTTEN WHAT YOU DID TO US DURING THE MUTANT MASSACRE. YOU TRIED TO EXTERMINATE US, SABRETOOTH.
CONSIDER THIS RIGHTEOUS PAYBACK!
STOP IT!

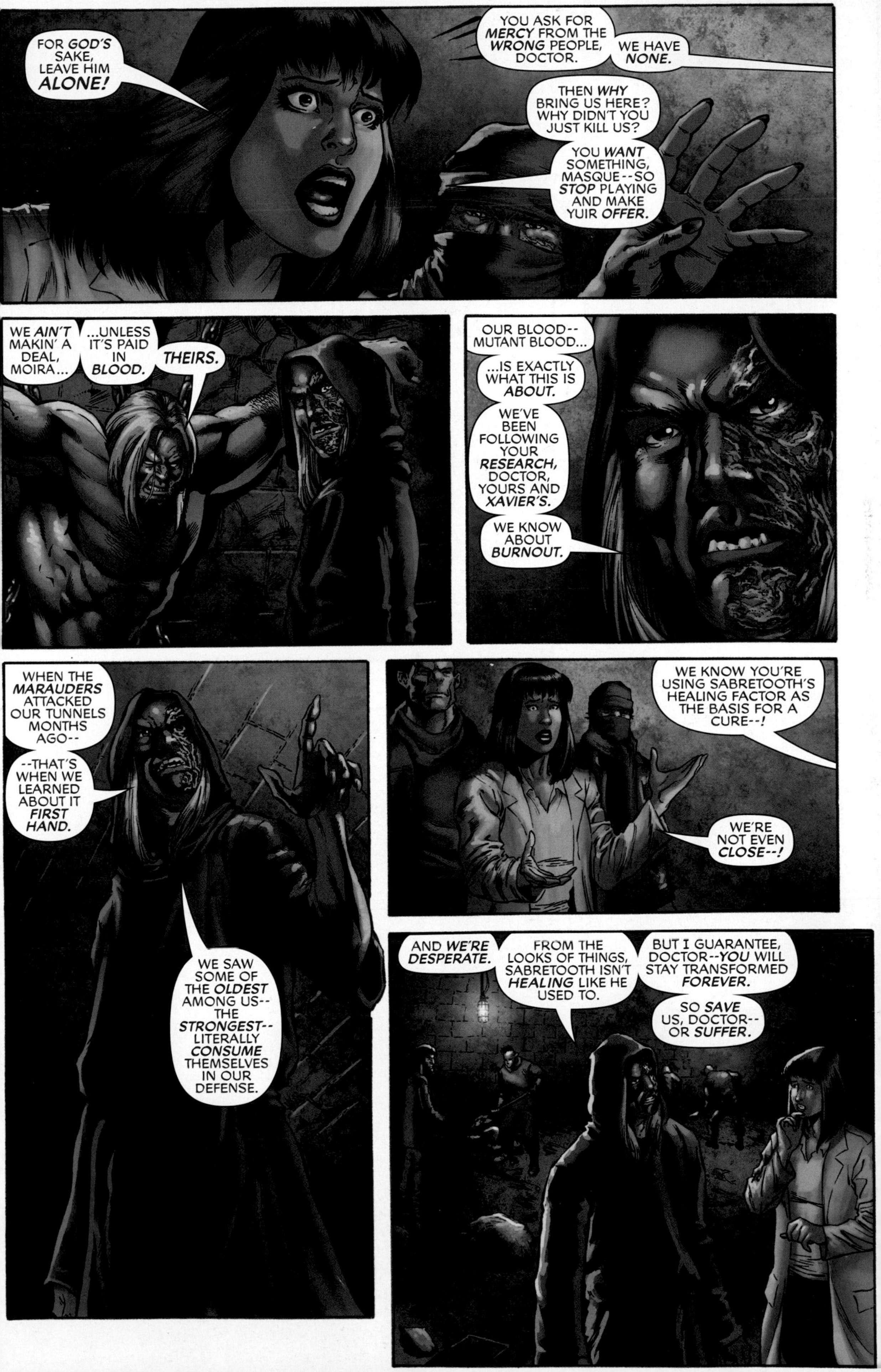
FOR GOD'S SAKE, LEAVE HIM ALONE!
YOU ASK FOR MERCY FROM THE WRONG PEOPLE, DOCTOR.
WE HAVE NONE.
THEN WHY BRING US HERE? WHY DIDN'T YOU JUST KILL US?
YOU WANT SOMETHING, MASQUE--SO STOP PLAYING AND MAKE YUIR OFFER.
WE AIN'T MAKIN' A DEAL, MOIRA...
...UNLESS IT'S PAID IN BLOOD.
THEIRS.
OUR BLOOD-- MUTANT BLOOD...
...IS EXACTLY WHAT THIS IS ABOUT.
WE'VE BEEN FOLLOWING YOUR RESEARCH, DOCTOR, YOURS AND XAVIER'S.
WE KNOW ABOUT BURNOUT.
WHEN THE MARAUDERS ATTACKED OUR TUNNELS MONTHS AGO--
--THAT'S WHEN WE LEARNED ABOUT IT FIRST HAND.
WE SAW SOME OF THE OLDEST AMONG US--THE STRONGEST--LITERALLY CONSUME THEMSELVES IN OUR DEFENSE.
WE KNOW YOU'RE USING SABRETOOTH'S HEALING FACTOR AS THE BASIS FOR A CURE--!
WE'RE NOT EVEN CLOSE--!
AND WE'RE DESPERATE.
FROM THE LOOKS OF THINGS, SABRETOOTH ISN'T HEALING LIKE HE USED TO.
BUT I GUARANTEE, DOCTOR--YOU WILL STAY TRANSFORMED FOREVER.
SO SAVE US, DOCTOR-- OR SUFFER.

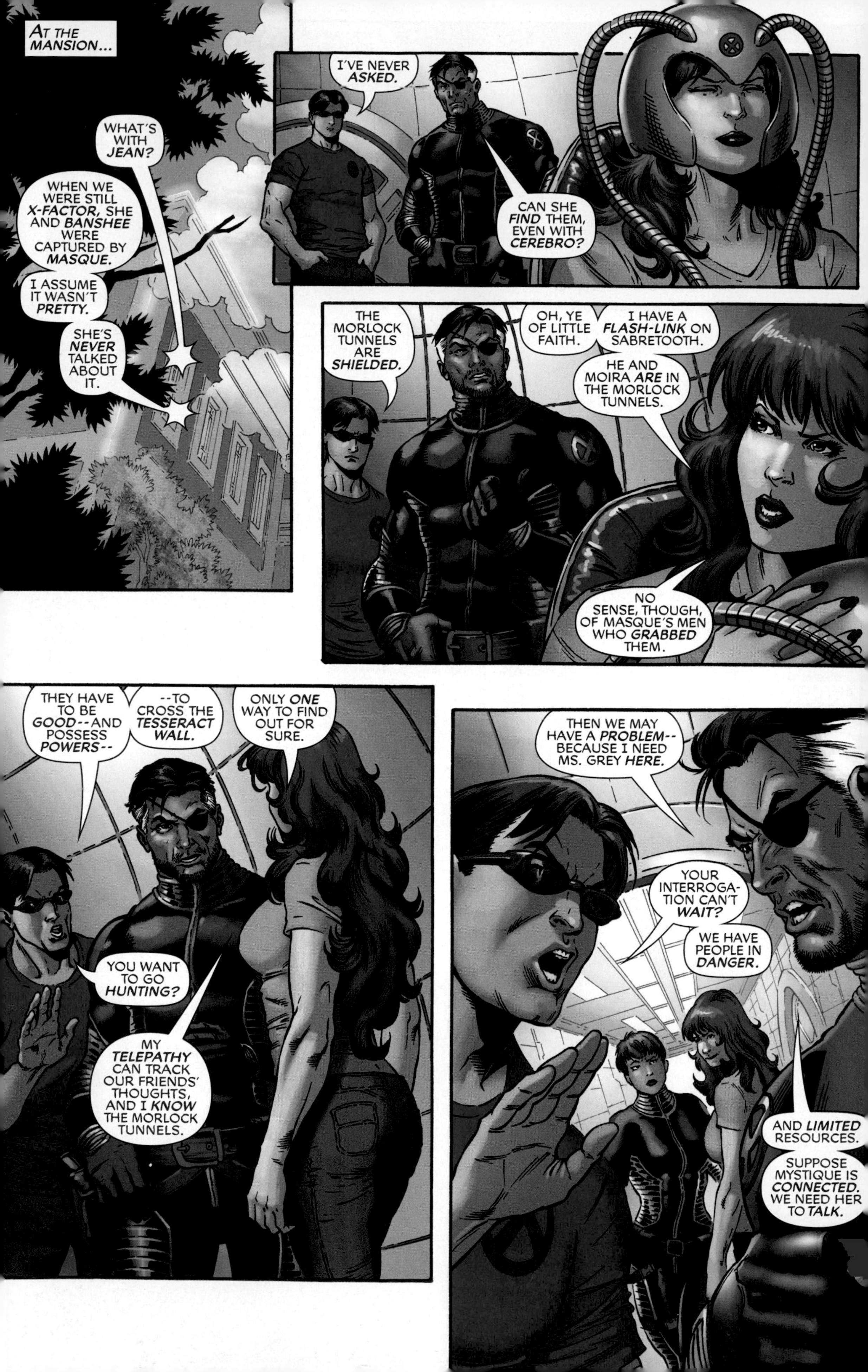

AT THE MANSION...
WHAT'S WITH JEAN?
WHEN WE WERE STILL X-FACTOR, SHE AND BANSHEE WERE CAPTURED BY MASQUE.
I ASSUME IT WASN'T PRETTY.
SHE'S NEVER TALKED ABOUT IT.
I'VE NEVER ASKED.
CAN SHE FIND THEM, EVEN WITH CEREBRO?
THE MORLOCK TUNNELS ARE SHIELDED.
OH, YE OF LITTLE FAITH.
I HAVE A FLASH-LINK ON SABRETOOTH.
HE AND MOIRA ARE IN THE MORLOCK TUNNELS.
NO SENSE, THOUGH, OF MASQUE'S MEN WHO GRABBED THEM.
THEY HAVE TO BE GOOD--AND POSSESS POWERS--
--TO CROSS THE TESSERACT WALL.
ONLY ONE WAY TO FIND OUT FOR SURE.
YOU WANT TO GO HUNTING?
MY TELEPATHY CAN TRACK OUR FRIENDS' THOUGHTS, AND I KNOW THE MORLOCK TUNNELS.
THEN WE MAY HAVE A PROBLEM--BECAUSE I NEED MS. GREY HERE.
YOUR INTERROGATION CAN'T WAIT?
WE HAVE PEOPLE IN DANGER.
AND LIMITED RESOURCES.
SUPPOSE MYSTIQUE IS CONNECTED. WE NEED HER TO TALK.

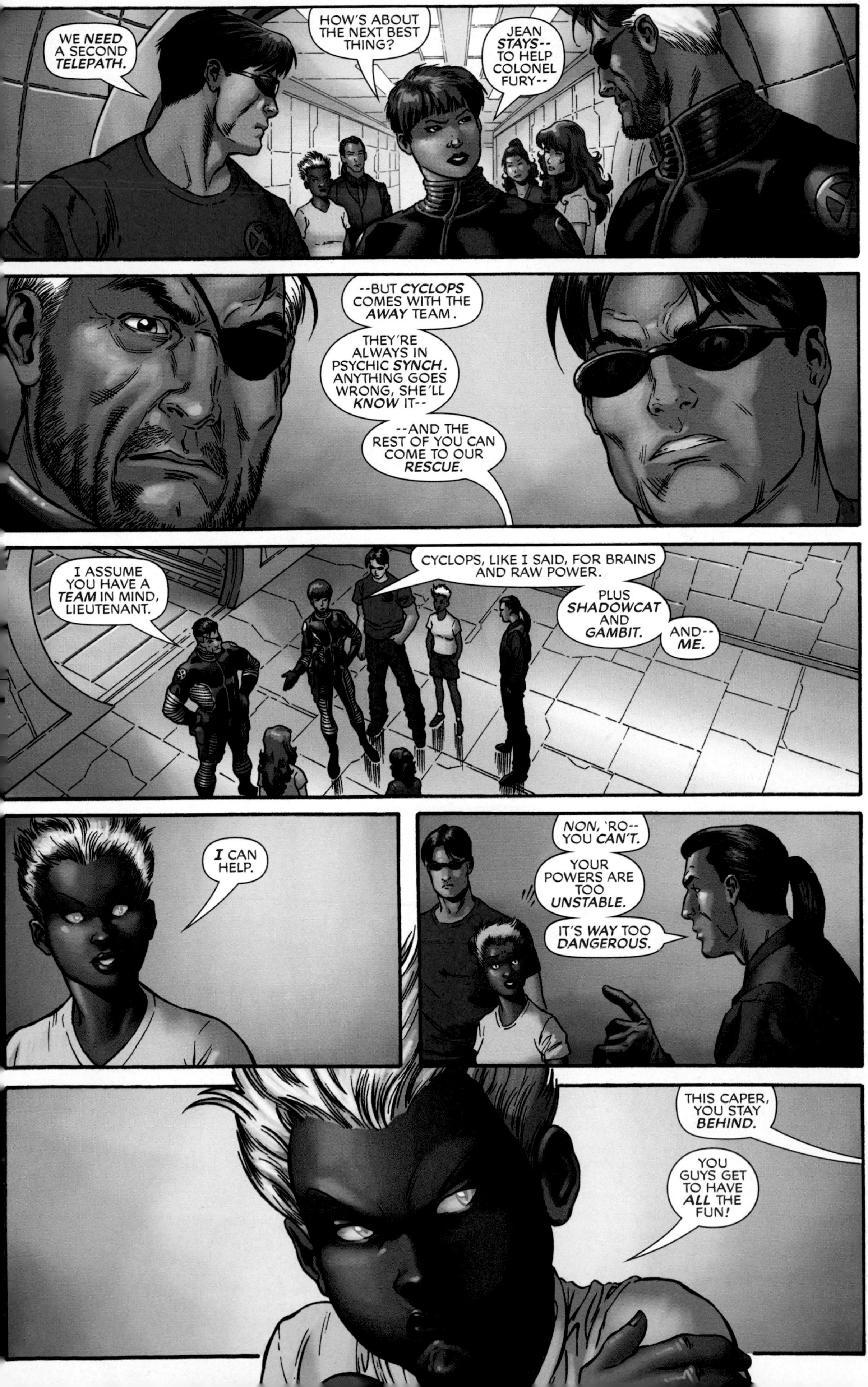
WE NEED A SECOND TELEPATH.
HOW'S ABOUT THE NEXT BEST THING?
JEAN STAYS-- TO HELP COLONEL FURY--
--BUT CYCLOPS COMES WITH THE AWAY TEAM.
THEY'RE ALWAYS IN PSYCHIC SYNCH. ANYTHING GOES WRONG, SHE'LL KNOW IT--
--AND THE REST OF YOU CAN COME TO OUR RESCUE.
I ASSUME YOU HAVE A TEAM IN MIND, LIEUTENANT.
CYCLOPS, LIKE I SAID, FOR BRAINS AND RAW POWER.
PLUS SHADOWCAT AND GAMBIT.
AND-- ME.
I CAN HELP.
NON, 'RO-- YOU CAN'T.
YOUR POWERS ARE TOO UNSTABLE.
IT'S WAY TOO DANGEROUS.
THIS CAPER, YOU STAY BEHIND.
YOU GUYS GET TO HAVE ALL THE FUN!

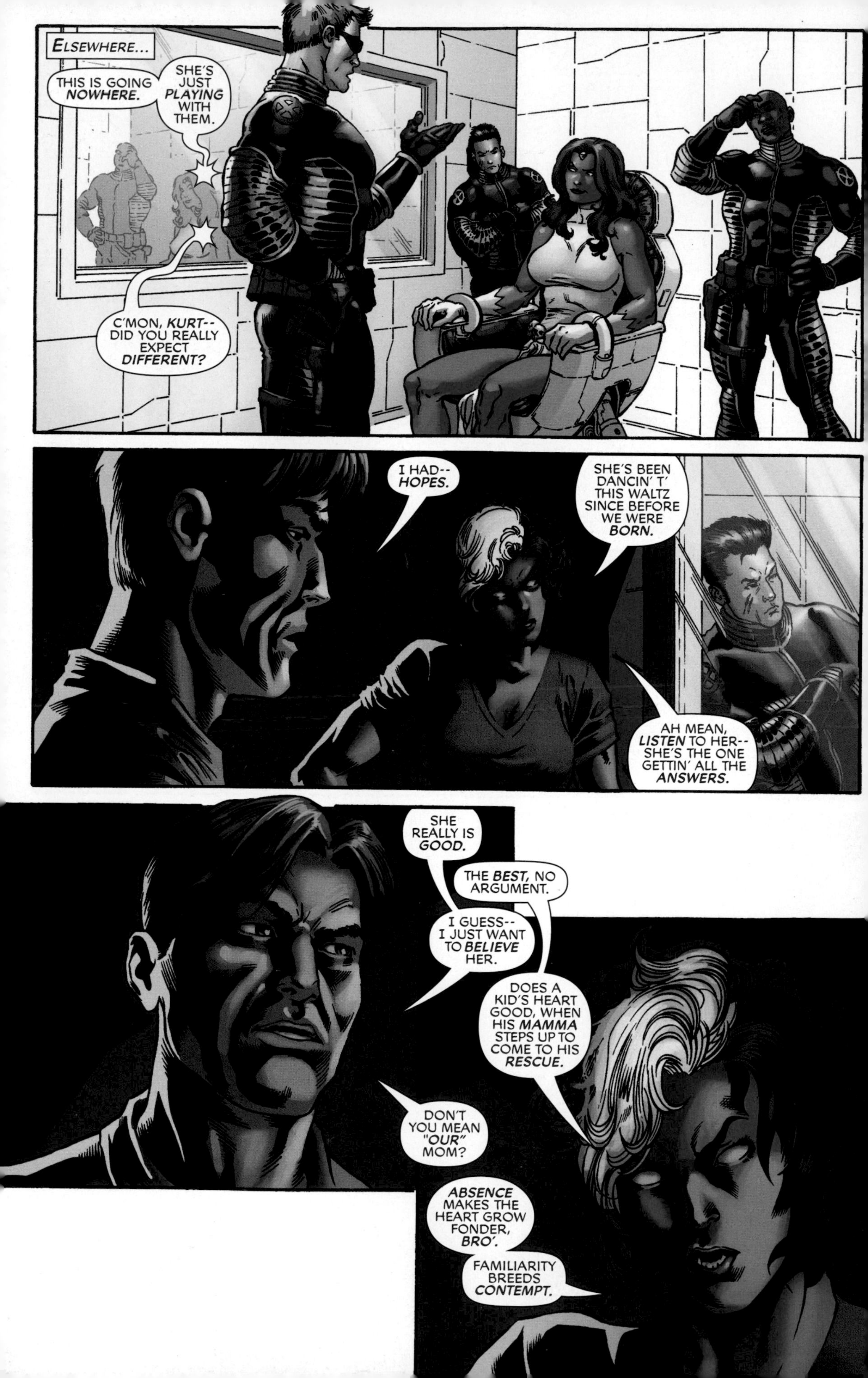

ELSEWHERE...
THIS IS GOING NOWHERE.
SHE'S JUST PLAYING WITH THEM.
C'MON, KURT-- DID YOU REALLY EXPECT DIFFERENT?
I HAD-- HOPES.
SHE'S BEEN DANCIN' T' THIS WALTZ SINCE BEFORE WE WERE BORN.
AH MEAN, LISTEN TO HER-- SHE'S THE ONE GETTIN' ALL THE ANSWERS.
SHE REALLY IS GOOD.
THE BEST, NO ARGUMENT.
I GUESS-- I JUST WANT TO BELIEVE HER.
DOES A KID'S HEART GOOD, WHEN HIS MAMMA STEPS UP TO COME TO HIS RESCUE.
DON'T YOU MEAN "OUR" MOM?
ABSENCE MAKES THE HEART GROW FONDER, BRO'.
FAMILIARITY BREEDS CONTEMPT.

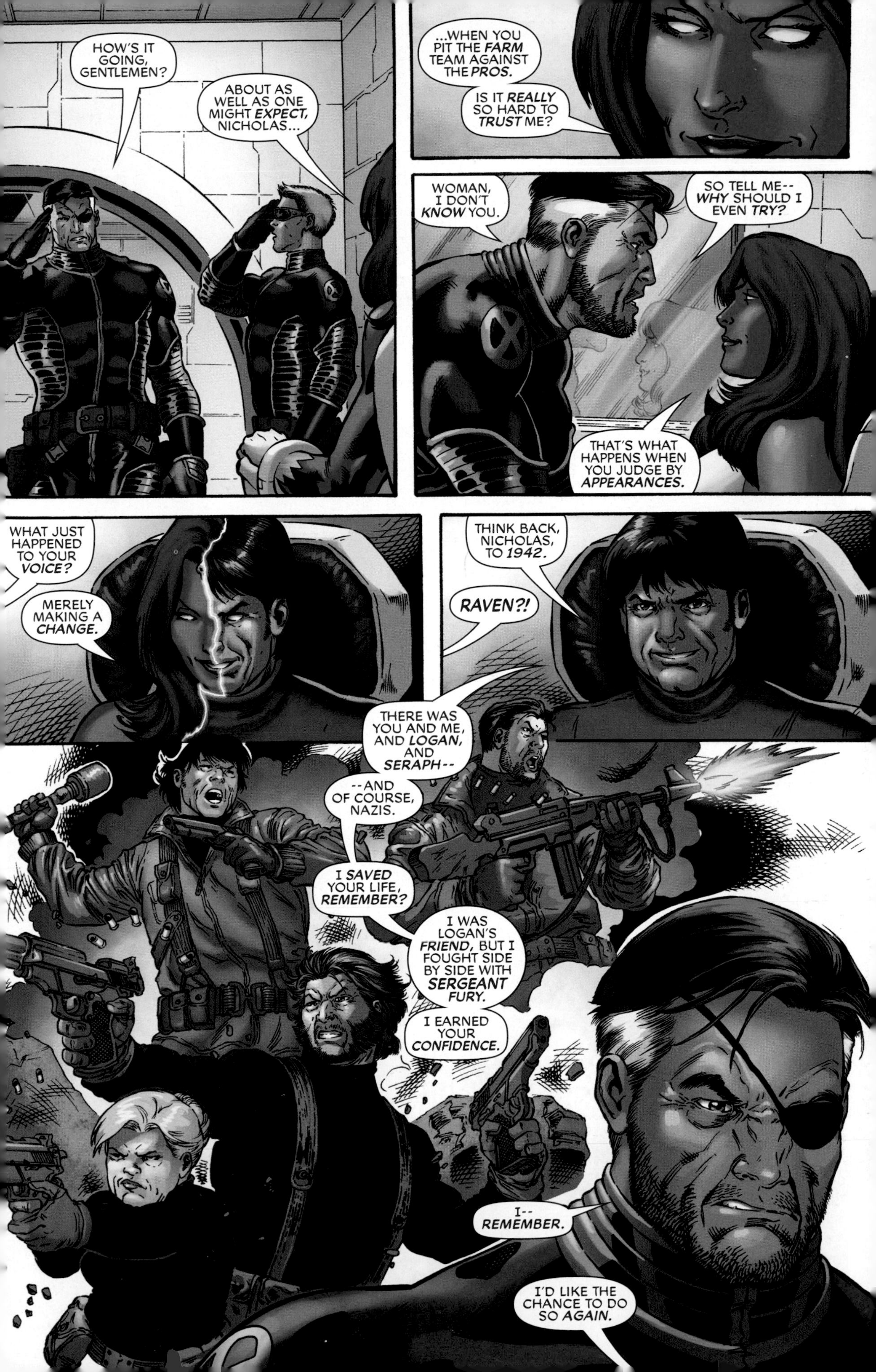
HOW'S IT GOING, GENTLEMEN?
ABOUT AS WELL AS ONE MIGHT EXPECT, NICHOLAS...
...WHEN YOU PIT THE FARM TEAM AGAINST THE PROS.
IS IT REALLY SO HARD TO TRUST ME?
WOMAN, I DON'T KNOW YOU.
SO TELL ME-- WHY SHOULD I EVEN TRY?
THAT'S WHAT HAPPENS WHEN YOU JUDGE BY APPEARANCES.
WHAT JUST HAPPENED TO YOUR VOICE?
MERELY MAKING A CHANGE.
THINK BACK, NICHOLAS, TO 1942.
RAVEN?!
THERE WAS YOU AND ME, AND LOGAN, AND SERAPH--
--AND OF COURSE, NAZIS.
I SAVED YOUR LIFE, REMEMBER?
I WAS LOGAN'S FRIEND, BUT I FOUGHT SIDE BY SIDE WITH SERGEANT FURY.
I EARNED YOUR CONFIDENCE.
I-- REMEMBER.
I'D LIKE THE CHANCE TO DO SO AGAIN.

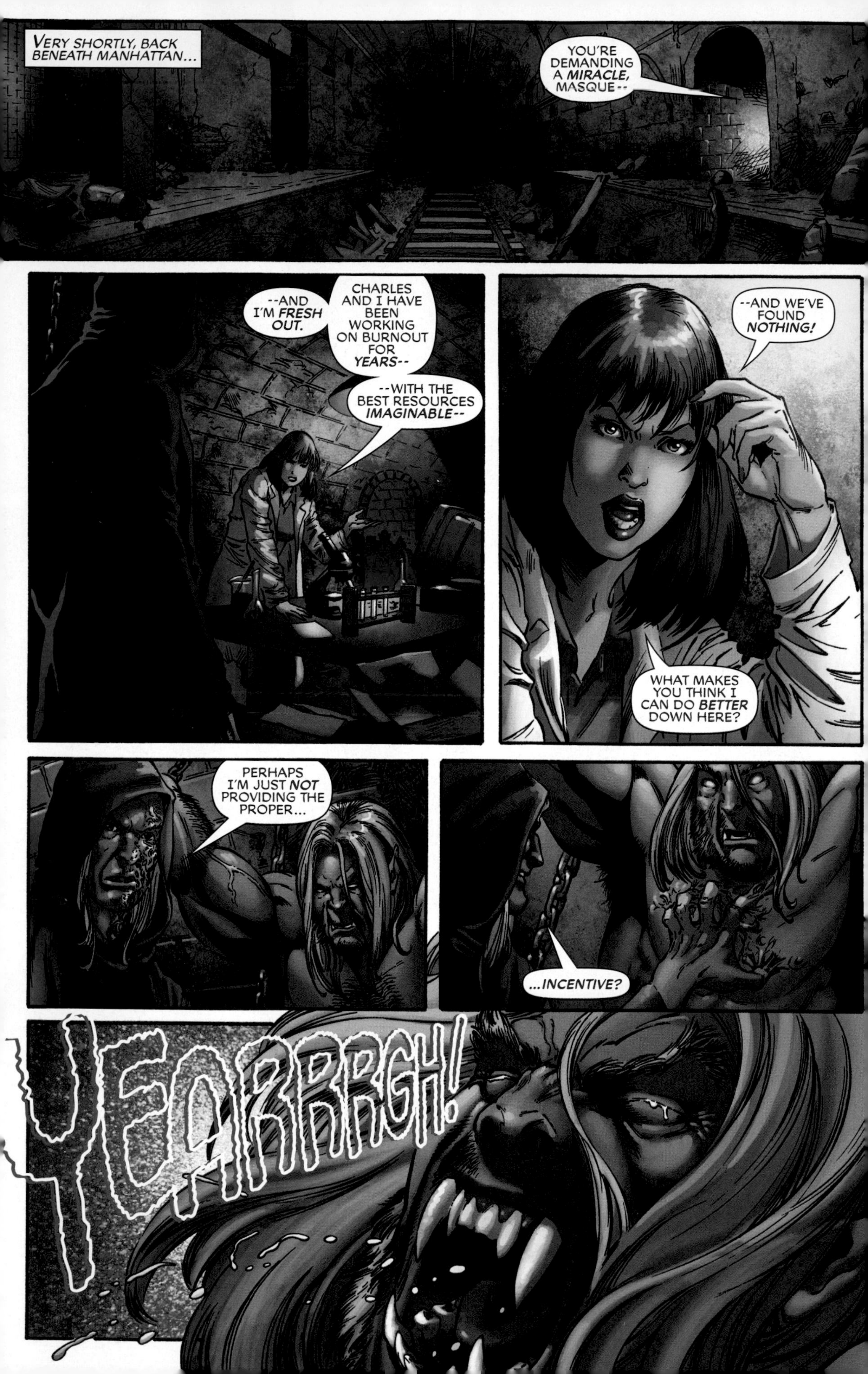
VERY SHORTLY, BACK BENEATH MANHATTAN...
YOU'RE DEMANDING A MIRACLE, MASQUE--
--AND I'M FRESH OUT.
CHARLES AND I HAVE BEEN WORKING ON BURNOUT FOR YEARS--
--WITH THE BEST RESOURCES IMAGINABLE--
--AND WE'VE FOUND NOTHING!
WHAT MAKES YOU THINK I CAN DO BETTER DOWN HERE?
PERHAPS I'M JUST NOT PROVIDING THE PROPER...
...INCENTIVE?
YEARRRGH!

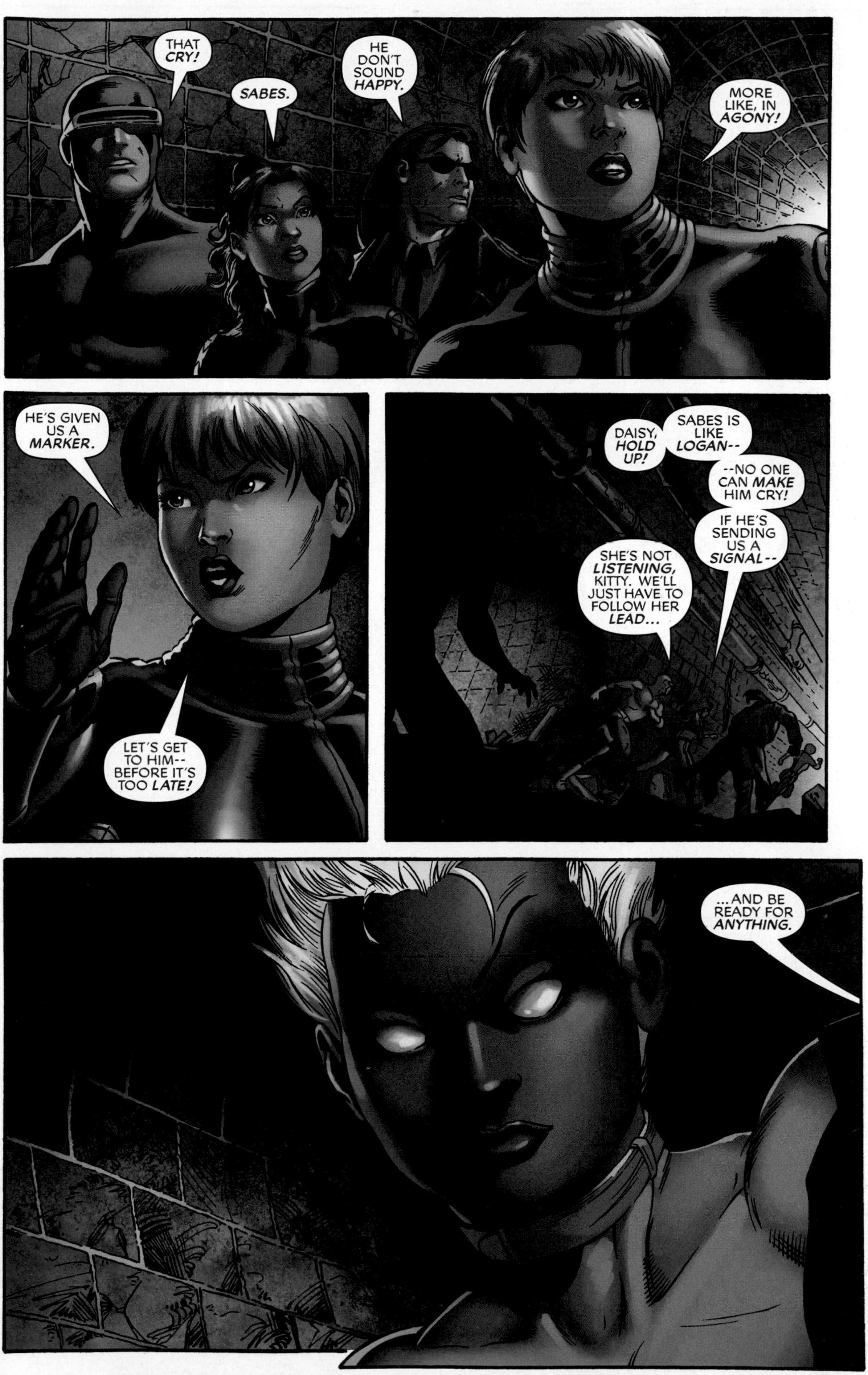
THAT CRY!
SABES.
HE DON'T SOUND HAPPY.
MORE LIKE, IN AGONY!
HE'S GIVEN US A MARKER.
LET'S GET TO HIM-- BEFORE IT'S TOO LATE!
DAISY, HOLD UP!
SABES IS LIKE LOGAN--
--NO ONE CAN MAKE HIM CRY!
IF HE'S SENDING US A SIGNAL--
SHE'S NOT LISTENING, KITTY. WE'LL JUST HAVE TO FOLLOW HER LEAD...
...AND BE READY FOR ANYTHING.

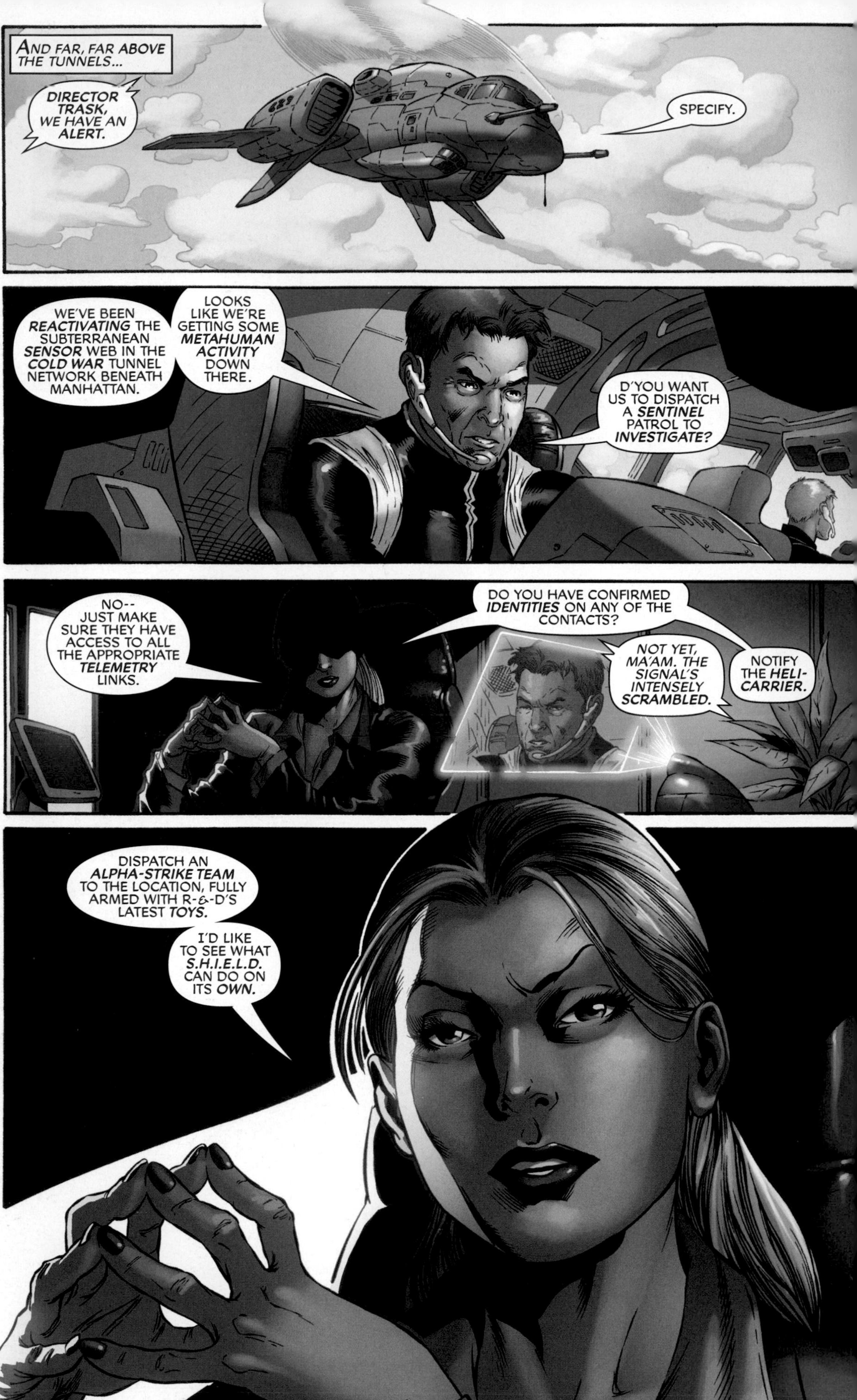
AND FAR, FAR ABOVE THE TUNNELS...
DIRECTOR TRASK, WE HAVE AN ALERT.
SPECIFY.
WE'VE BEEN REACTIVATING THE SUBTERRANEAN SENSOR WEB IN THE COLD WAR TUNNEL NETWORK BENEATH MANHATTAN.
LOOKS LIKE WE'RE GETTING SOME METAHUMAN ACTIVITY DOWN THERE.
D'YOU WANT US TO DISPATCH A SENTINEL PATROL TO INVESTIGATE?
NO-- JUST MAKE SURE THEY HAVE ACCESS TO ALL THE APPROPRIATE TELEMETRY LINKS.
DO YOU HAVE CONFIRMED IDENTITIES ON ANY OF THE CONTACTS?
NOT YET, MA'AM. THE SIGNAL'S INTENSELY SCRAMBLED.
NOTIFY THE HELI-CARRIER.
DISPATCH AN ALPHA-STRIKE TEAM TO THE LOCATION, FULLY ARMED WITH R-&-D'S LATEST TOYS.
I'D LIKE TO SEE WHAT S.H.I.E.L.D. CAN DO ON ITS OWN.

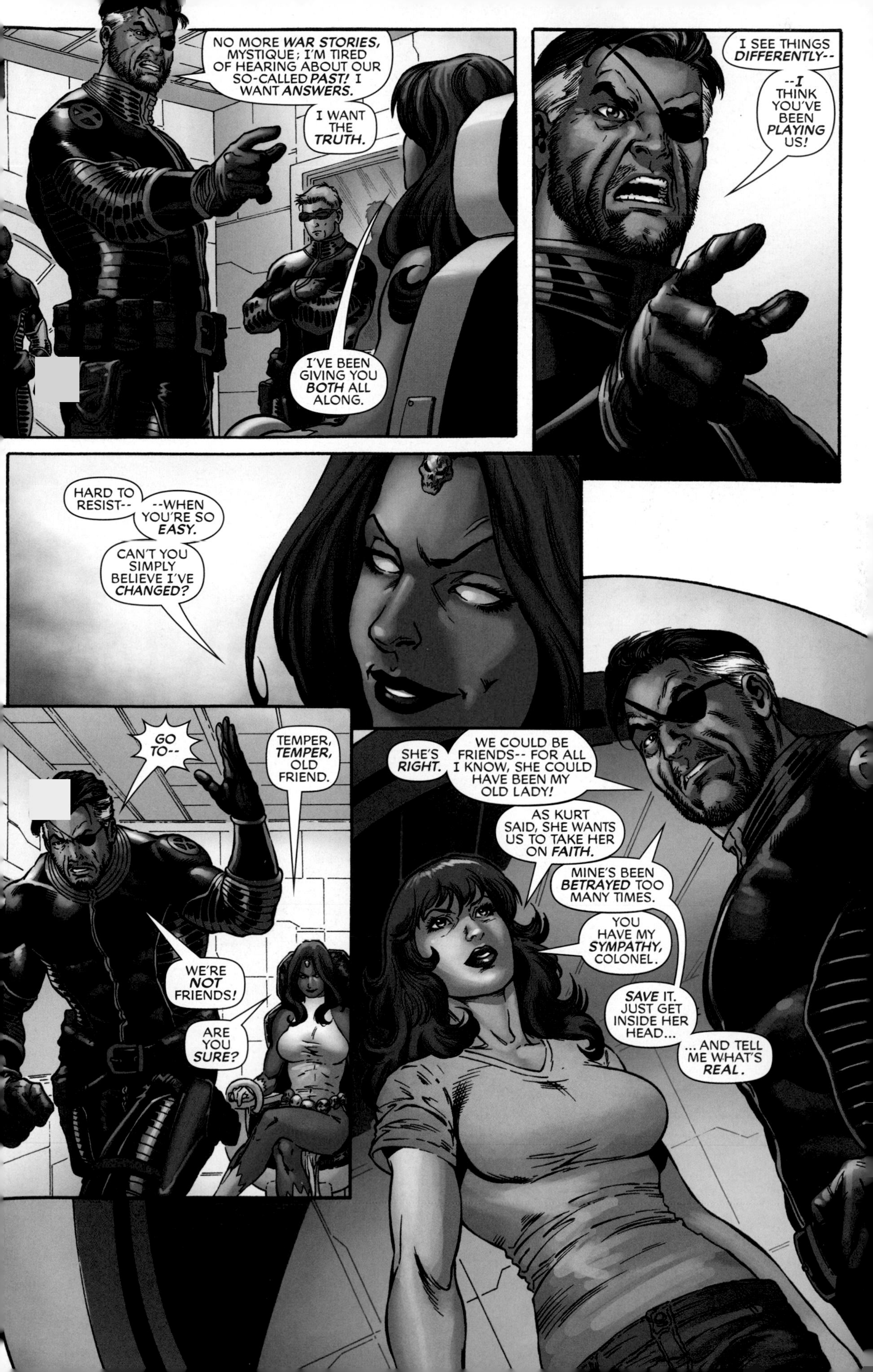
NO MORE *WAR STORIES,* MYSTIQUE; I'M TIRED OF HEARING ABOUT OUR SO-CALLED *PAST!* I WANT *ANSWERS.*
I WANT THE *TRUTH.*
I'VE BEEN GIVING YOU *BOTH* ALL ALONG.
I SEE THINGS *DIFFERENTLY--*
--*I* THINK YOU'VE BEEN *PLAYING* US!
HARD TO RESIST--
--WHEN YOU'RE SO *EASY.*
CAN'T YOU SIMPLY BELIEVE I'VE *CHANGED?*
GO TO--
TEMPER, *TEMPER,* OLD FRIEND.
WE'RE *NOT* FRIENDS!
ARE YOU *SURE?*
SHE'S *RIGHT.*
WE COULD BE FRIENDS-- FOR ALL I KNOW, SHE COULD HAVE BEEN MY OLD LADY!
AS KURT SAID, SHE WANTS US TO TAKE HER ON *FAITH.*
MINE'S BEEN *BETRAYED* TOO MANY TIMES.
YOU HAVE MY *SYMPATHY,* COLONEL.
SAVE IT. JUST GET INSIDE HER HEAD...
...AND TELL ME WHAT'S *REAL.*

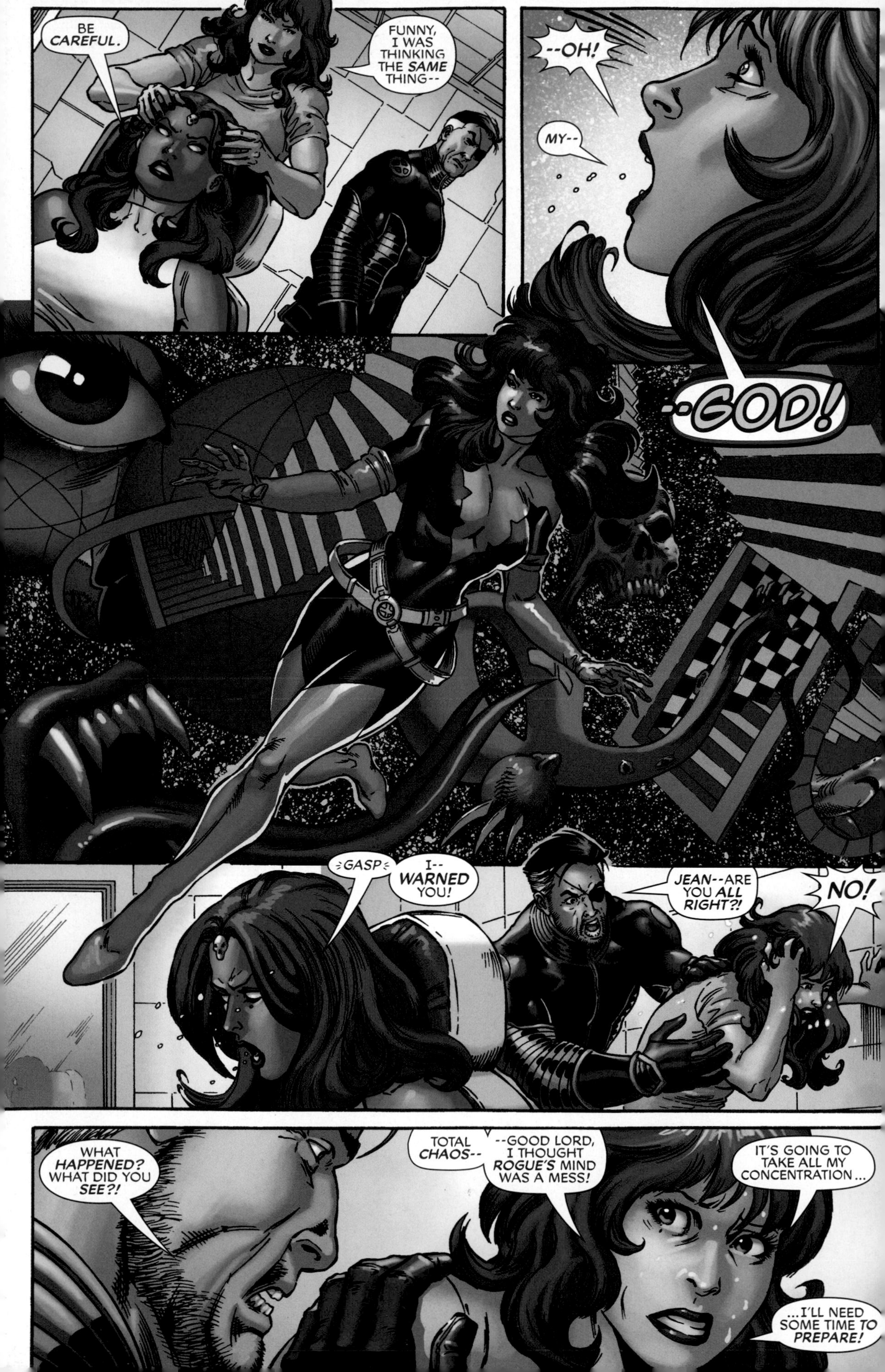
BE CAREFUL.
FUNNY, I WAS THINKING THE SAME THING--
--OH!
MY--
--GOD!
GASP
I-- WARNED YOU!
JEAN--ARE YOU ALL RIGHT?!
NO!
WHAT HAPPENED? WHAT DID YOU SEE?!
TOTAL CHAOS--
--GOOD LORD, I THOUGHT ROGUE'S MIND WAS A MESS!
IT'S GOING TO TAKE ALL MY CONCENTRATION...
...I'LL NEED SOME TIME TO PREPARE!

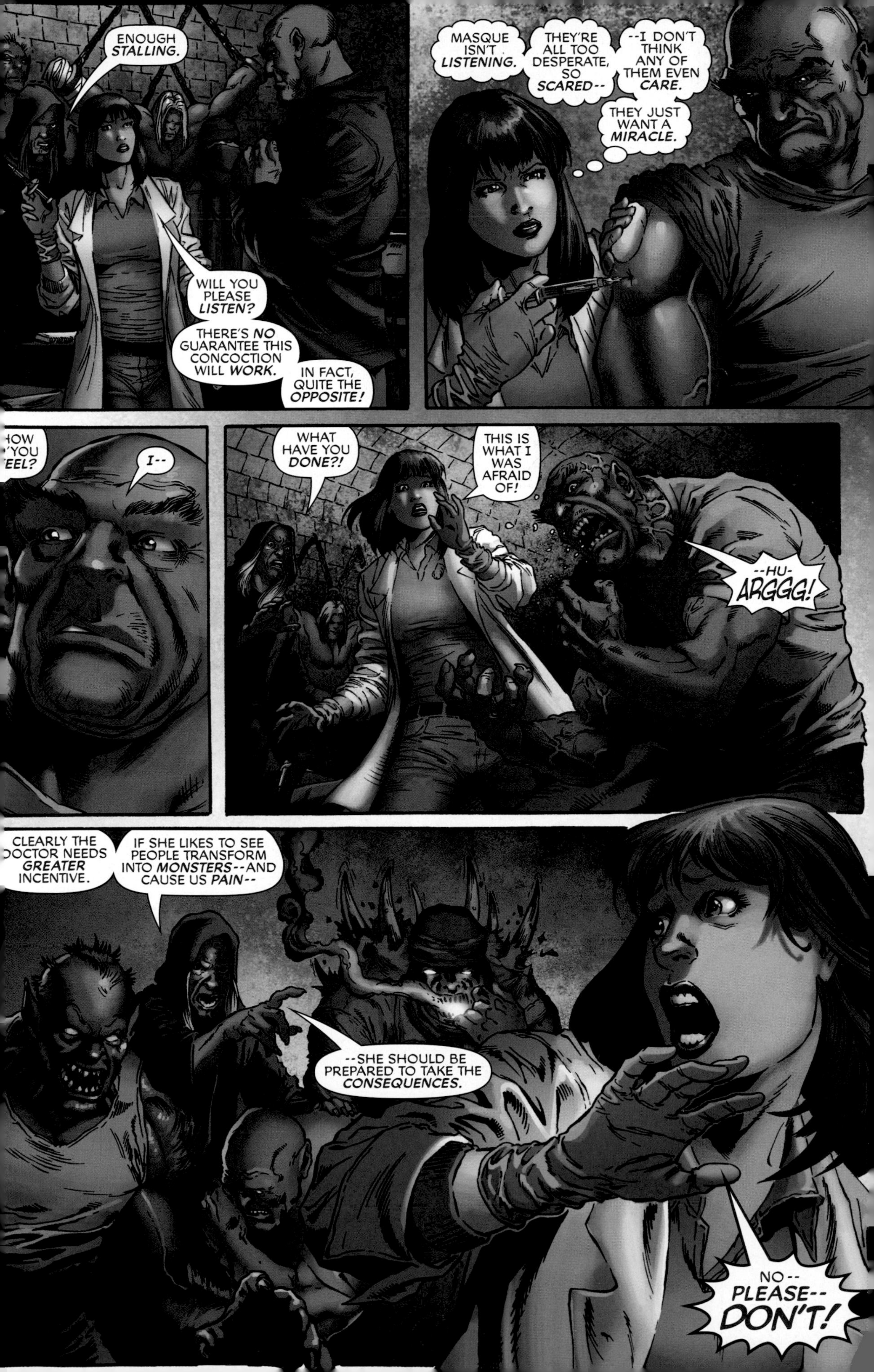
ENOUGH STALLING.
WILL YOU PLEASE LISTEN?
THERE'S NO GUARANTEE THIS CONCOCTION WILL WORK.
IN FACT, QUITE THE OPPOSITE!
MASQUE ISN'T LISTENING.
THEY'RE ALL TOO DESPERATE, SO SCARED--
--I DON'T THINK ANY OF THEM EVEN CARE.
THEY JUST WANT A MIRACLE.
HOW 'YOU EEL?
I--
WHAT HAVE YOU DONE?!
THIS IS WHAT I WAS AFRAID OF!
--HU-ARGGG!
CLEARLY THE DOCTOR NEEDS GREATER INCENTIVE.
IF SHE LIKES TO SEE PEOPLE TRANSFORM INTO MONSTERS--AND CAUSE US PAIN--
--SHE SHOULD BE PREPARED TO TAKE THE CONSEQUENCES.
NO-- PLEASE-- DON'T!

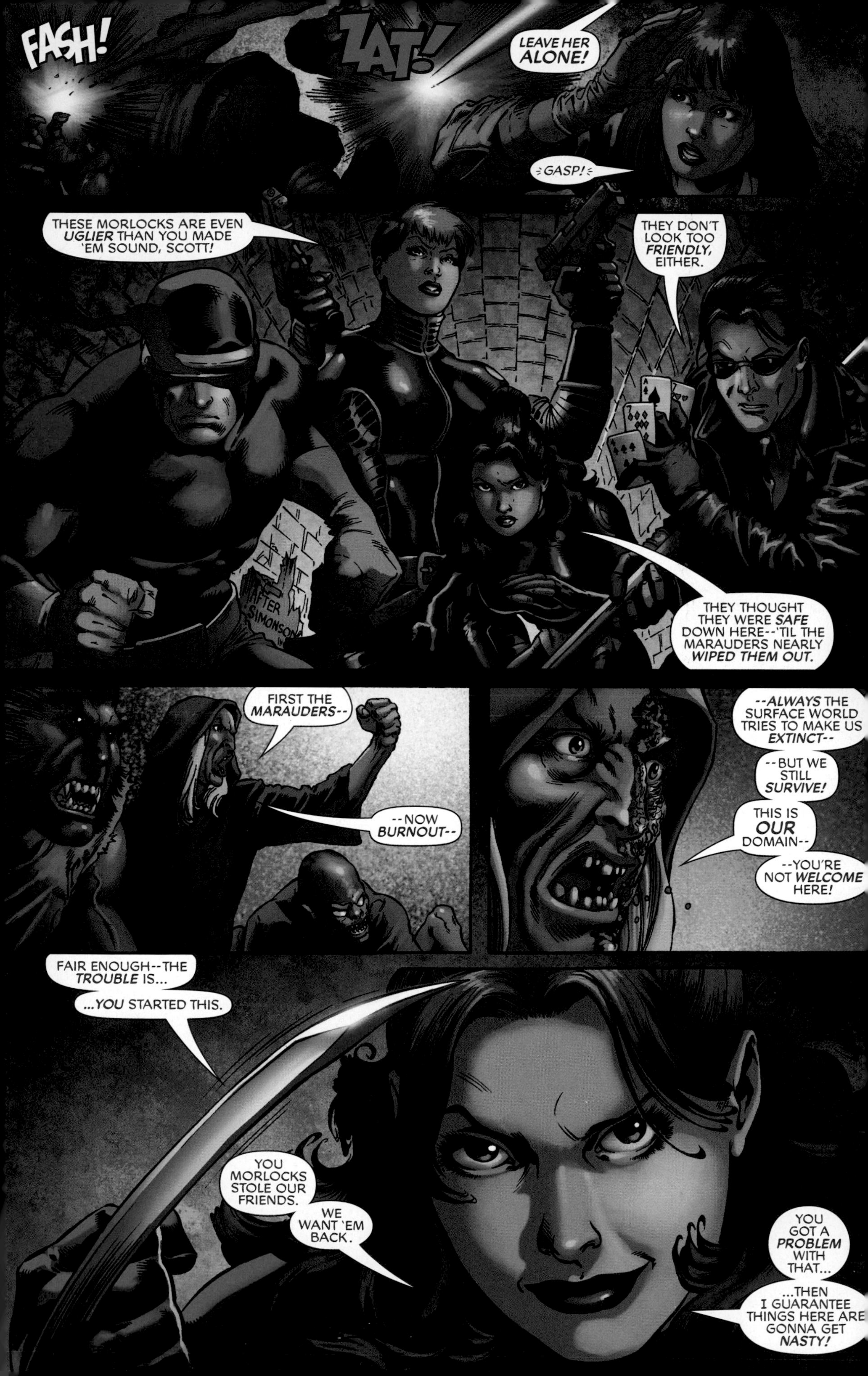
FASH!
ZAT!
LEAVE HER ALONE!
GASP!
THESE MORLOCKS ARE EVEN UGLIER THAN YOU MADE 'EM SOUND, SCOTT!
THEY DON'T LOOK TOO FRIENDLY, EITHER.
AFTER SIMONSON
THEY THOUGHT THEY WERE SAFE DOWN HERE--'TIL THE MARAUDERS NEARLY WIPED THEM OUT.
FIRST THE MARAUDERS--
--NOW BURNOUT--
--ALWAYS THE SURFACE WORLD TRIES TO MAKE US EXTINCT--
--BUT WE STILL SURVIVE!
THIS IS OUR DOMAIN--
--YOU'RE NOT WELCOME HERE!
FAIR ENOUGH--THE TROUBLE IS...
...YOU STARTED THIS.
YOU MORLOCKS STOLE OUR FRIENDS.
WE WANT 'EM BACK.
YOU GOT A PROBLEM WITH THAT...
...THEN I GUARANTEE THINGS HERE ARE GONNA GET NASTY!

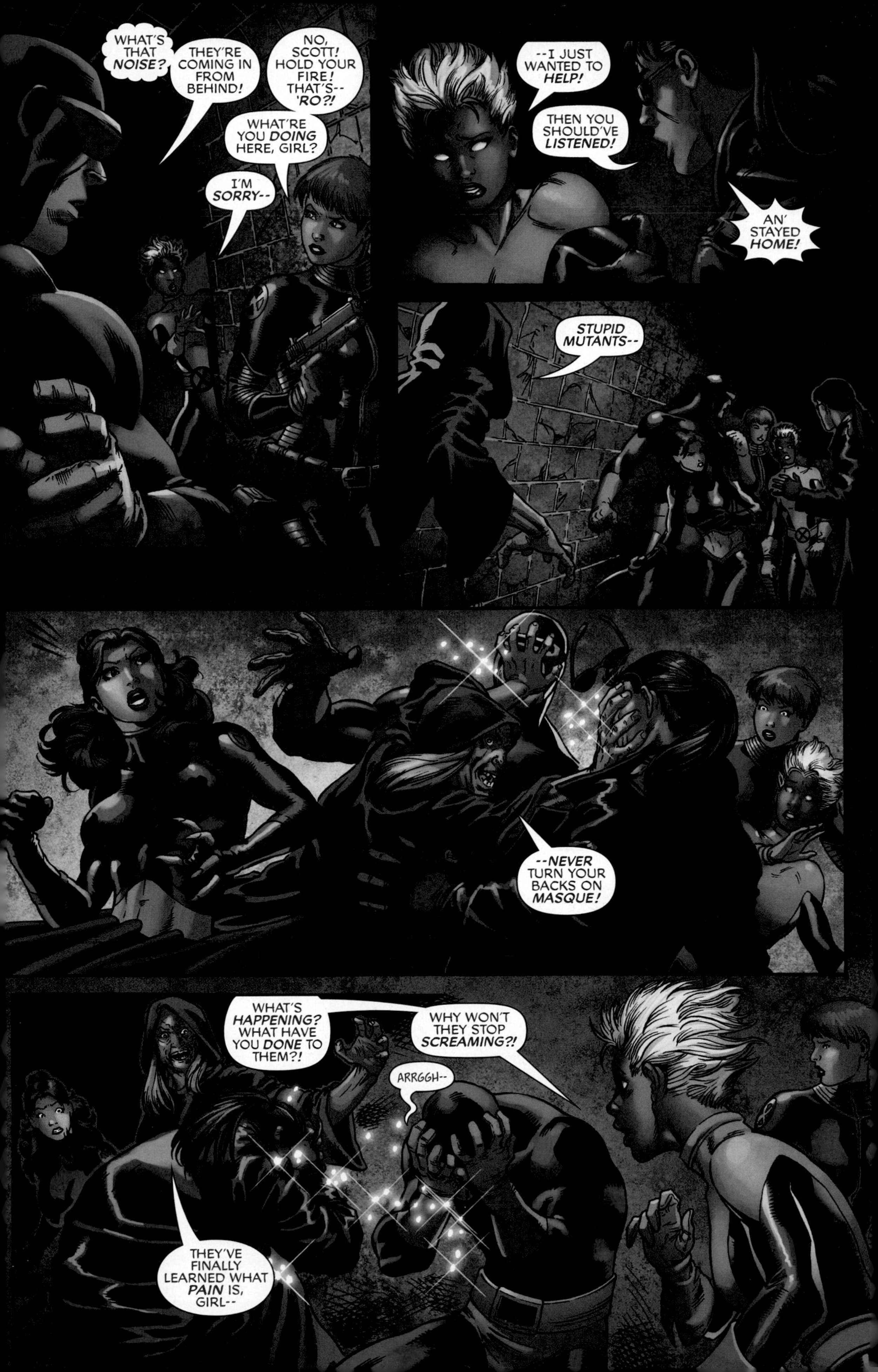
WHAT'S THAT NOISE?
THEY'RE COMING IN FROM BEHIND!
NO, SCOTT! HOLD YOUR FIRE! THAT'S-- 'RO?!
WHAT'RE YOU DOING HERE, GIRL?
I'M SORRY--
--I JUST WANTED TO HELP!
THEN YOU SHOULD'VE LISTENED!
AN' STAYED HOME!
STUPID MUTANTS--
--NEVER TURN YOUR BACKS ON MASQUE!
WHAT'S HAPPENING? WHAT HAVE YOU DONE TO THEM?!
WHY WON'T THEY STOP SCREAMING?!
ARRGGH--
THEY'VE FINALLY LEARNED WHAT PAIN IS, GIRL--

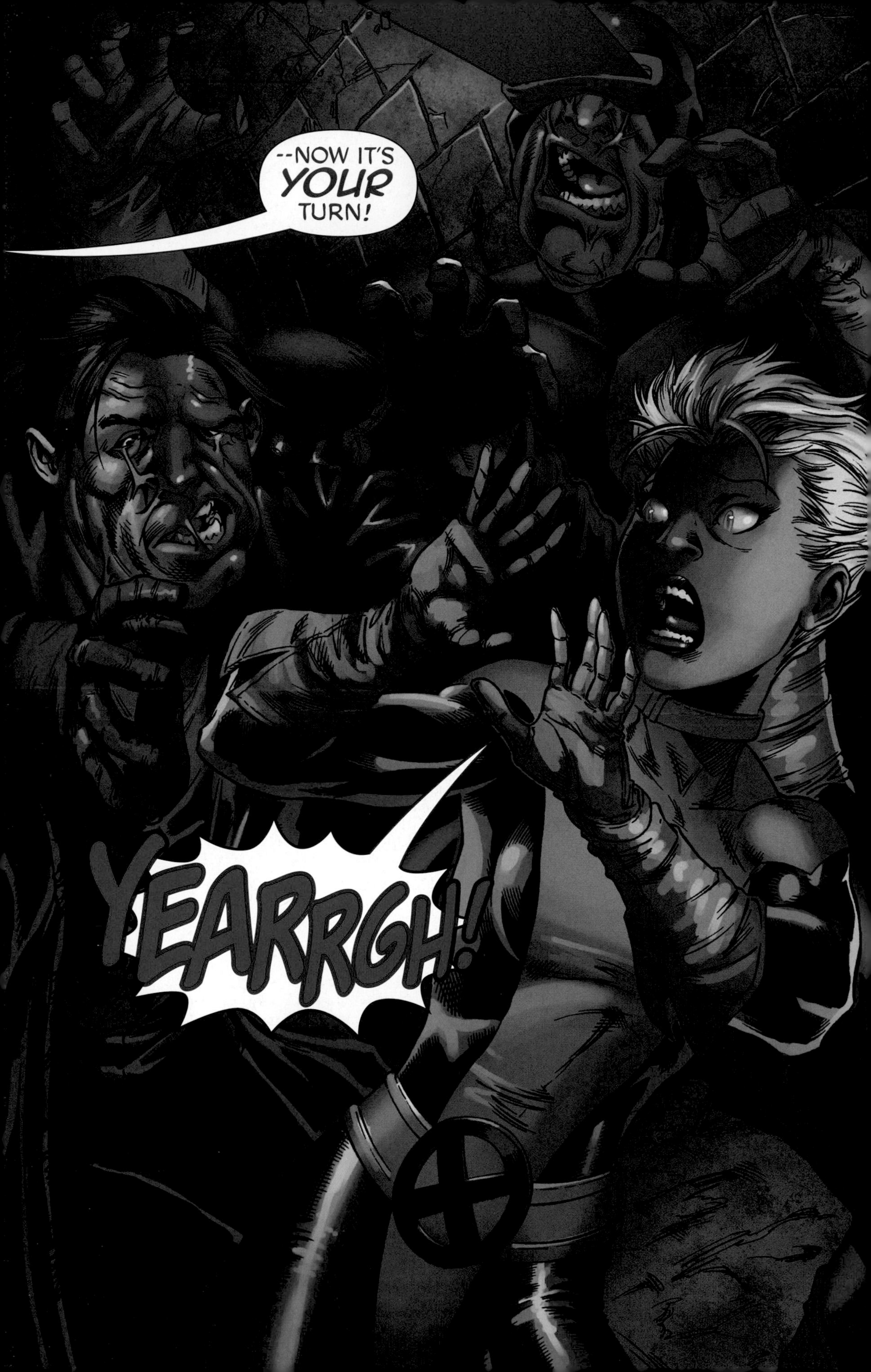
--NOW IT'S YOUR TURN!
YEARRGH!

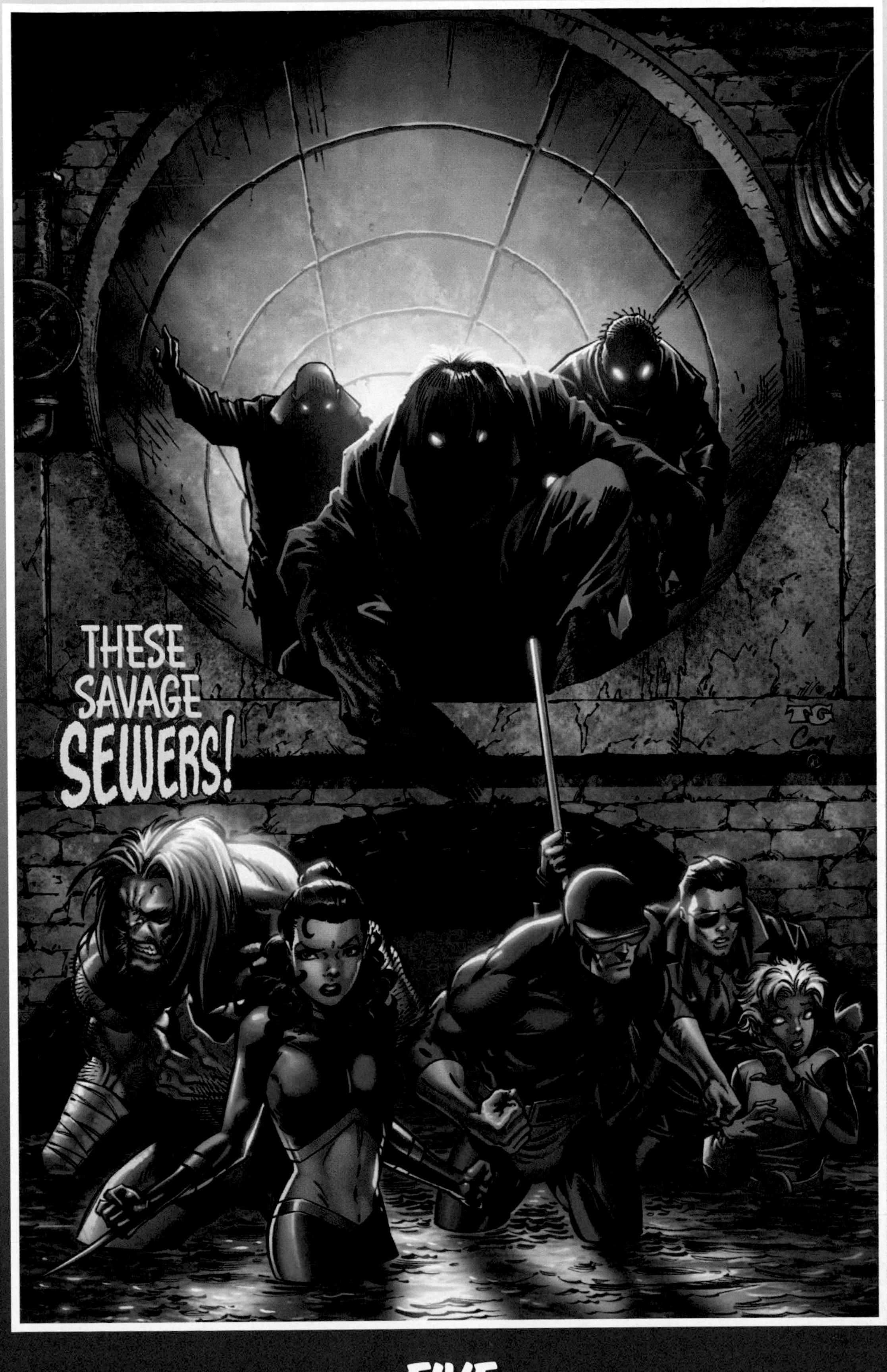
THESE SAVAGE SEWERS!
TG
Cary

FIVE

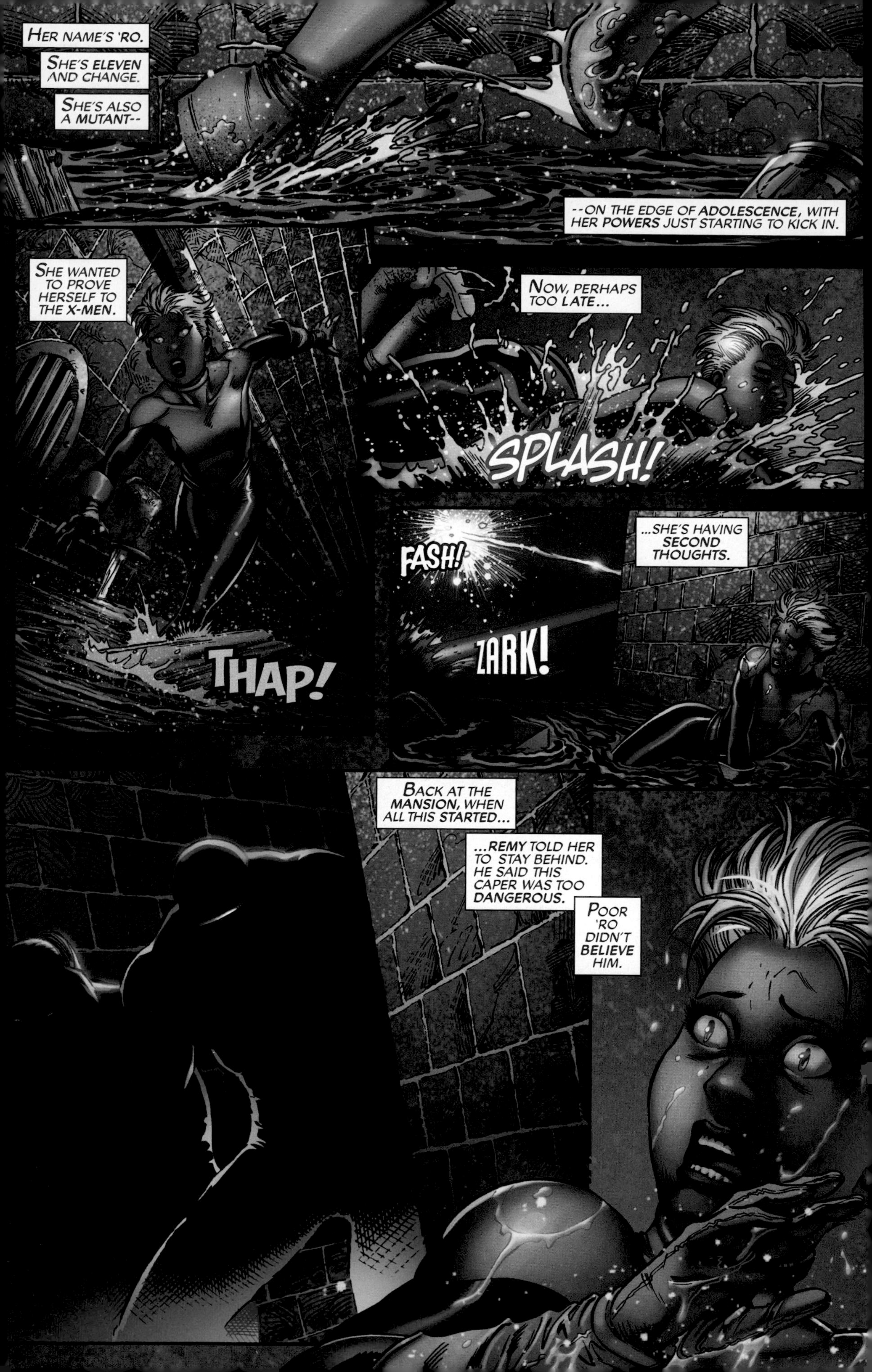

HER NAME'S 'RO.
SHE'S ELEVEN AND CHANGE.
SHE'S ALSO A MUTANT--
--ON THE EDGE OF ADOLESCENCE, WITH HER POWERS JUST STARTING TO KICK IN.
SHE WANTED TO PROVE HERSELF TO THE X-MEN.
THAP!
NOW, PERHAPS TOO LATE...
SPLASH!
FASH!
ZARK!
...SHE'S HAVING SECOND THOUGHTS.
BACK AT THE MANSION, WHEN ALL THIS STARTED...
...REMY TOLD HER TO STAY BEHIND. HE SAID THIS CAPER WAS TOO DANGEROUS.
POOR 'RO DIDN'T BELIEVE HIM.

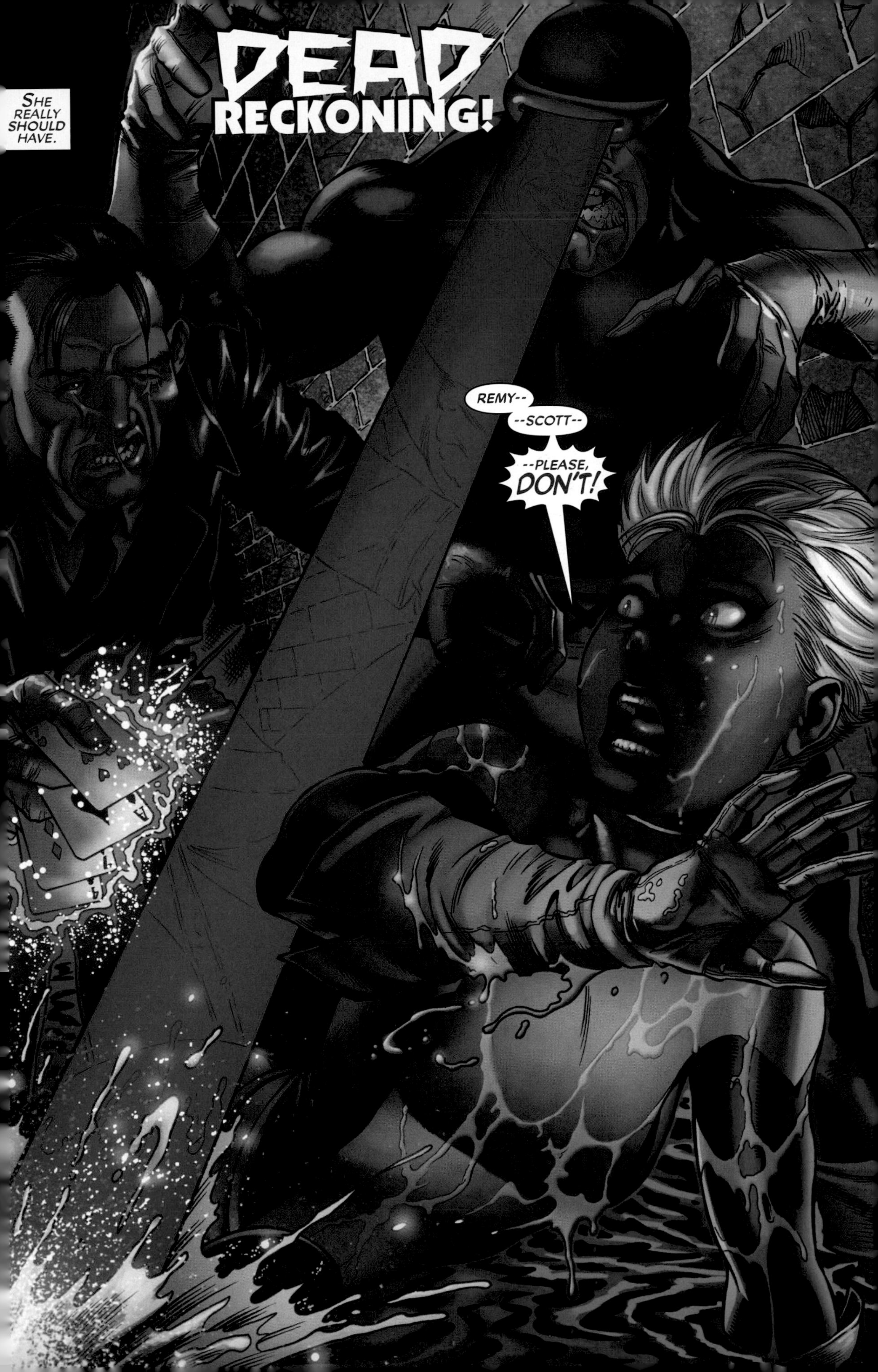
She really should have.
DEAD RECKONING!
REMY--
--SCOTT--
--PLEASE, DON'T!

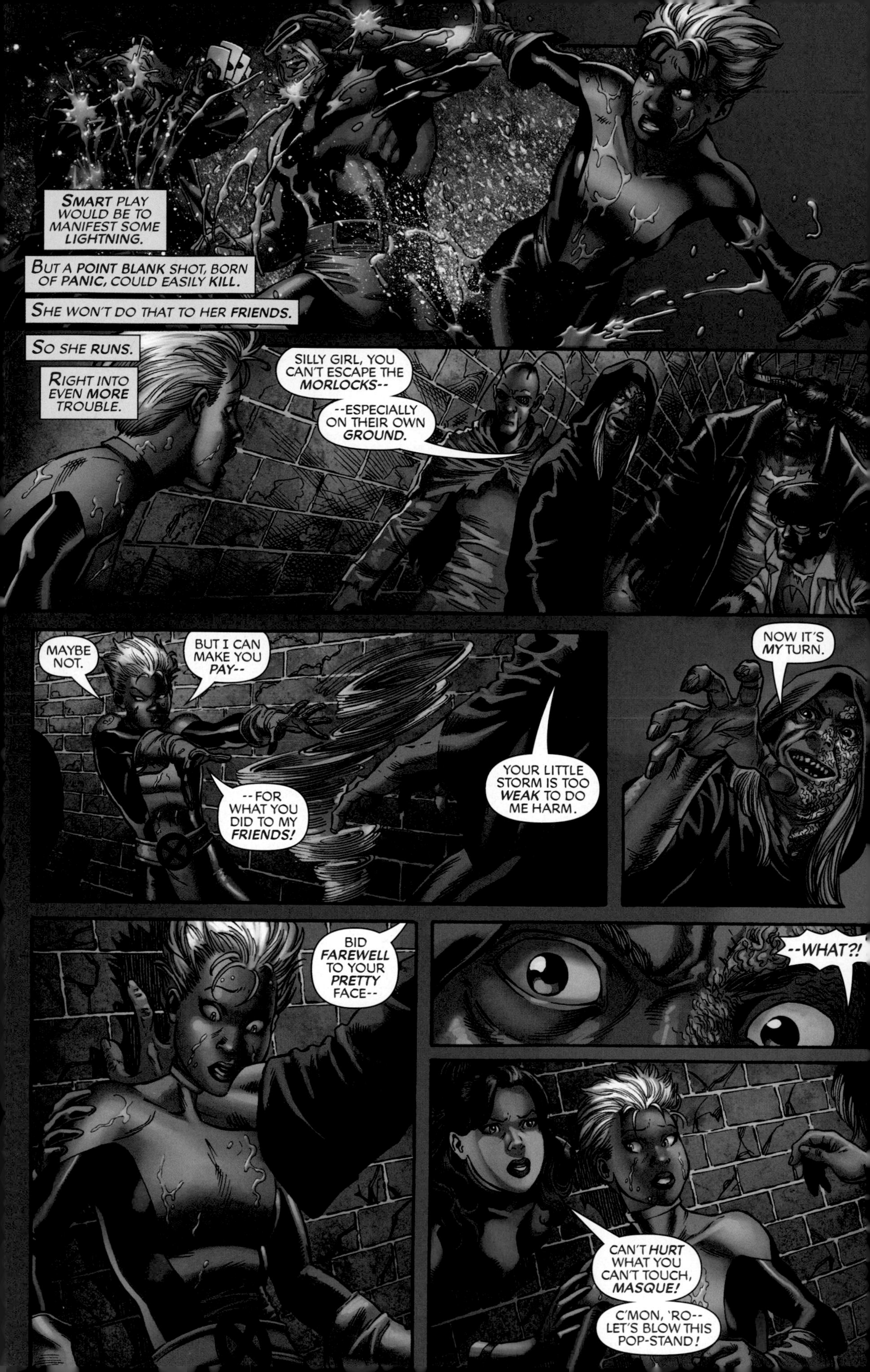
SMART PLAY WOULD BE TO MANIFEST SOME LIGHTNING.
BUT A POINT BLANK SHOT, BORN OF PANIC, COULD EASILY KILL.
SHE WON'T DO THAT TO HER FRIENDS.
SO SHE RUNS.
RIGHT INTO EVEN MORE TROUBLE.
SILLY GIRL, YOU CAN'T ESCAPE THE MORLOCKS--
--ESPECIALLY ON THEIR OWN GROUND.
MAYBE NOT.
BUT I CAN MAKE YOU PAY--
--FOR WHAT YOU DID TO MY FRIENDS!
YOUR LITTLE STORM IS TOO WEAK TO DO ME HARM.
NOW IT'S MY TURN.
BID FAREWELL TO YOUR PRETTY FACE--
--WHAT?!
CAN'T HURT WHAT YOU CAN'T TOUCH, MASQUE!
C'MON, 'RO-- LET'S BLOW THIS POP-STAND!

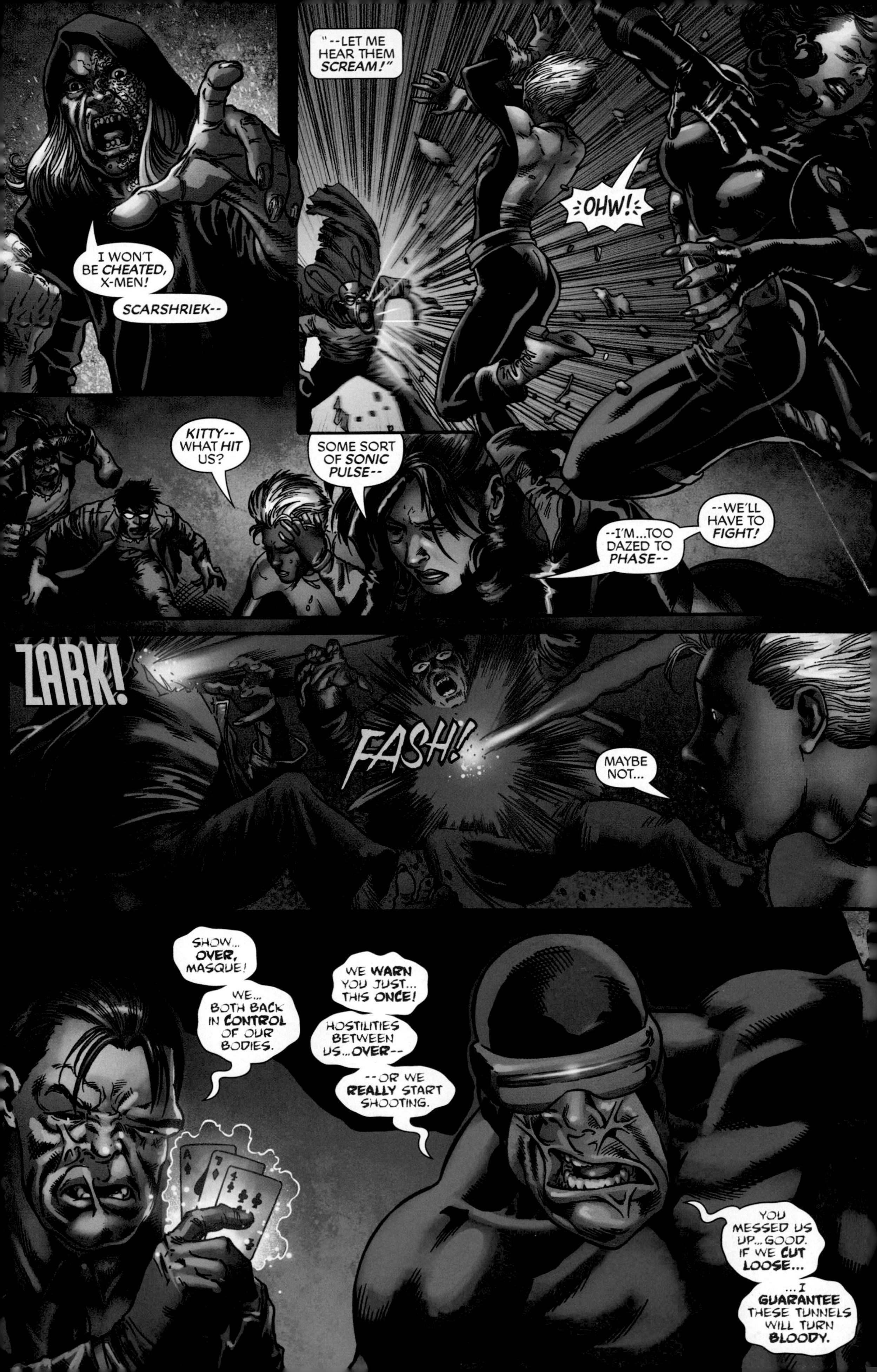
I WON'T BE CHEATED, X-MEN!
SCARSHRIEK--
"--LET ME HEAR THEM SCREAM!"
OHW!
KITTY--WHAT HIT US?
SOME SORT OF SONIC PULSE--
--I'M...TOO DAZED TO PHASE--
--WE'LL HAVE TO FIGHT!
ZARK!
FASH!
MAYBE NOT...
SHOW... OVER, MASQUE!
WE... BOTH BACK IN CONTROL OF OUR BODIES.
WE WARN YOU JUST... THIS ONCE!
HOSTILITIES BETWEEN US...OVER--
--OR WE REALLY START SHOOTING.
YOU MESSED US UP...GOOD. IF WE CUT LOOSE...
...I GUARANTEE THESE TUNNELS WILL TURN BLOODY.

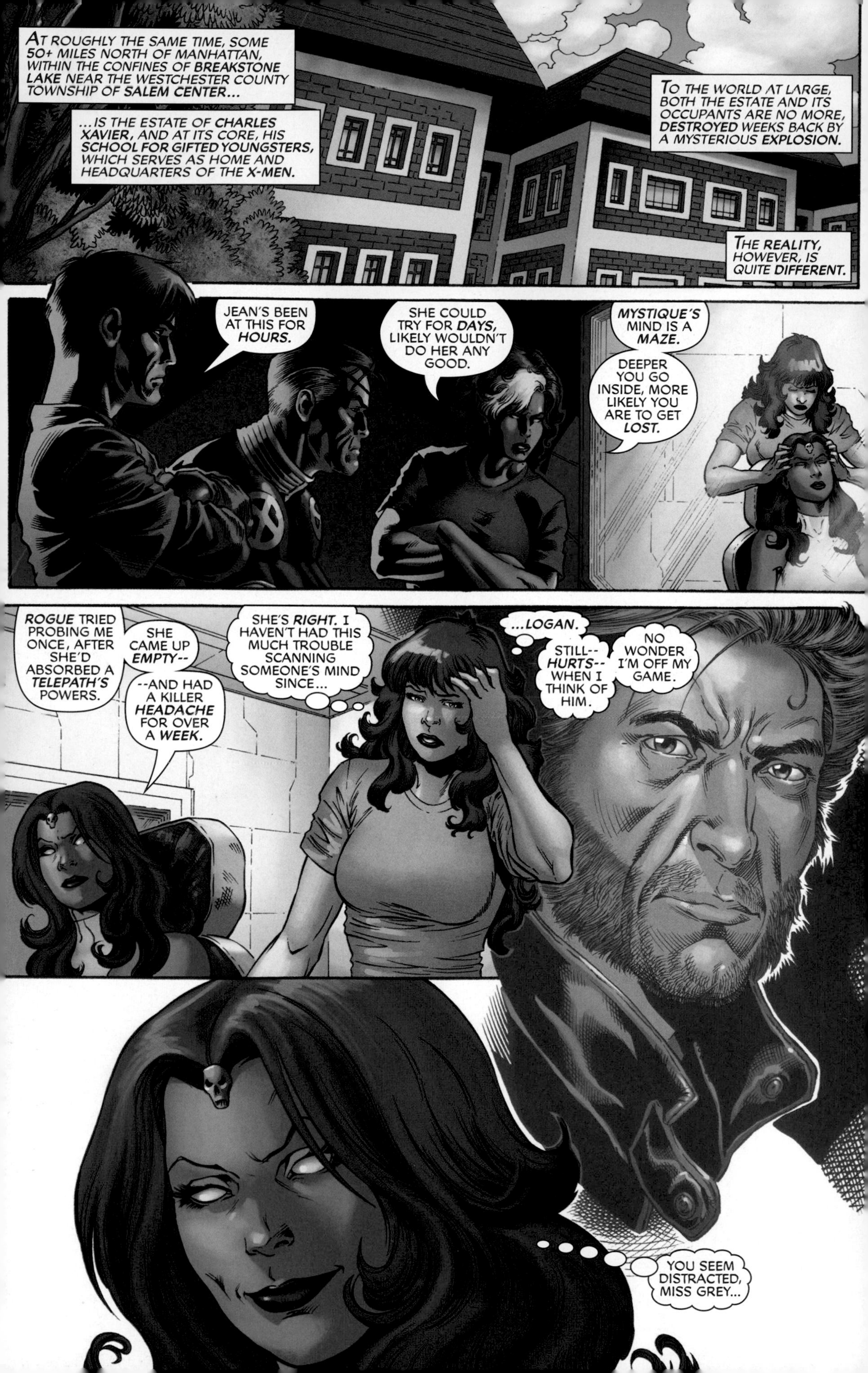
AT ROUGHLY THE SAME TIME, SOME 50+ MILES NORTH OF MANHATTAN, WITHIN THE CONFINES OF BREAKSTONE LAKE NEAR THE WESTCHESTER COUNTY TOWNSHIP OF SALEM CENTER...
...IS THE ESTATE OF CHARLES XAVIER, AND AT ITS CORE, HIS SCHOOL FOR GIFTED YOUNGSTERS, WHICH SERVES AS HOME AND HEADQUARTERS OF THE X-MEN.
TO THE WORLD AT LARGE, BOTH THE ESTATE AND ITS OCCUPANTS ARE NO MORE, DESTROYED WEEKS BACK BY A MYSTERIOUS EXPLOSION.
THE REALITY, HOWEVER, IS QUITE DIFFERENT.
JEAN'S BEEN AT THIS FOR HOURS.
SHE COULD TRY FOR DAYS, LIKELY WOULDN'T DO HER ANY GOOD.
MYSTIQUE'S MIND IS A MAZE.
DEEPER YOU GO INSIDE, MORE LIKELY YOU ARE TO GET LOST.
ROGUE TRIED PROBING ME ONCE, AFTER SHE'D ABSORBED A TELEPATH'S POWERS.
SHE CAME UP EMPTY--
--AND HAD A KILLER HEADACHE FOR OVER A WEEK.
SHE'S RIGHT. I HAVEN'T HAD THIS MUCH TROUBLE SCANNING SOMEONE'S MIND SINCE...
...LOGAN.
STILL--HURTS--WHEN I THINK OF HIM.
NO WONDER I'M OFF MY GAME.
YOU SEEM DISTRACTED, MISS GREY...

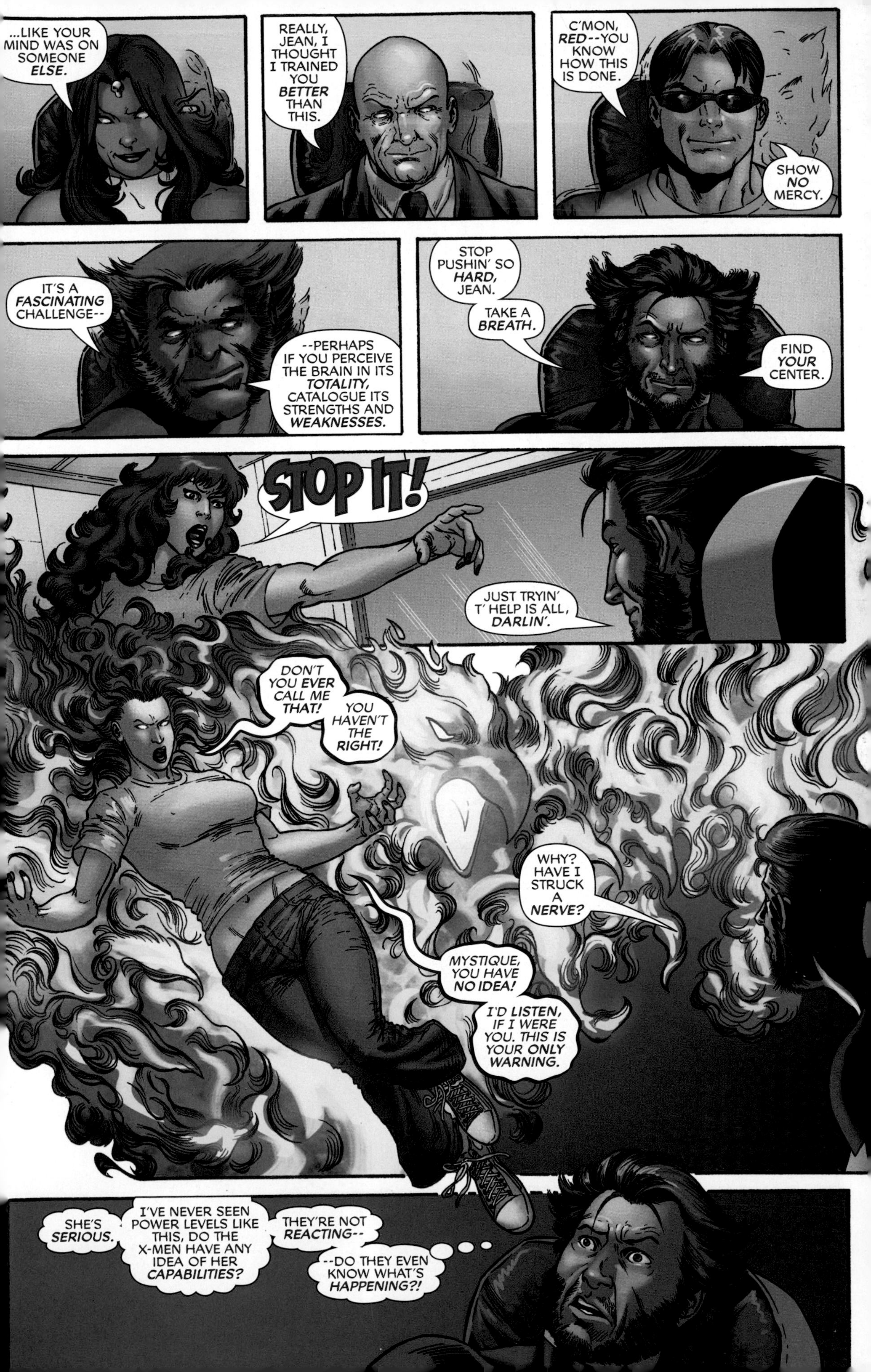
...LIKE YOUR MIND WAS ON SOMEONE ELSE.
REALLY, JEAN, I THOUGHT I TRAINED YOU BETTER THAN THIS.
C'MON, RED--YOU KNOW HOW THIS IS DONE.
SHOW NO MERCY.
IT'S A FASCINATING CHALLENGE--
--PERHAPS IF YOU PERCEIVE THE BRAIN IN ITS TOTALITY, CATALOGUE ITS STRENGTHS AND WEAKNESSES.
STOP PUSHIN' SO HARD, JEAN.
TAKE A BREATH.
FIND YOUR CENTER.
STOP IT!
JUST TRYIN' T' HELP IS ALL, DARLIN'.
DON'T YOU EVER CALL ME THAT!
YOU HAVEN'T THE RIGHT!
WHY? HAVE I STRUCK A NERVE?
MYSTIQUE, YOU HAVE NO IDEA!
I'D LISTEN, IF I WERE YOU. THIS IS YOUR ONLY WARNING.
SHE'S SERIOUS.
I'VE NEVER SEEN POWER LEVELS LIKE THIS, DO THE X-MEN HAVE ANY IDEA OF HER CAPABILITIES?
THEY'RE NOT REACTING--
--DO THEY EVEN KNOW WHAT'S HAPPENING?!

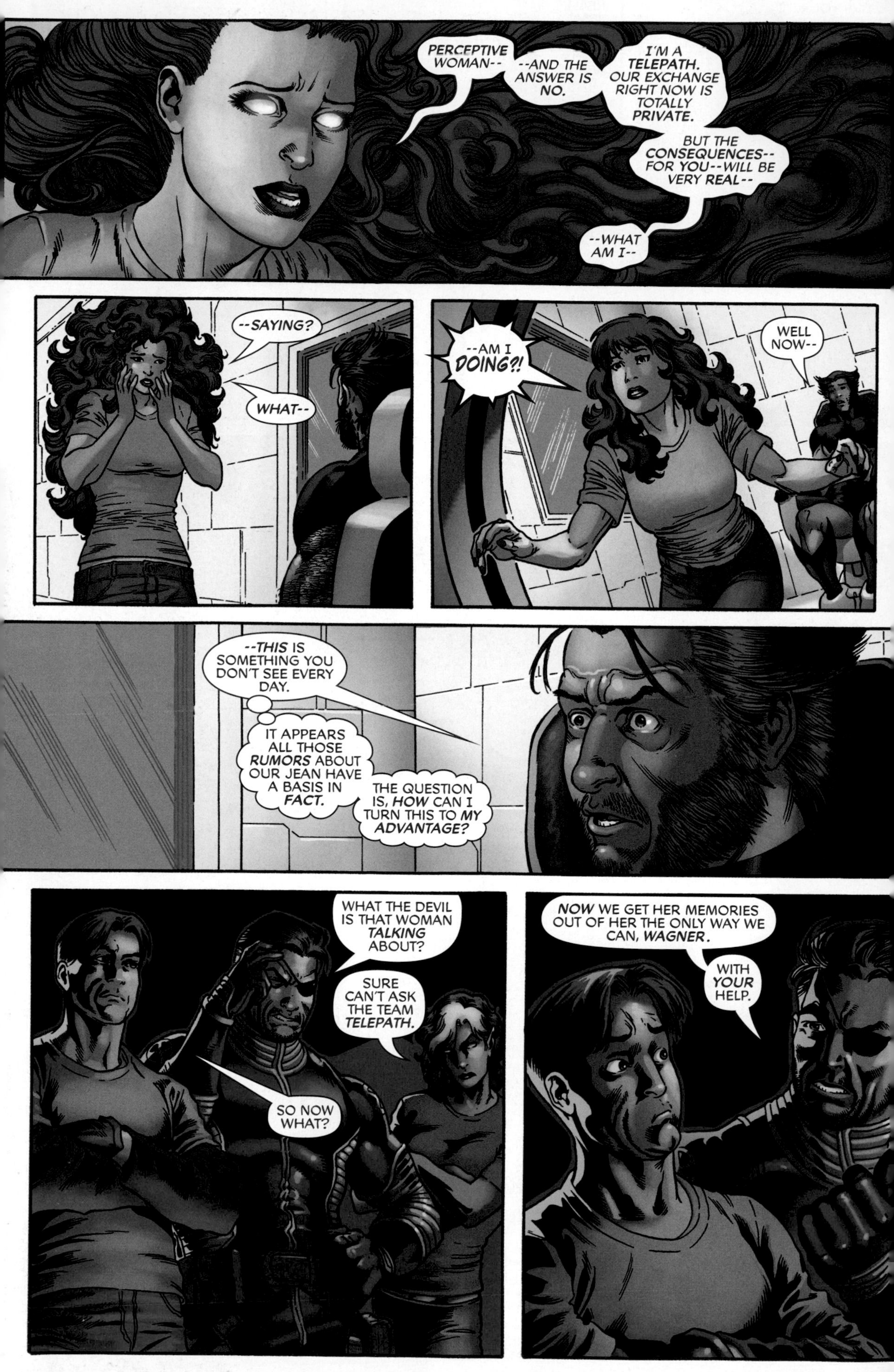
PERCEPTIVE WOMAN--
--AND THE ANSWER IS NO.
I'M A TELEPATH. OUR EXCHANGE RIGHT NOW IS TOTALLY PRIVATE.
BUT THE CONSEQUENCES-- FOR YOU--WILL BE VERY REAL--
--WHAT AM I--
--SAYING?
WHAT--
--AM I DOING?!
WELL NOW--
--THIS IS SOMETHING YOU DON'T SEE EVERY DAY.
IT APPEARS ALL THOSE RUMORS ABOUT OUR JEAN HAVE A BASIS IN FACT.
THE QUESTION IS, HOW CAN I TURN THIS TO MY ADVANTAGE?
WHAT THE DEVIL IS THAT WOMAN TALKING ABOUT?
SURE CAN'T ASK THE TEAM TELEPATH.
SO NOW WHAT?
NOW WE GET HER MEMORIES OUT OF HER THE ONLY WAY WE CAN, WAGNER.
WITH YOUR HELP.

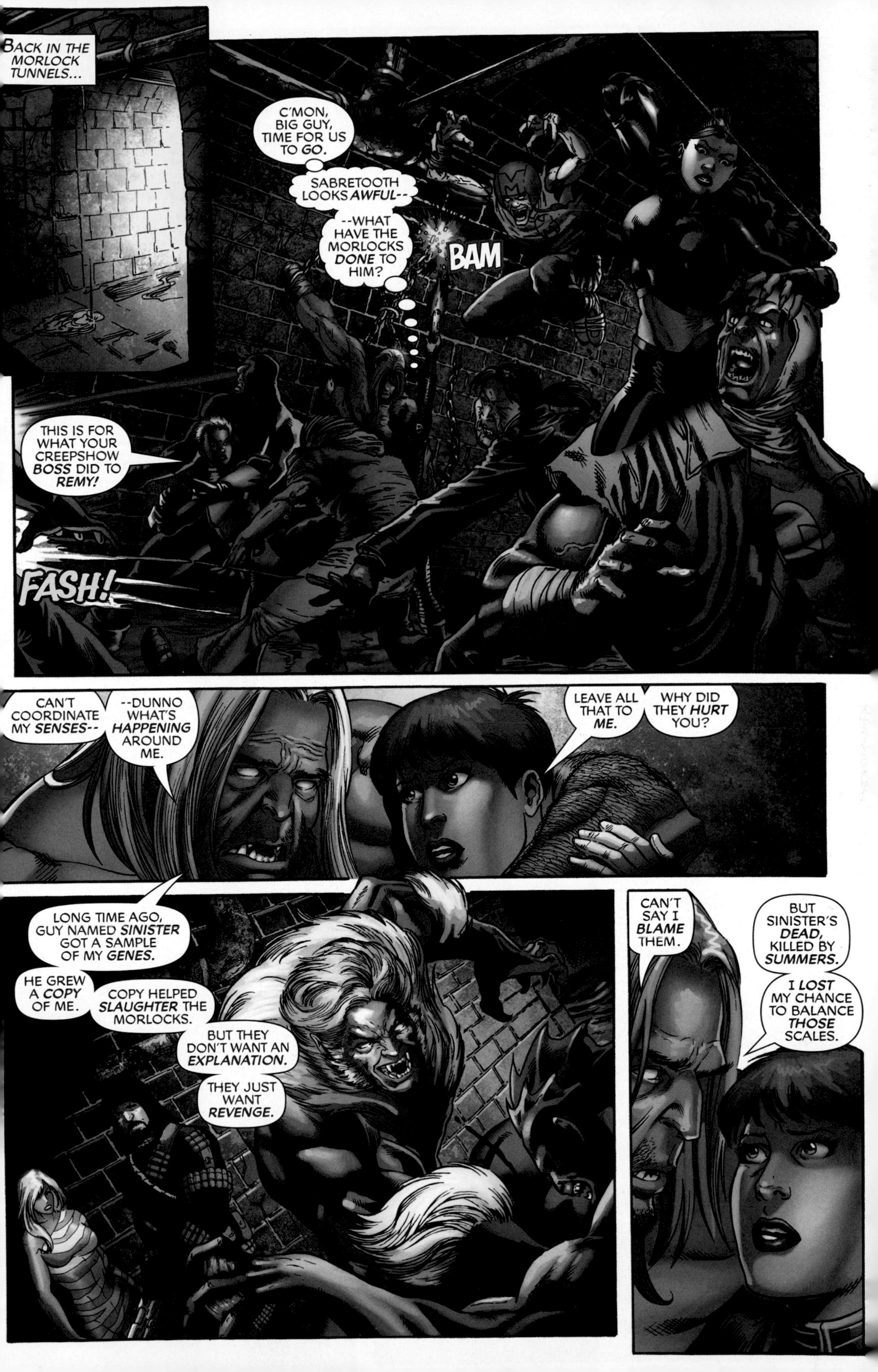

BACK IN THE MORLOCK TUNNELS...
C'MON, BIG GUY, TIME FOR US TO GO.
SABRETOOTH LOOKS AWFUL--
--WHAT HAVE THE MORLOCKS DONE TO HIM?
BAM
THIS IS FOR WHAT YOUR CREEPSHOW BOSS DID TO REMY!
FASH!
CAN'T COORDINATE MY SENSES--
--DUNNO WHAT'S HAPPENING AROUND ME.
LEAVE ALL THAT TO ME.
WHY DID THEY HURT YOU?
LONG TIME AGO, GUY NAMED SINISTER GOT A SAMPLE OF MY GENES.
HE GREW A COPY OF ME.
COPY HELPED SLAUGHTER THE MORLOCKS.
BUT THEY DON'T WANT AN EXPLANATION.
THEY JUST WANT REVENGE.
CAN'T SAY I BLAME THEM.
BUT SINISTER'S DEAD, KILLED BY SUMMERS.
I LOST MY CHANCE TO BALANCE THOSE SCALES.

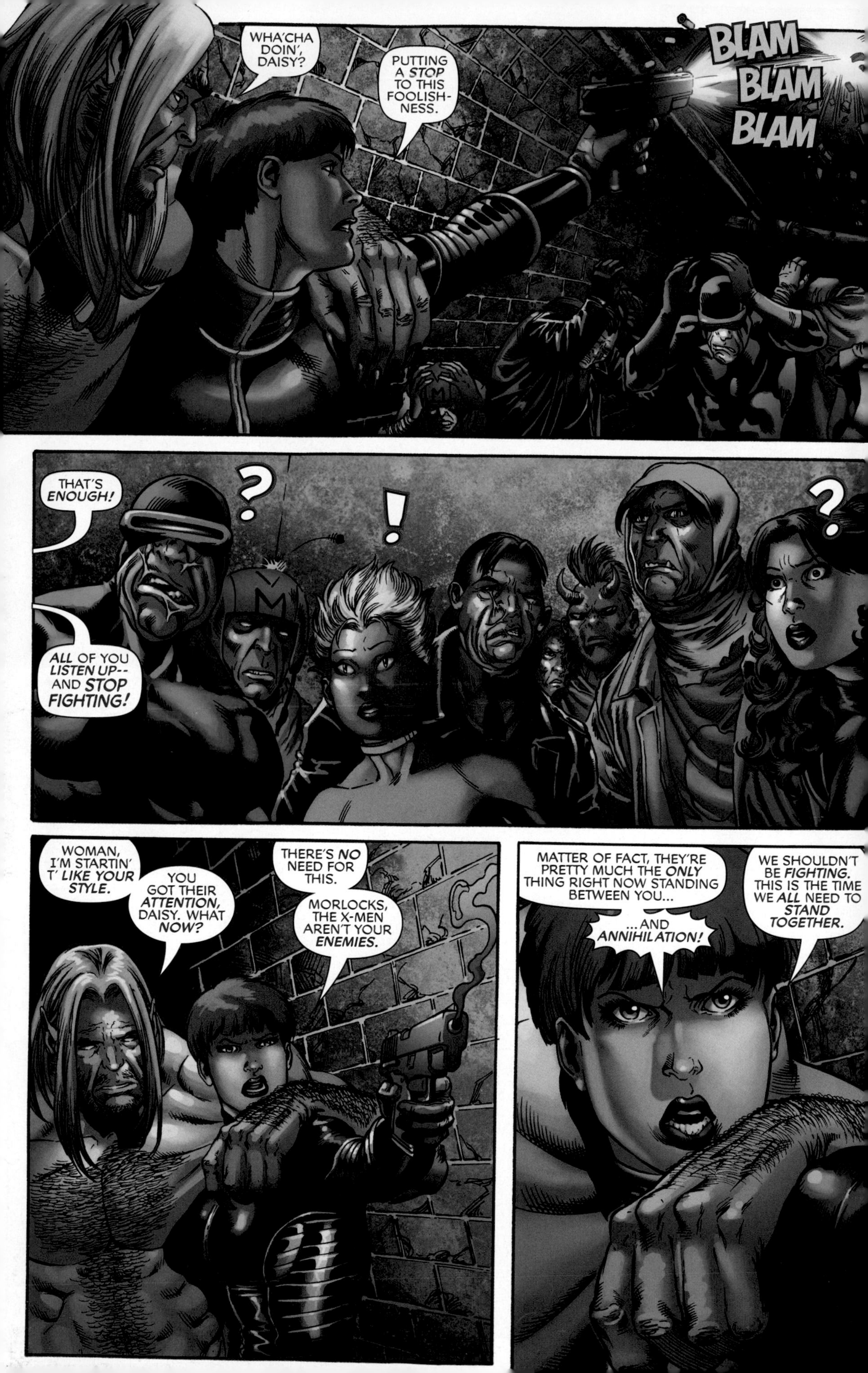
WHA'CHA DOIN', DAISY?
PUTTING A STOP TO THIS FOOLISHNESS.
BLAM BLAM BLAM
THAT'S ENOUGH!
?
!
?
ALL OF YOU LISTEN UP-- AND STOP FIGHTING!
WOMAN, I'M STARTIN' T' LIKE YOUR STYLE.
YOU GOT THEIR ATTENTION, DAISY. WHAT NOW?
THERE'S NO NEED FOR THIS.
MORLOCKS, THE X-MEN AREN'T YOUR ENEMIES.
MATTER OF FACT, THEY'RE PRETTY MUCH THE ONLY THING RIGHT NOW STANDING BETWEEN YOU...
...AND ANNIHILATION!
WE SHOULDN'T BE FIGHTING. THIS IS THE TIME WE ALL NEED TO STAND TOGETHER.

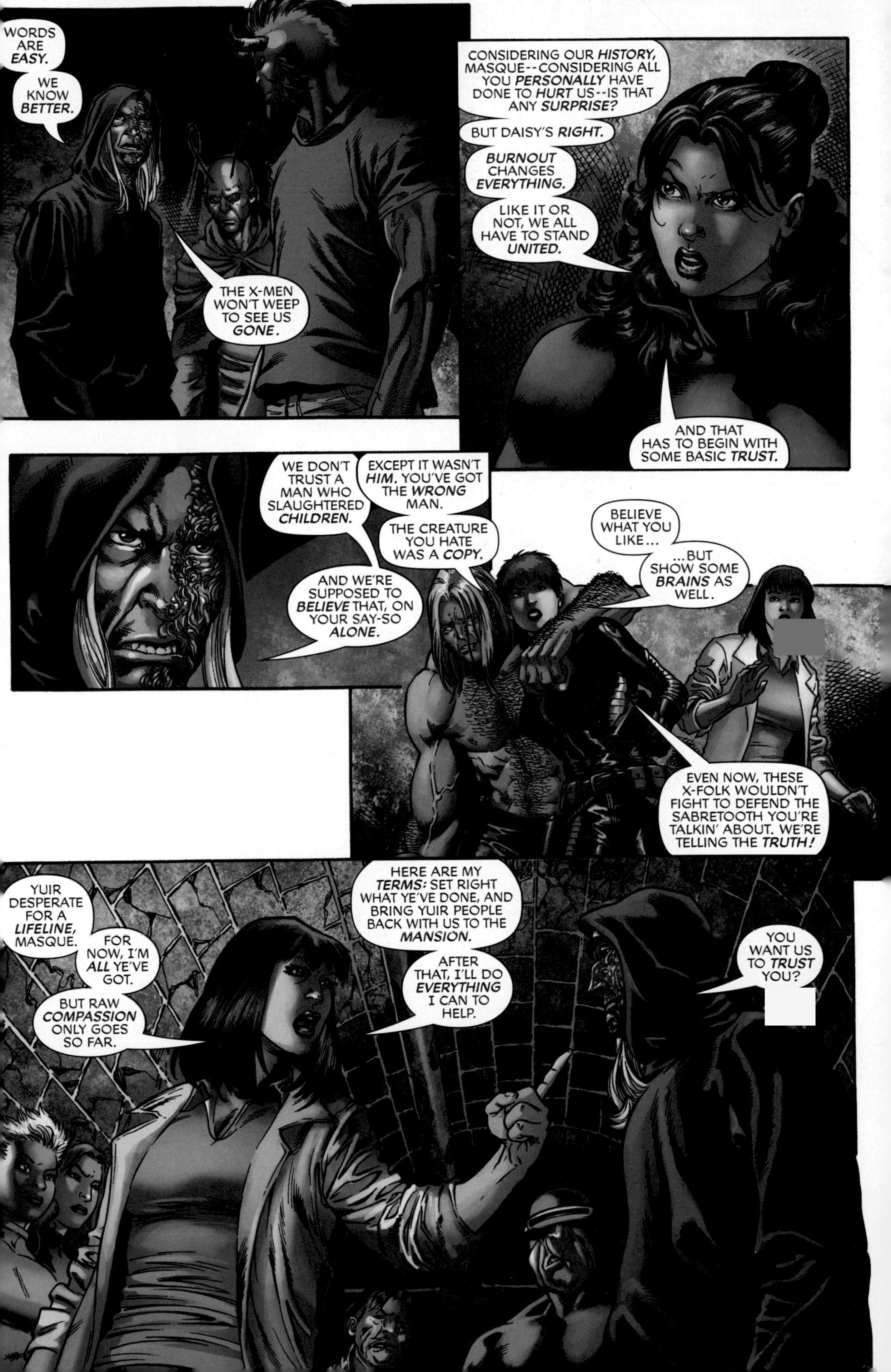

WORDS ARE *EASY.*
WE KNOW *BETTER.*
THE X-MEN WON'T WEEP TO SEE US *GONE.*
CONSIDERING OUR *HISTORY,* MASQUE--CONSIDERING ALL YOU *PERSONALLY* HAVE DONE TO *HURT* US--IS THAT ANY *SURPRISE?*
BUT DAISY'S *RIGHT.*
BURNOUT CHANGES *EVERYTHING.*
LIKE IT OR NOT, WE ALL HAVE TO STAND *UNITED.*
AND THAT HAS TO BEGIN WITH SOME BASIC *TRUST.*
WE DON'T TRUST A MAN WHO SLAUGHTERED *CHILDREN.*
EXCEPT IT WASN'T *HIM.* YOU'VE GOT THE *WRONG* MAN.
THE CREATURE YOU HATE WAS A *COPY.*
AND WE'RE SUPPOSED TO *BELIEVE* THAT, ON YOUR SAY-SO *ALONE.*
BELIEVE WHAT YOU LIKE...
...BUT SHOW SOME *BRAINS* AS WELL.
EVEN NOW, THESE X-FOLK WOULDN'T FIGHT TO DEFEND THE SABRETOOTH YOU'RE TALKIN' ABOUT. WE'RE TELLING THE *TRUTH!*
YUIR DESPERATE FOR A *LIFELINE,* MASQUE.
FOR NOW, I'M *ALL* YE'VE GOT.
BUT RAW *COMPASSION* ONLY GOES SO FAR.
HERE ARE MY *TERMS:* SET RIGHT WHAT YE'VE DONE, AND BRING YUIR PEOPLE BACK WITH US TO THE *MANSION.*
AFTER THAT, I'LL DO *EVERYTHING* I CAN TO HELP.
YOU WANT US TO *TRUST* YOU?

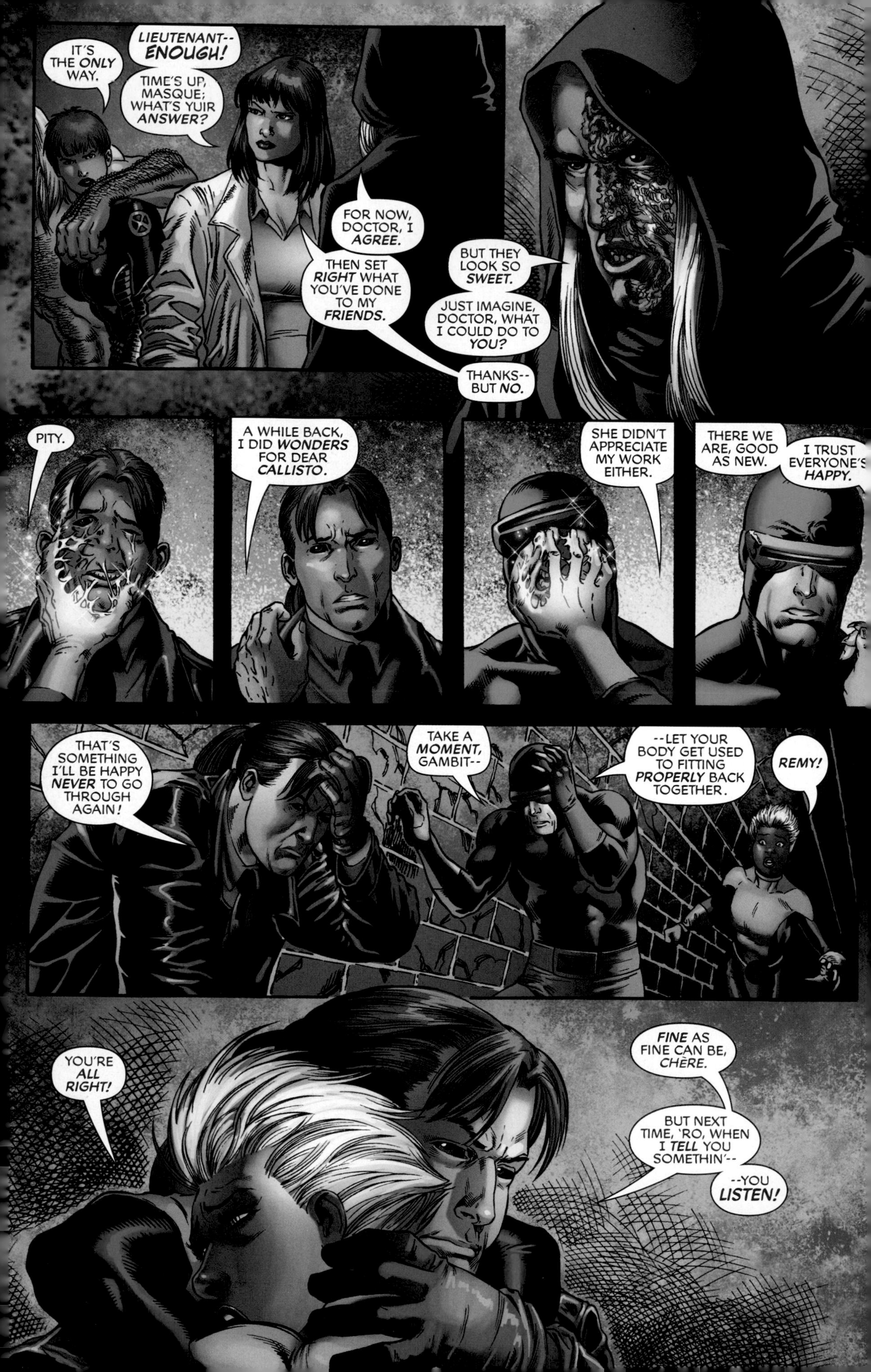
IT'S THE ONLY WAY.
LIEUTENANT-- ENOUGH!
TIME'S UP, MASQUE; WHAT'S YUIR ANSWER?
FOR NOW, DOCTOR, I AGREE.
THEN SET RIGHT WHAT YOU'VE DONE TO MY FRIENDS.
BUT THEY LOOK SO SWEET.
JUST IMAGINE, DOCTOR, WHAT I COULD DO TO YOU?
THANKS-- BUT NO.
PITY.
A WHILE BACK, I DID WONDERS FOR DEAR CALLISTO.
SHE DIDN'T APPRECIATE MY WORK EITHER.
THERE WE ARE, GOOD AS NEW.
I TRUST EVERYONE'S HAPPY.
THAT'S SOMETHING I'LL BE HAPPY NEVER TO GO THROUGH AGAIN!
TAKE A MOMENT, GAMBIT--
--LET YOUR BODY GET USED TO FITTING PROPERLY BACK TOGETHER.
REMY!
YOU'RE ALL RIGHT!
FINE AS FINE CAN BE, CHÈRE.
BUT NEXT TIME, 'RO, WHEN I TELL YOU SOMETHIN'--
--YOU LISTEN!

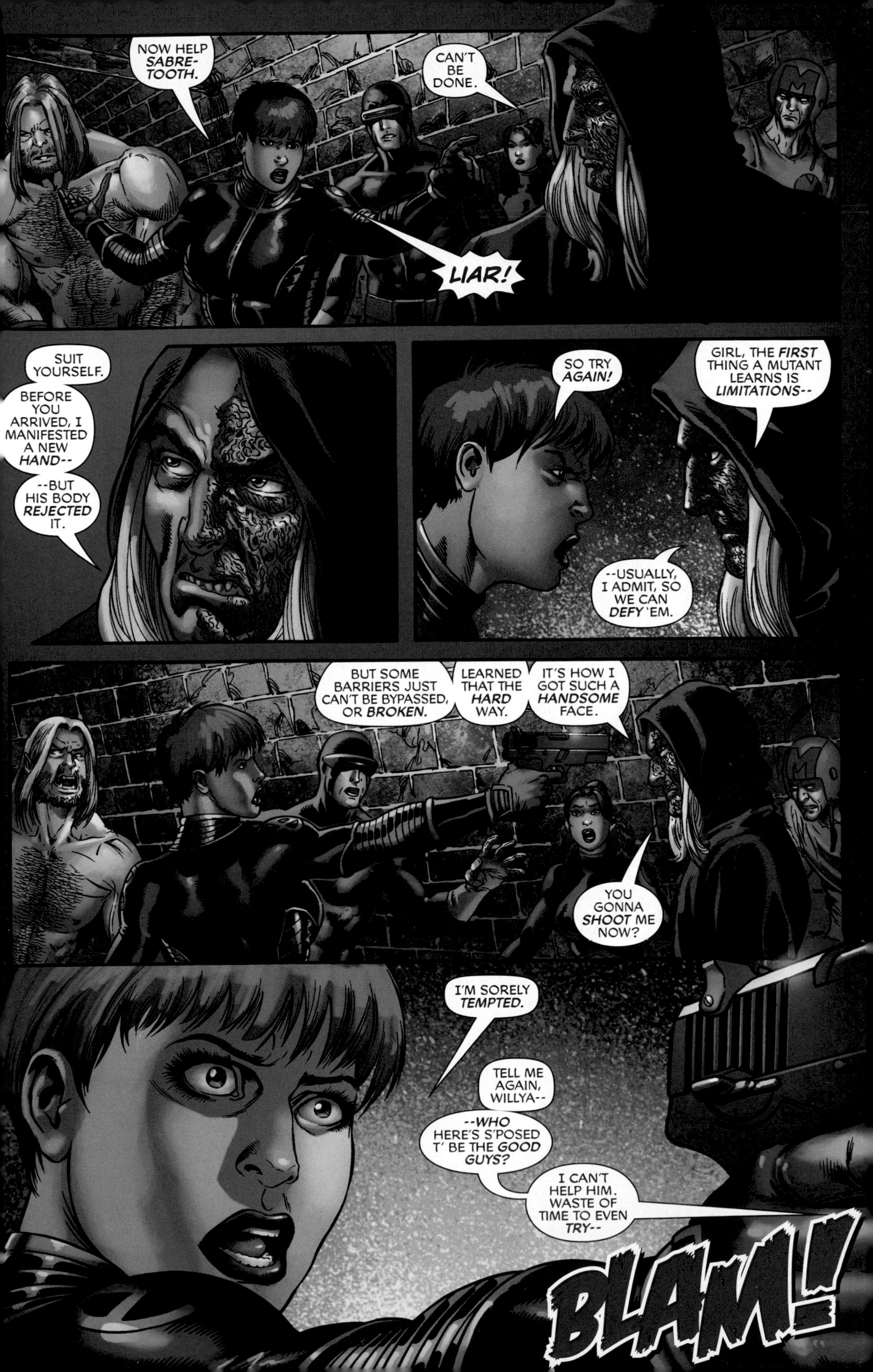
NOW HELP SABRE-TOOTH.
CAN'T BE DONE.
LIAR!
SUIT YOURSELF.
BEFORE YOU ARRIVED, I MANIFESTED A NEW HAND--
--BUT HIS BODY REJECTED IT.
SO TRY AGAIN!
GIRL, THE FIRST THING A MUTANT LEARNS IS LIMITATIONS--
--USUALLY, I ADMIT, SO WE CAN DEFY 'EM.
BUT SOME BARRIERS JUST CAN'T BE BYPASSED, OR BROKEN.
LEARNED THAT THE HARD WAY.
IT'S HOW I GOT SUCH A HANDSOME FACE.
YOU GONNA SHOOT ME NOW?
I'M SORELY TEMPTED.
TELL ME AGAIN, WILLYA--
--WHO HERE'S S'POSED T' BE THE GOOD GUYS?
I CAN'T HELP HIM. WASTE OF TIME TO EVEN TRY--
BLAM!

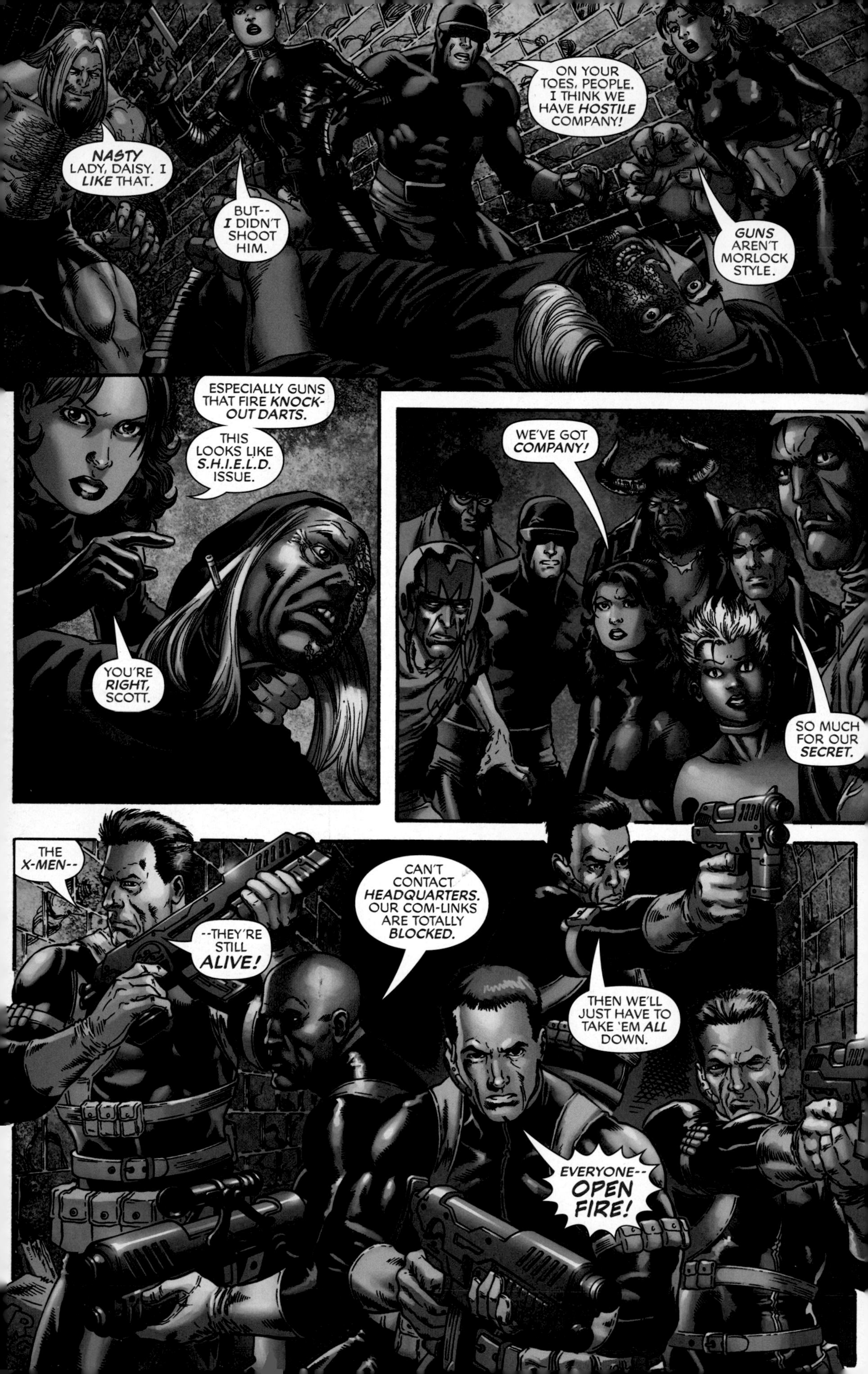

NASTY LADY, DAISY. I LIKE THAT.
BUT-- I DIDN'T SHOOT HIM.
ON YOUR TOES, PEOPLE. I THINK WE HAVE HOSTILE COMPANY!
GUNS AREN'T MORLOCK STYLE.
ESPECIALLY GUNS THAT FIRE KNOCK-OUT DARTS.
THIS LOOKS LIKE S.H.I.E.L.D. ISSUE.
YOU'RE RIGHT, SCOTT.
WE'VE GOT COMPANY!
SO MUCH FOR OUR SECRET.
THE X-MEN--
--THEY'RE STILL ALIVE!
CAN'T CONTACT HEADQUARTERS. OUR COM-LINKS ARE TOTALLY BLOCKED.
THEN WE'LL JUST HAVE TO TAKE 'EM ALL DOWN.
EVERYONE-- OPEN FIRE!

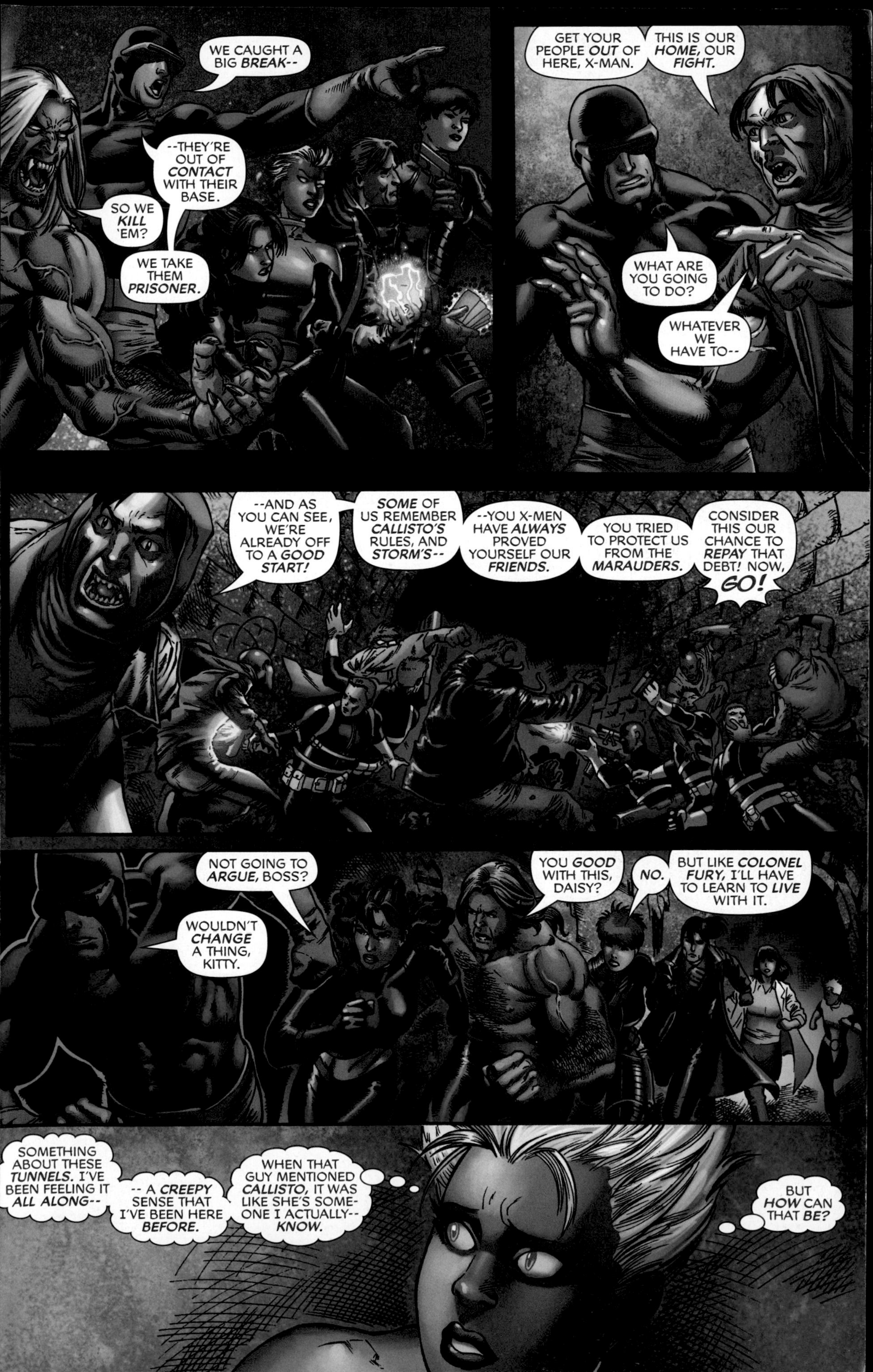
WE CAUGHT A BIG BREAK--
--THEY'RE OUT OF CONTACT WITH THEIR BASE.
SO WE KILL 'EM?
WE TAKE THEM PRISONER.
GET YOUR PEOPLE OUT OF HERE, X-MAN.
THIS IS OUR HOME, OUR FIGHT.
WHAT ARE YOU GOING TO DO?
WHATEVER WE HAVE TO--
--AND AS YOU CAN SEE, WE'RE ALREADY OFF TO A GOOD START!
SOME OF US REMEMBER CALLISTO'S RULES, AND STORM'S--
--YOU X-MEN HAVE ALWAYS PROVED YOURSELF OUR FRIENDS.
YOU TRIED TO PROTECT US FROM THE MARAUDERS.
CONSIDER THIS OUR CHANCE TO REPAY THAT DEBT! NOW, GO!
NOT GOING TO ARGUE, BOSS?
WOULDN'T CHANGE A THING, KITTY.
YOU GOOD WITH THIS, DAISY?
NO.
BUT LIKE COLONEL FURY, I'LL HAVE TO LEARN TO LIVE WITH IT.
SOMETHING ABOUT THESE TUNNELS. I'VE BEEN FEELING IT ALL ALONG--
-- A CREEPY SENSE THAT I'VE BEEN HERE BEFORE.
WHEN THAT GUY MENTIONED CALLISTO, IT WAS LIKE SHE'S SOME-ONE I ACTUALLY-- KNOW.
BUT HOW CAN THAT BE?

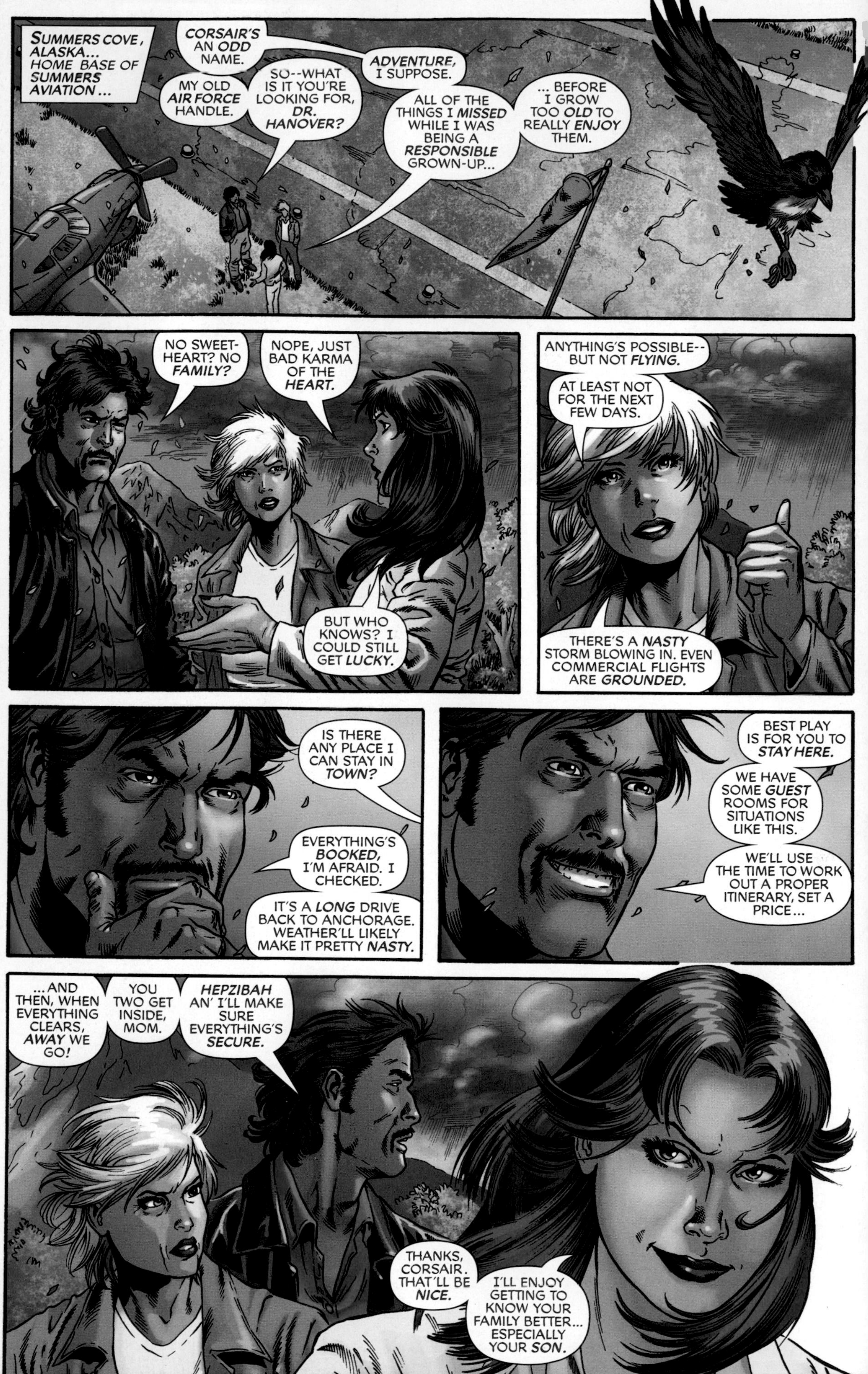
SUMMERS COVE, ALASKA... HOME BASE OF SUMMERS AVIATION...
CORSAIR'S AN ODD NAME.
MY OLD AIR FORCE HANDLE.
SO--WHAT IS IT YOU'RE LOOKING FOR, DR. HANOVER?
ADVENTURE, I SUPPOSE.
ALL OF THE THINGS I MISSED WHILE I WAS BEING A RESPONSIBLE GROWN-UP...
... BEFORE I GROW TOO OLD TO REALLY ENJOY THEM.
NO SWEET-HEART? NO FAMILY?
NOPE, JUST BAD KARMA OF THE HEART.
BUT WHO KNOWS? I COULD STILL GET LUCKY.
ANYTHING'S POSSIBLE-- BUT NOT FLYING.
AT LEAST NOT FOR THE NEXT FEW DAYS.
THERE'S A NASTY STORM BLOWING IN. EVEN COMMERCIAL FLIGHTS ARE GROUNDED.
IS THERE ANY PLACE I CAN STAY IN TOWN?
EVERYTHING'S BOOKED, I'M AFRAID. I CHECKED.
IT'S A LONG DRIVE BACK TO ANCHORAGE. WEATHER'LL LIKELY MAKE IT PRETTY NASTY.
BEST PLAY IS FOR YOU TO STAY HERE.
WE HAVE SOME GUEST ROOMS FOR SITUATIONS LIKE THIS.
WE'LL USE THE TIME TO WORK OUT A PROPER ITINERARY, SET A PRICE...
...AND THEN, WHEN EVERYTHING CLEARS, AWAY WE GO!
YOU TWO GET INSIDE, MOM.
HEPZIBAH AN' I'LL MAKE SURE EVERYTHING'S SECURE.
THANKS, CORSAIR. THAT'LL BE NICE.
I'LL ENJOY GETTING TO KNOW YOUR FAMILY BETTER... ESPECIALLY YOUR SON.

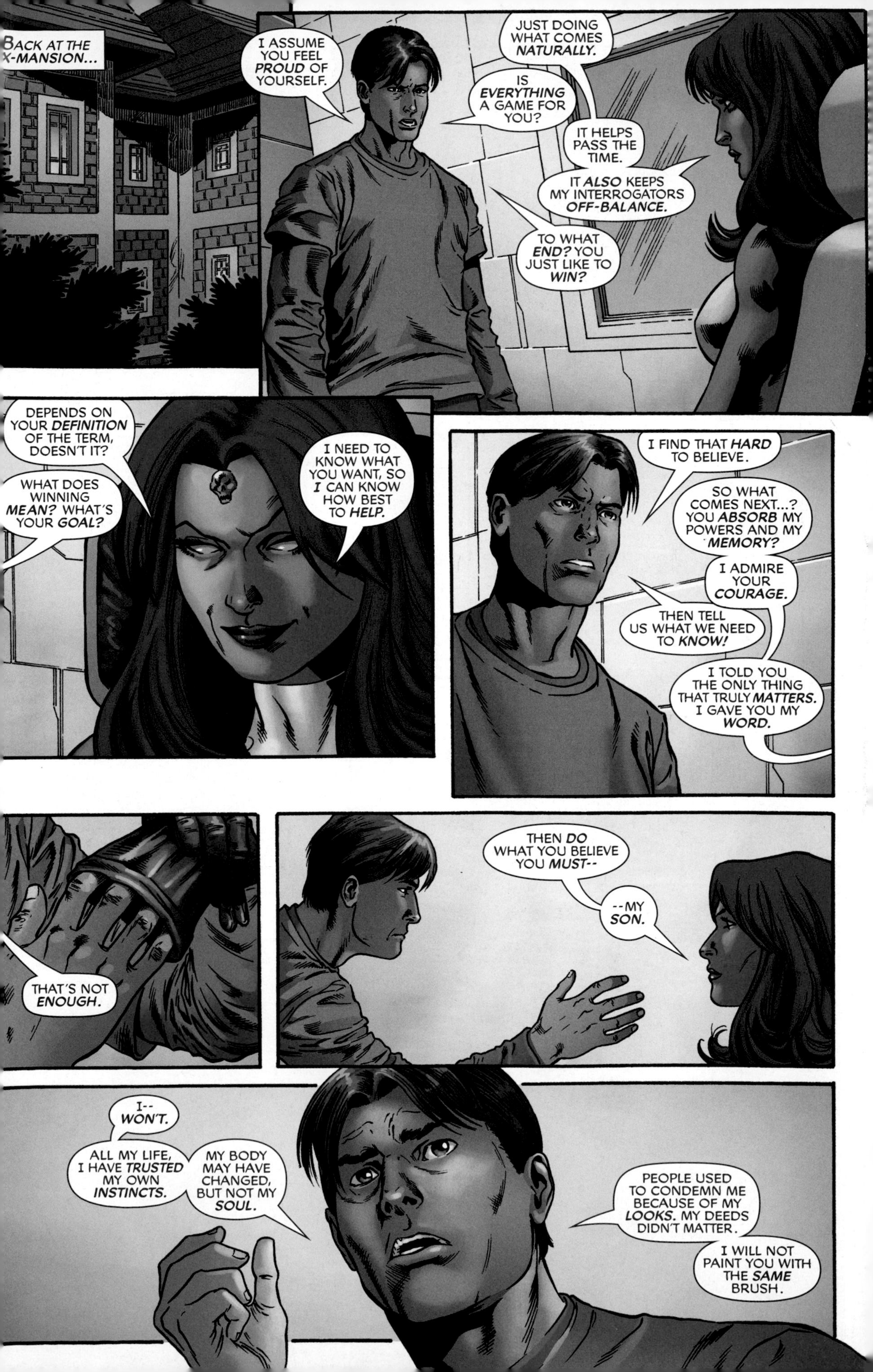
BACK AT THE X-MANSION...
I ASSUME YOU FEEL PROUD OF YOURSELF.
JUST DOING WHAT COMES NATURALLY.
IS EVERYTHING A GAME FOR YOU?
IT HELPS PASS THE TIME.
IT ALSO KEEPS MY INTERROGATORS OFF-BALANCE.
TO WHAT END? YOU JUST LIKE TO WIN?
DEPENDS ON YOUR DEFINITION OF THE TERM, DOESN'T IT?
WHAT DOES WINNING MEAN? WHAT'S YOUR GOAL?
I NEED TO KNOW WHAT YOU WANT, SO I CAN KNOW HOW BEST TO HELP.
I FIND THAT HARD TO BELIEVE.
SO WHAT COMES NEXT...? YOU ABSORB MY POWERS AND MY MEMORY?
I ADMIRE YOUR COURAGE.
THEN TELL US WHAT WE NEED TO KNOW!
I TOLD YOU THE ONLY THING THAT TRULY MATTERS. I GAVE YOU MY WORD.
THAT'S NOT ENOUGH.
THEN DO WHAT YOU BELIEVE YOU MUST--
--MY SON.
I-- WON'T.
ALL MY LIFE, I HAVE TRUSTED MY OWN INSTINCTS.
MY BODY MAY HAVE CHANGED, BUT NOT MY SOUL.
PEOPLE USED TO CONDEMN ME BECAUSE OF MY LOOKS. MY DEEDS DIDN'T MATTER.
I WILL NOT PAINT YOU WITH THE SAME BRUSH.

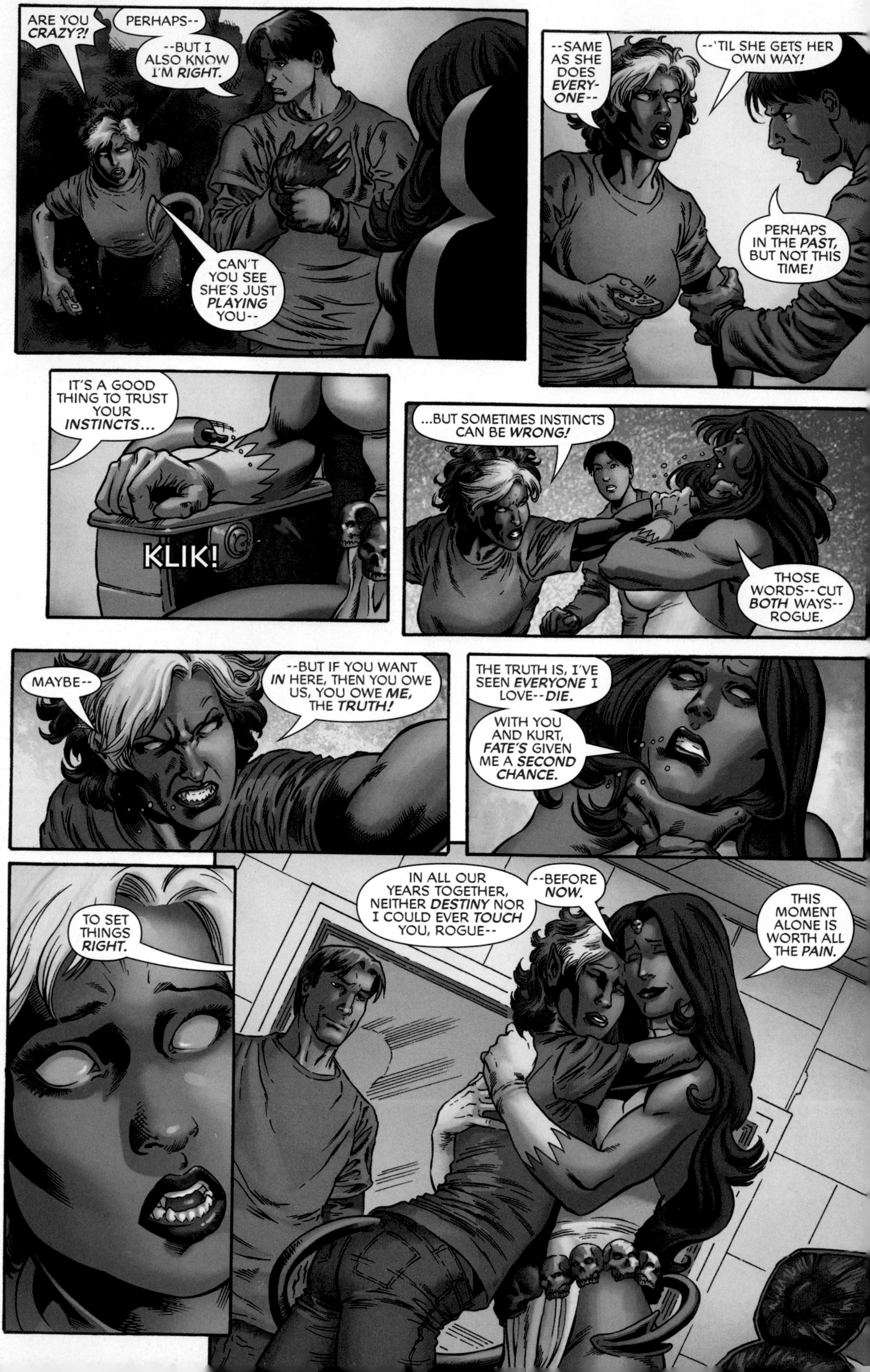
ARE YOU CRAZY?!
PERHAPS--
--BUT I ALSO KNOW I'M RIGHT.
CAN'T YOU SEE SHE'S JUST PLAYING YOU--
--SAME AS SHE DOES EVERY-ONE--
--'TIL SHE GETS HER OWN WAY!
PERHAPS IN THE PAST, BUT NOT THIS TIME!
IT'S A GOOD THING TO TRUST YOUR INSTINCTS...
KLIK!
...BUT SOMETIMES INSTINCTS CAN BE WRONG!
THOSE WORDS--CUT BOTH WAYS--ROGUE.
MAYBE--
--BUT IF YOU WANT IN HERE, THEN YOU OWE US, YOU OWE ME, THE TRUTH!
THE TRUTH IS, I'VE SEEN EVERYONE I LOVE--DIE.
WITH YOU AND KURT, FATE'S GIVEN ME A SECOND CHANCE.
TO SET THINGS RIGHT.
IN ALL OUR YEARS TOGETHER, NEITHER DESTINY NOR I COULD EVER TOUCH YOU, ROGUE--
--BEFORE NOW.
THIS MOMENT ALONE IS WORTH ALL THE PAIN.

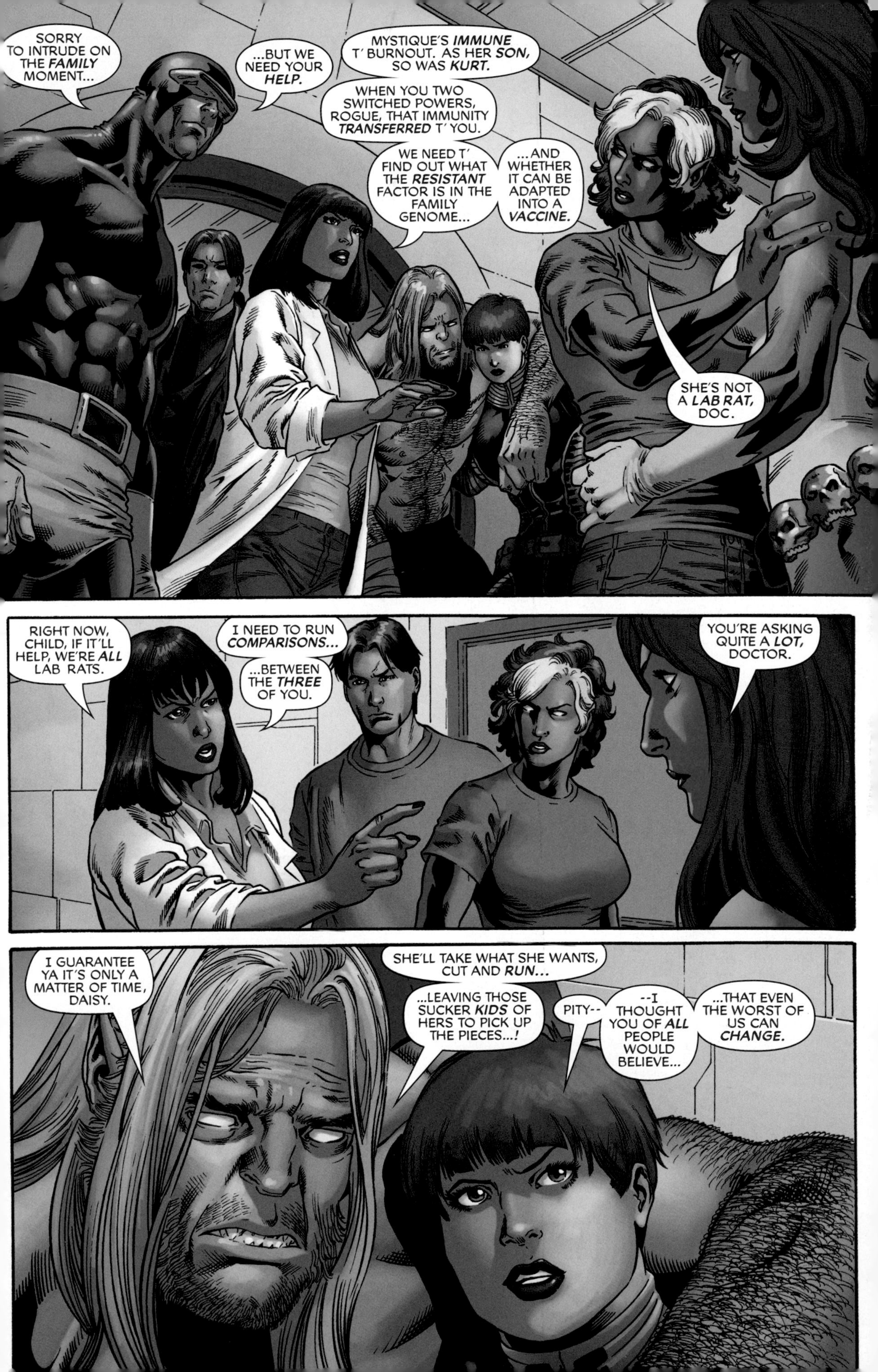
SORRY TO INTRUDE ON THE FAMILY MOMENT...
...BUT WE NEED YOUR HELP.
MYSTIQUE'S IMMUNE T' BURNOUT. AS HER SON, SO WAS KURT.
WHEN YOU TWO SWITCHED POWERS, ROGUE, THAT IMMUNITY TRANSFERRED T' YOU.
WE NEED T' FIND OUT WHAT THE RESISTANT FACTOR IS IN THE FAMILY GENOME...
...AND WHETHER IT CAN BE ADAPTED INTO A VACCINE.
SHE'S NOT A LAB RAT, DOC.
RIGHT NOW, CHILD, IF IT'LL HELP, WE'RE ALL LAB RATS.
I NEED TO RUN COMPARISONS...
...BETWEEN THE THREE OF YOU.
YOU'RE ASKING QUITE A LOT, DOCTOR.
I GUARANTEE YA IT'S ONLY A MATTER OF TIME, DAISY.
SHE'LL TAKE WHAT SHE WANTS, CUT AND RUN...
...LEAVING THOSE SUCKER KIDS OF HERS TO PICK UP THE PIECES...!
PITY--
--I THOUGHT YOU OF ALL PEOPLE WOULD BELIEVE...
...THAT EVEN THE WORST OF US CAN CHANGE.

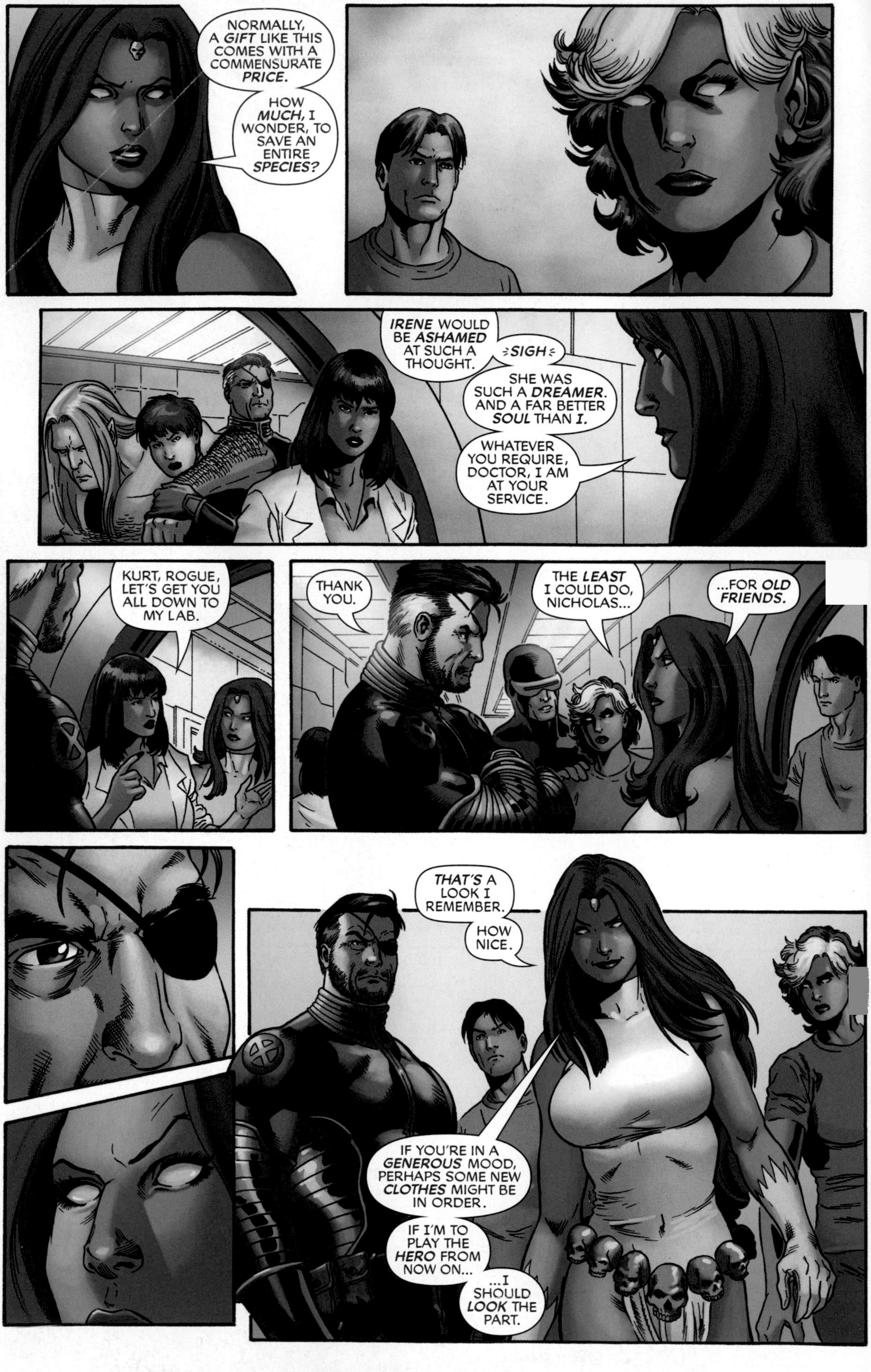
NORMALLY, A GIFT LIKE THIS COMES WITH A COMMENSURATE PRICE.
HOW MUCH, I WONDER, TO SAVE AN ENTIRE SPECIES?
IRENE WOULD BE ASHAMED AT SUCH A THOUGHT.
SIGH
SHE WAS SUCH A DREAMER. AND A FAR BETTER SOUL THAN I.
WHATEVER YOU REQUIRE, DOCTOR, I AM AT YOUR SERVICE.
KURT, ROGUE, LET'S GET YOU ALL DOWN TO MY LAB.
THANK YOU.
THE LEAST I COULD DO, NICHOLAS...
...FOR OLD FRIENDS.
THAT'S A LOOK I REMEMBER.
HOW NICE.
IF YOU'RE IN A GENEROUS MOOD, PERHAPS SOME NEW CLOTHES MIGHT BE IN ORDER.
IF I'M TO PLAY THE HERO FROM NOW ON...
...I SHOULD LOOK THE PART.

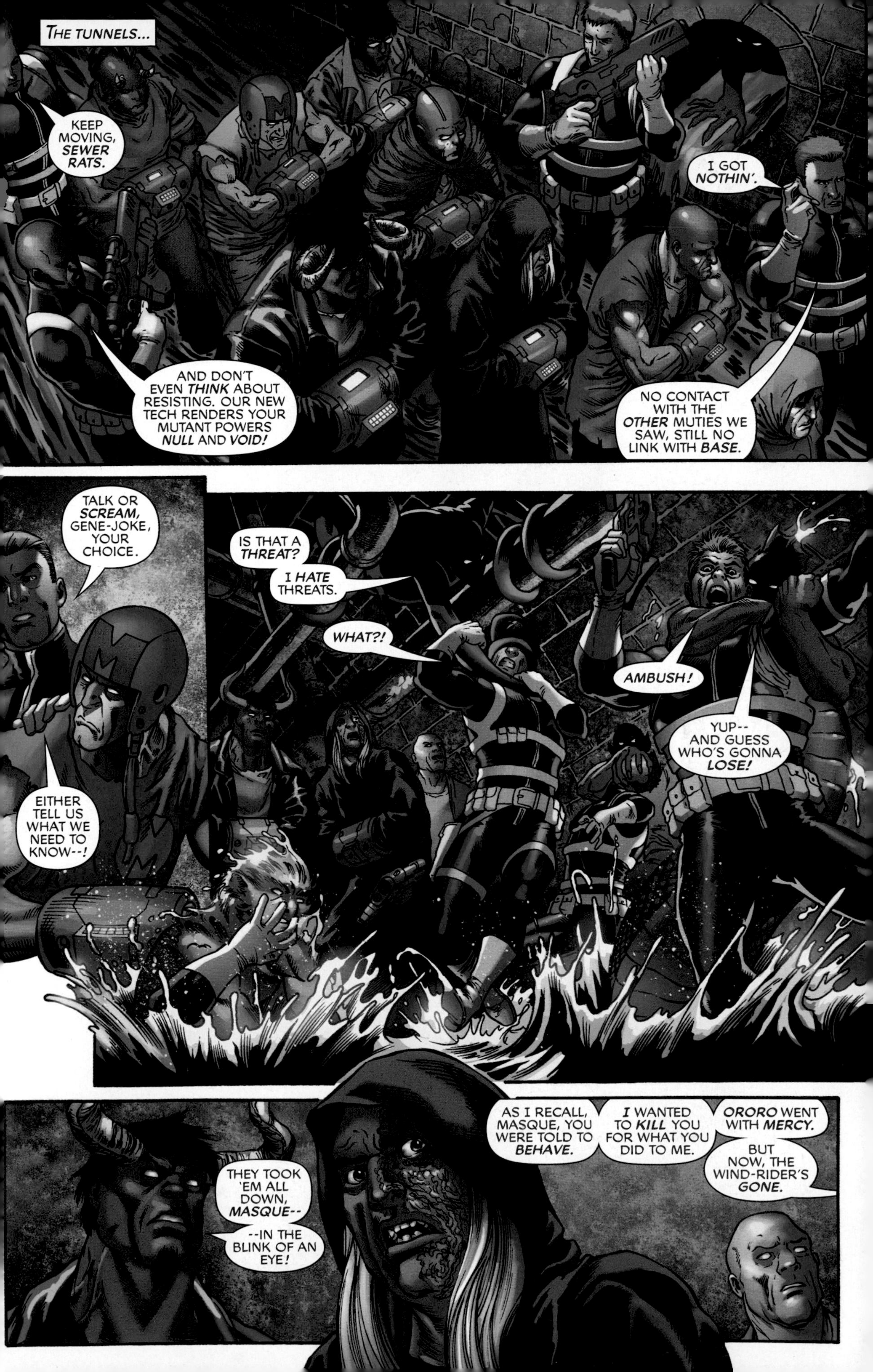
THE TUNNELS...
KEEP MOVING, SEWER RATS.
AND DON'T EVEN THINK ABOUT RESISTING. OUR NEW TECH RENDERS YOUR MUTANT POWERS NULL AND VOID!
I GOT NOTHIN'.
NO CONTACT WITH THE OTHER MUTIES WE SAW, STILL NO LINK WITH BASE.
TALK OR SCREAM, GENE-JOKE, YOUR CHOICE.
EITHER TELL US WHAT WE NEED TO KNOW--!
IS THAT A THREAT? I HATE THREATS.
WHAT?!
AMBUSH!
YUP-- AND GUESS WHO'S GONNA LOSE!
THEY TOOK 'EM ALL DOWN, MASQUE--
--IN THE BLINK OF AN EYE!
AS I RECALL, MASQUE, YOU WERE TOLD TO BEHAVE.
I WANTED TO KILL YOU FOR WHAT YOU DID TO ME.
ORORO WENT WITH MERCY.
BUT NOW, THE WIND-RIDER'S GONE.

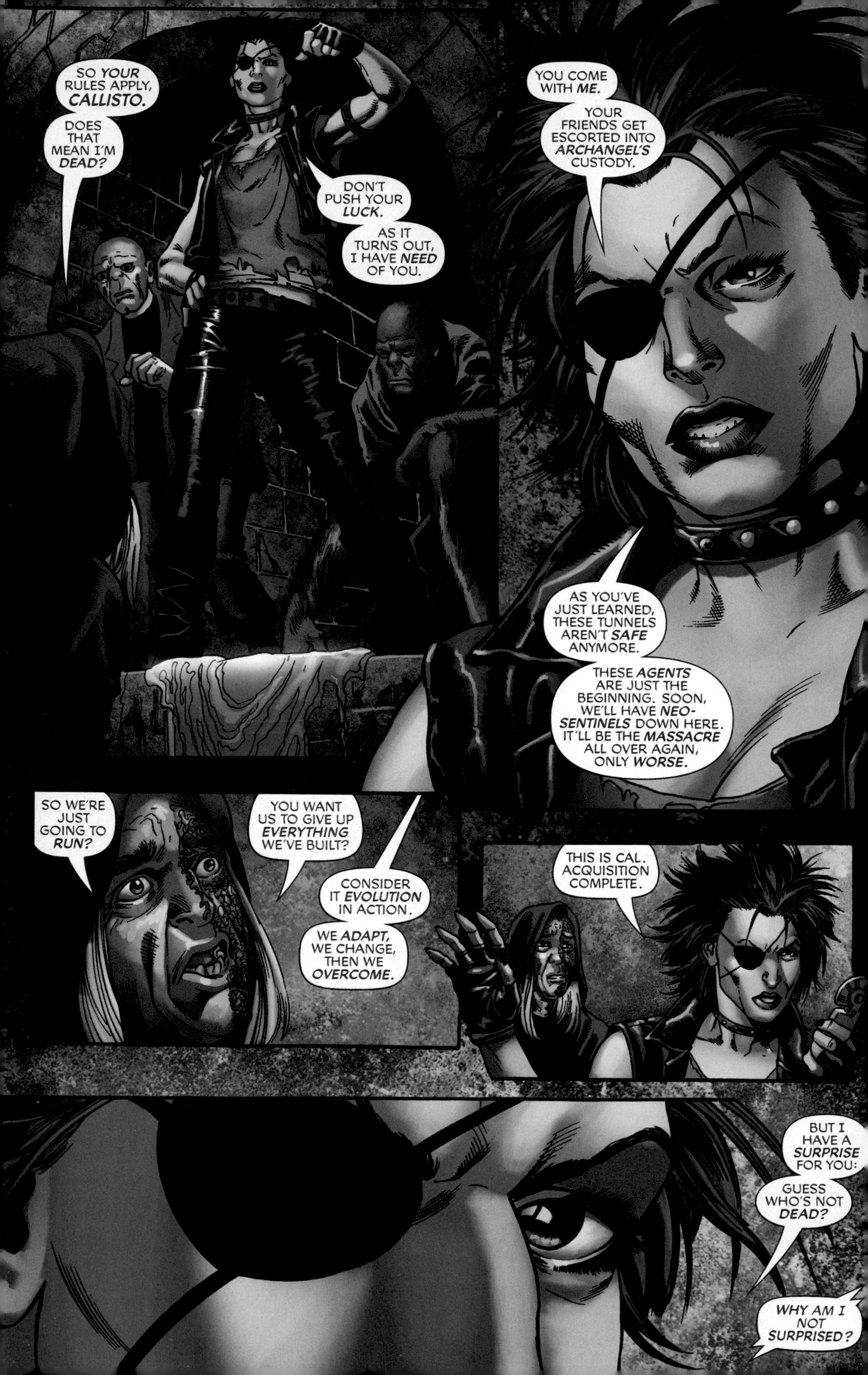
SO *YOUR* RULES APPLY, *CALLISTO.*
DOES THAT MEAN I'M *DEAD?*
DON'T PUSH YOUR *LUCK.*
AS IT TURNS OUT, I HAVE *NEED* OF YOU.
YOU COME WITH *ME.*
YOUR FRIENDS GET ESCORTED INTO *ARCHANGEL'S* CUSTODY.
AS YOU'VE JUST LEARNED, THESE TUNNELS AREN'T *SAFE* ANYMORE.
THESE *AGENTS* ARE JUST THE BEGINNING. SOON, WE'LL HAVE *NEO-SENTINELS* DOWN HERE. IT'LL BE THE *MASSACRE* ALL OVER AGAIN, ONLY *WORSE.*
SO WE'RE JUST GOING TO *RUN?*
YOU WANT US TO GIVE UP *EVERYTHING* WE'VE BUILT?
CONSIDER IT *EVOLUTION* IN ACTION.
WE *ADAPT,* WE CHANGE, THEN WE *OVERCOME.*
THIS IS CAL. ACQUISITION COMPLETE.
BUT I HAVE A *SURPRISE* FOR YOU:
GUESS WHO'S NOT *DEAD?*
WHY AM I NOT SURPRISED?

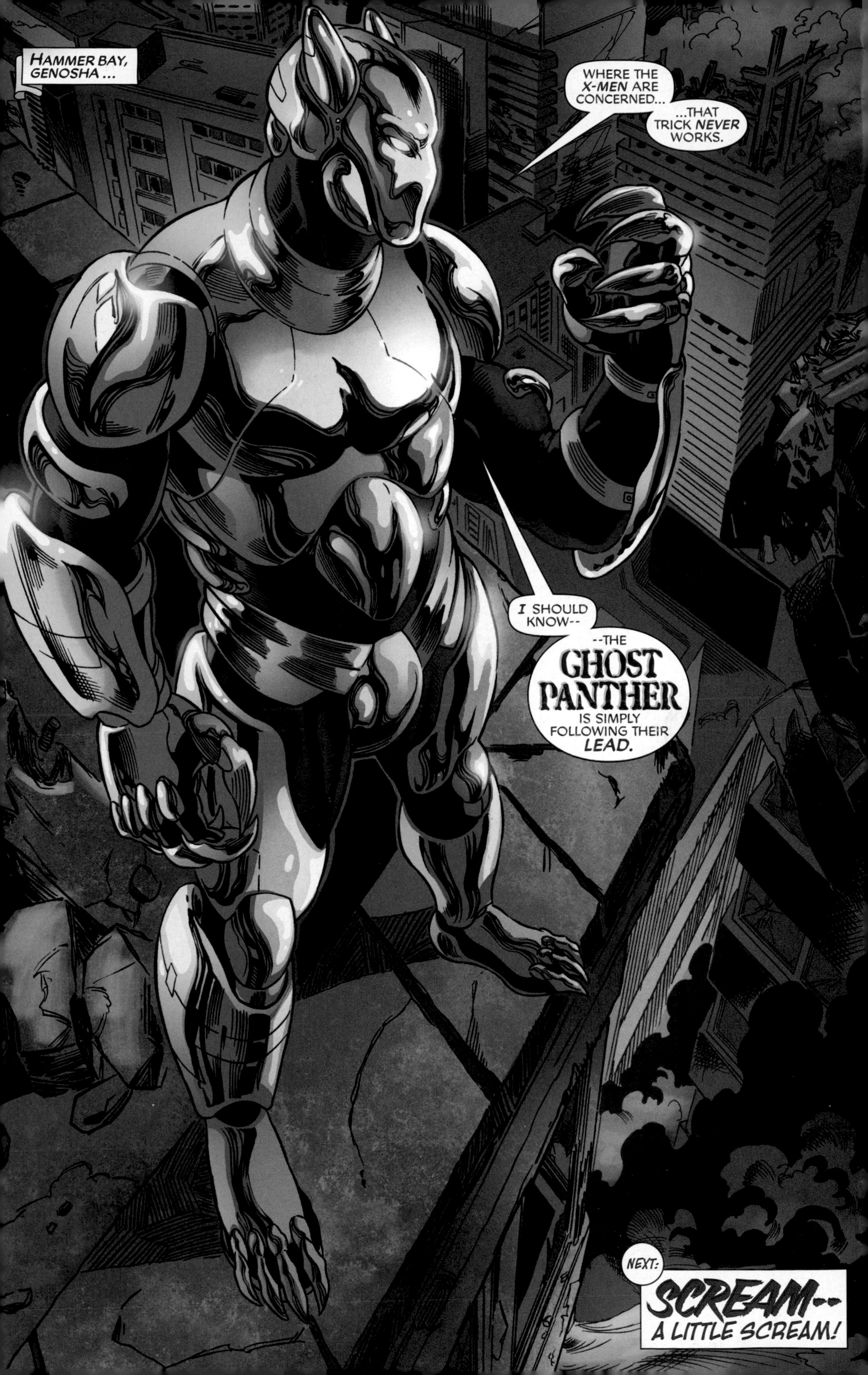
HAMMER BAY, GENOSHA...
WHERE THE X-MEN ARE CONCERNED...
...THAT TRICK NEVER WORKS.
I SHOULD KNOW--
--THE GHOST PANTHER IS SIMPLY FOLLOWING THEIR LEAD.
NEXT:
SCREAM-- A LITTLE SCREAM!